MARKETING STRATEGY FOR INDIAN RURAL BANKS IN NEW MILLENNIUM

MARKETING STRATEGY FOR INDIAN RURAL BANKS IN NEW MILLENNIUM

By

GURJEET KAUR

ANMOL PUBLICATIONS PVT. LTD.
NEW DELHI - 110 002 (INDIA)

ANMOL PUBLICATIONS PVT. LTD.
4374/4B, Ansari Road, Daryaganj
New Delhi - 110 002
Ph.: 3261597, 3278000
www.anmolbooks.com

Marketing Strategy for Indian Rural Banks in New Millennium

First Edition, 2002

ISBN 81-261-1191-7

PRINTED IN INDIA

Published by J.L. Kumar for Anmol Publications Pvt. Ltd., New Delhi - 110 002 and Printed at Mehra Offset Press, Delhi.

Contents

Preface

The Regional Rural Banks (RRBs) started working in 1975 with the primary objective of providing banking services in the rural area of the country, particularly to those sections of rural society where commercial banking facilities had not reached. The RRBs have become an integral part of the rural banking system of the country. Though they started playing a commendable role in providing credit and banking services to the rural areas, still there is a need to reorient a qualitative and quantitative change in their structure, philosophy, planning operations within the domain of marketing orientation relevant to local rural conditions.

The extent of marketing orientation has been measured through five-point Likert scale, for two RRBs viz., Jammu Rural Bank (JRB) and Shivalik Kshetriya Gramin Bank (SKGB) as the case studies. The adequate application of marketing concept in actual practice by rural banks will be of much help to achieve customer-satisfaction, growth and profitability. The present study was taken up to evolve a suitable and effective strategy for marketing orientation in RRBs. This study has been divided into eleven chapters viz. 'Inbuilt Marketing Orientation in Indian Rural Banking', 'Review of Literature', 'Research Design and Methodology', 'Measurement of Marketing Orientation in Jammu Rural Bank— With Reference to Underdeveloped, Developing and Developed Rural Areas', 'Measurement of Marketing Orientation in Shivalik Kshetriya Gramin Bank— With Reference to Underdeveloped, Developing and Developed

Rural Areas'. 'Measurement of Marketing Orientation in Rural Banks Through Management Opinion' and 'Marketing Orientation Strategy for RRBs'.

—Dr. Gurjeet Kaur

Acknowledgements

I express my sincerest gratitude and indebtedness to Prof. R.D. Sharma, Department of Commerce and Prof. Desh Bandhu, Directorate of Distance Education, University of Jammu, whose constant guidance, encouragement, unflinching support enabled me to complete this difficult task.

I extend sincere thanks to Dr. S.K. Gupta, Senior Manager JRB; Mr. B.K. Handa and Mr. Charanjit Kumar, Senior Managers SKGB. I am also thankful to the branch managers of JRB and SKGB, viz., Mr. C.S. Toor, Mr. Rattan Singh, Mr. Sudheep Singh, Mr. C.S. Arora, Mr. H.S. Uppal and Mr. Satnam Singh, who supplied all the relevant information and provided me requisite assistance while conducting surveys.

I acknowledge my thanks to Dr. Rahul Gupta, Lecturer, Department of Statistics and Mr. Raman Gupta, Programmer, Computer Centre, University of Jammu, who helped me in the application of different statistical techniques.

I would be failing if I don't acknowledge my gratitude to my parents, brothers and sister-in-law, whose affection, encouragement and benediction remained the constant source of inspiration in the completion of the work.

—Gurjeet Kaur

List of Exhibits

List of Tables

Abbreviations

G.O.I.	=	Government of India
J&K Bank Ltd.	=	Jammu and Kashmir Bank Ltd.
JRB	=	Jammu Rural Bank
MKTORIENT	=	Marketing Orientation
NABARD	=	National Bank for Agriculture and Rural Development
P.N.B.	=	Punjab National Bank
R.B.I.	=	Reserve Bank of India
RRBs	=	Regional Rural Banks
S.B.I.	=	State Bank of India
SKGB	=	Shivalik Kshetriya Gramin Bank

Chapter—1

Inbuilt Marketing Orientation in Indian Rural Banking

The inbuilt marketing orientation in the Indian rural banking services, the procedures followed by the banks in rural sector *vis-a-vis* government programmes regulated through the banks, ensure the achievement of institutional objectives and customer satisfaction. Government and Reserve Bank of India (R.B.I.) have been playing a vital role in injuncting the concept of marketing orientation by creating form, place, time and ownership utilities (Bhattacharya, 1989) in Indian rural banking. Both G.O.I. and R.B.I. have been paying regular attention from time to time towards the promotion and upliftment of rural development through various agencies established with the main objective to cater to the financial needs of the rural people. The establishment of Regional Rural Banks (RRBs) may be viewed in the historical perspective of marketing orientation in Indian rural credit. Several committees/commissions have been set up by R.B.I. and the government in order to study the extent to which the existing institutions and agencies have been able to effectively meet the credit needs of the rural sector (*R.B.I. Bulletin*, 1994).

Before the establishment of RRBs, the existing rural banking setup suffered from certain limitations for catering to the credit requirements of the small and marginal farmers, rural artisans and weaker sections. Co-operatives faced the problems of mounting overdues, lack of strength and managerial expertise and overall poor operations. The commercial banks also suffered from limited coverage in rural sector, inadequate appreciation of the rural problems, high cost of operations and urban orientation. The Banking Commission (1972), therefore, recommended the establishment of a chain of rural banks (G.O.I. 1972) and subsequently a Working Group on rural banks under the Chairmanship of M. Narasimham was appointed on July, 1, 1975 to examine in-depth the possibility of setting up the rural banks to bridge the credit gap in the rural areas. Narasimham Committee observed, what is needed is an institution which combines the local feel and familiarity with rural problems which the co-operatives possess and the degree of business organisation, ability to mobilise deposits, access to central money markets and a modernised outlook which the commercial banks have (G.O.I. 1975). The committee finally recommended the creation of rural banks to meet the rural credit needs.

The recommendations of Narasimham Committee were accepted by G.O.I. and accordingly RRBs Ordinance of 1975 was passed by the President on 26th Sept., 1975 which was subsequently replaced by the RRBs Act of 1976 on 9th Feb., 1976 (G.O.I. 1986). First five RRBs were inaugurated on 2nd Oct., 1975 at Jaipur in Rajasthan, Bhiwani in Haryana, Moradabad and Gorakhpur in U.P. and Malda in W. Bengal (*R.B.I. Bulletin*, 1976).

MAIN FEATURES OF RRBs

1. Objectives

To develop the rural economy by providing, for the purpose of development of agriculture trade, commerce, industry and other productive activities in the rural areas, credit and other facilities particularly to the small and marginal farmers, agricultural labourers, artisans and small entrepreneurs and for matters connected therewith and incidental thereto (*R.B.I. Bulletin* 1976; Singh 1976).

2. Share Capital

The authorised capital of each RRB is Rs. 5 crores and the issued capital is fixed by Central Government and is in no case less than Rs. 25 lakhs or exceed Rs. one crore (Sec. 6, RRBs Act 1976).

3. Sponsorship

RRBs are sponsored scheduled commercial banks. Of the issued capital, 50% is subscribed by G.O.I., 15% by the concerned state government and 35% by the sponsor bank (Sec. 6, RRB Act 1976).

4. Branch Expansion

RRBs have been successful in extending their operations through a network of increased branch expansion (Tables 1.1 and 1.2). On Dec. 1975, number of RRBs' branches was 17, which increased to 3279 as on Dec. 1980, followed by 12606 on Dec. 1985, 14443 on Mar. 1990, 14509 on Mar. 1995 and 14461 as on Mar. 1997 and 1998.

5. Financial Position

Financial position of RRBs (Table 1.1) reveals an attractive picture in absolute terms as such amount of deposits and advances increased year by year. But in relative term (C.D. ratio), which is considered more appropriate for comparison, financial position of RRBs reflects an unsound phenomenon as credit-deposit ratio increased from 1975 to 1978 but then onwards started declining year after year. C. D. ratio as on Mar. 1998 came out to be 44 which highlights that only 44% of deposits have been advanced by RRBs. Thus, it can be concluded that RRBs have been successful in attracting the savings of rural people through deposit mobilization but the spread of credit habit has yet to gain momentum.

Thus, an effort has been made to conceptually analyse the marketing orientation inbuilt in the rural banking

Table 1.1
Branch Expansion and Year-wise Financial Position of RRBs

Year	*Number of RRBs*	*Districts Covered*	*Number of Branches*	*Deposits (In lakhs)*	*Advance Outstanding (In lakhs)*	*C.D. Ratio*
Dec. 75	06	12	17	20	10	50
Dec. 76	40	84	489	772	702	91
Dec. 77	48	99	1187	3304	4235	128
Dec. 78	51	102	1753	7411	12202	165
Dec. 79	60	111	2420	12322	16741	136
Dec. 80	85	144	3279	19983	24338	122
Dec. 81	107	182	4795	33600	40659	121
Dec. 82	124	214	6191	50226	57711	115
Dec. 83	150	265	7795	67785	75084	111
Dec. 84	173	307	10245	95997	108077	113
Dec. 85	188	333	12606	128582	140767	109
Dec. 86	194	351	12838	171494	178484	104
Dec. 87	196	365	13353	230582	223226	97
Dec. 88	196	369	13920	296588	280429	95
Mar. 89	196	369	14079	311858	291825	94
Mar. 90	196	370	14443	415052	355404	86
Mar. 91	196	381	14527	498924	360927	72
Mar. 92	196	392	14539	586783	409086	70
Mar. 93	196	398	14543	693813	462673	67
Mar. 94	196	408	14542	882651	525302	60
Mar. 95	196	425	14509	1115001	629096	56
Mar. 96	196	427	14497	1418790	750502	53
Mar. 97	196	427	14461	1803201	871808	48
Mar. 98	196	427	14461	2218222	975858	44

Source: Statistics on RRBS (As on 31.3.98) NABARD Division, Mumbai.

scenario. Beside McCarthy's (1978) well established four Ps, other two Ps viz., people and process have also been studied in the context of rural banking. The bank personnel provide the crucial link between the services offered by the banks and the actual users of the services and similarly the procedures adopted by them have a direct bearing on the customer satisfaction (Thingalaya 1991). Thus in the banking industry, people and procedural aspects require adequate attention even though these Ps are the part of the universal four Ps of McCarthy (Kotler, 1996).

Table 1.2
State-wise Financial Position of RRBs

(Amt. in Lakh)

Name of the State	*Number of Branches*	*Accumulated Loss till 1996 (Rs.)*	*Profit/Loss for 1998 (in Lakhs)*
Andhra Pradesh	1128	10867.35	+ 3226.48
Arunachal Pradesh	19	148.74	+ 8.03
Assam	404	7658.10	– 239.85
Bihar	1887	32528.14	– 5280.08
Gujarat	411	6186.66	+ 540.09
Haryana	291	3144.15	+ 1488.60
Himachal Pradesh	129	1053.10	+ 156.51
Jammu & Kashmir	274	3874.58	– 400.18
Karnataka	1073	9184.81	+ 43.10
Kerala	273	0.00	+ 34.59
Madhya Pradesh	1586	31809.23	– 2761.45
Maharashtra	587	10763.15	– 317.80
Manipur	29	562.06	– 64.13
Meghalaya	51	0.00	+ 312.99
Mizoram	54	527.10	+ 64.51
Nagaland	8	128.15	+ 5.33
Orissa	815	20961.62	– 4087.11
Punjab	201	880.37	+ 876.14
Rajasthan	1061	16833.95	– 1010.02
Tamilnadu	206	3085.49	+ 581.75
Tripura	90	6486.34	– 1122.90
Uttar Pradesh	3020	31827.57	+ 9643.41
West Bengal	864	16698.66	– 2899.78

Source: Key Statistics on RRBs (as on 31.03.1998), NABARD Division.

MARKETING ORIENTATION AT PRODUCT-MIX LEVEL

Here marketing orientation means that all major product decisions should begin with an understanding of the needs of the consumers (Cundiff, Still and Govoni 1980; Enis 1980; Hughes 1980). In this regard many steps have been taken by government and R.B.I. to satisfy the banking product requirements of different rural sectors of the economy. Initially only the lending aspect of rural banking was given prime importance as compared to deposit mobilisation phenomenon. From the view point of loan disbursement, the primary focus has been laid on agricultural credit requirements of the rural people (Co-operative Credit Societies 1904; Agricultural Credit Department 1935; Standing Advisory Committee on Agricultural Credit 1951; National Agricultural Credit Fund 1956; Agricultural Refinance and Development Corporation 1968; College of Agricultural Banking 1969; and National Bank for Agriculture and Rural Development 1982), whereas the needs relating to trade, commerce, industry and agricultural allied activities received secondary importance. Short-term agricultural demands have been successfully looked after by the government and R.B.I. through the establishment of co-operative banks, commercial banks and RRBs and long-term agricultural needs by Agricultural Refinance and Development Corporation renamed as NABARD in 1982.

Due to the fact that only agricultural sector received significant attention in past, government decided to impose social control over banks in 1967 to ensure that credit be distributed equitably and purposefully among the different sectors (both urban and rural) of the economy. Subsequently the nationalisation of 14 major commercial banks further accelerated the pace of rural credit designed to meet the banking requirements of various sectors of rural community. Furthermore Large Sized Adivasi Multipurpose Co-operative Societies (LAMPS) were organised in 1971 for providing an appropriate institutional framework in tribal areas. Similarly in pursuance of Government's 15-point programme for the welfare of minority communities, a number of steps were taken by the banks for ensuring adequate credit facilities to these rural communities (*R.B.I. Bulletin* 1995). The introduction of Multipurpose Scheme (1972) and establishment of RRBs (1975) strengthened the concept.

Many institutions viz., Co-operative Banks, State Bank of India, Commercial banks and RRBs have been catering to the credit needs of rural people through the provision of call loans, term loans, cash credit, overdraft, personal loan for durable consumer goods, construction of residential houses, loans to road transport operators, loans to small scale industry, loans to self-employed persons, loans to technicians, loans to retail trade, green card loan schemes (Maheshwari 1991; Mithani 1989), Kisan Credit Cards Scheme and new subsidy scheme for cold storage/godowns (Budget 1999). These institutions have also been playing active role in mobilising the savings of rural population thereby inculcating the habits of saving and thrift. Large number of need-based deposit schemes have also been introduced by R.B.I. from time to time viz., saving deposits, fixed deposits, current deposits, cash certificates, daily saving schemes, minor saving schemes, monthly interest income scheme, annuity or retirement schemes, farmers' schemes, insurance linked deposit schemes etc. (Maheshwari 1991; Mithani 1989).

MARKETING ORIENTATION AT PLACE-MIX LEVEL

The products/services should be offered at the right places (Mark 1988) which are easily accessible (Madhukar 1991) in order to make the physical distribution outlet of an institution marketing oriented (Ross 1997; Sharma 1995; Gupta 1992). This aspect of bank marketing mix has also received due consideration of government and R.B.I. through the branch expansion of aforesaid existing agencies in the rural areas. First effort in this direction has been the setting up of Co-operative Credit Societies (1904), followed by the establishment of Primary Agricultural Credit Societies and Land Development Banks. Further on the recommendation of Rural Credit Survey Committee (1954), State Bank of India (1955) was established to facilitate the banking services in rural areas through its extensive branch network and thereafter the nationalisation of 14 major commercial banks in 1969 and 6 banks in 1980 provided much stimuli and sense of direction to expand their operations by opening branches in the rural areas as well. Lastly the introduction of RRBs (1975) led to a massive increase in the number of rural bank branches in the hitherto neglected areas of the rural economy. The branch expansion programme in the rural areas has also been emphasised by Agricultural Finance Corporation (1981) and CRAFICARD (1981). A Committee on Financial System (1992) headed by M. Narasimham suggested that branch licensing be abolished and the matter of opening branches be left to the commercial judgement of an individual bank. However, R.B.I. decided to give freedom to banks to rationalise their existing branch network by relocating branches, setting up of controlling offices and establishing extension counters. In this context, RRBs were given liberty in 1994 to relocate their loss making branches within service area only. They were also allowed to open the extension counters, so as to ensure the provision of uninterrupted and satisfactory banking services on an ongoing basis to the clientele in their area of operation (*R.B.I. Bulletin* 1995). Furthermore 70 RRBs were freed (1996) from the service area obligations and were permitted to relocate their loss making branches at taluka/block headquarters, village markets, mandis and agricultural produce centres. They were also freed to consider merging of two loss making branches operating within the close proximity of about 5 kms into one branch. Subsequently they had been given operational liberty (1997) to open and relocate branches at semi-urban and urban centres subject to the prior approval of their respective boards.

MARKETING ORIENTATION AT PRICE-MIX LEVEL

Marketing Orientation demands delivery of superior products/services at reasonable prices (Kotler 1996) and thus for ensuring overall economic development of rural sector, it is imperative that timely and adequate institutional credit at affordable cost is made available (*R.B.I. Bulletin* 1997). The price-mix in banking, being important to both bankers and their customers, has to be designed in the light of socio-economic profile of the target market (Sharma 1995). Beside other factors, the major reason behind the establishment of banks in rural sector was the exorbitant rate of interest charged by unscrupulous private money lenders (G.O.I. 1945; All India Rural Credit Survey 1954; Wadhwa 1980; Kanvinde 1984; Verma 1988 and Patnaik and Mishra 1993) and therefore government started the credit movement with the passing of Co-operative Credit Societies Act in 1904 (Gupta and Singh 1985; Thingalaya 1993) in order to provide banking services and facilities to rural people at the reasonable cost. Further in order to remove the non-institutional money lenders from rural scenario, S.B.I., Commercial Banks and RRBs were introduced. In July 1972 the Ministry of Finance introduced a 'Differential Rate of Interest Scheme' under which the public sector banks were asked to render financial assistance to weaker sections of the community at a concessional rate of interest (4% p.a.). Among other financial institutions set up by the government, RRBs' have been established especially for lending only to weaker sections and that too at a low rate of interest (Steering Committee on RRBs 1981). Keeping in view the socio-economic status of the rural population R.B.I. has recently increased interest rates on deposits (*R.B.I. Bulletin* 1995; 1992; 1991) and decreased interest rates on advances (*R.B.I. Bulletin* 1994; 1993; 1992) of commercial, cooperative and RRBs. Last step in this direction has been the 'deregulation of the interest rates' recommended by Narasimham Committee (1992) which provided for fixing of the minimum and maximum rate of interest by R.B.I. In between these limits, banks have been freed to quote the interest rates as per their banking requirements (*R.B.I. Bulletin* 1998; 1996; 1995).

MARKETING ORIENTATION AT PROMOTION-MIX LEVEL

Banks should adopt an approach by which the wider expectations of the customers can be met and different promotional tools should be employed, to educate the customers about the nature of banking services, to meet these expectations (Sarkar 1983) instead of simply trying to sell (Mark 1988) what R.B.I. introduces. This aspect of marketing-mix has not received much attention of policy-makers and administrators of rural banks as compared to other Ps. Till date, on the counter services are quite common among rural banks but field selling of banking schemes has not become very popular. Rural banking business can be promoted by making bank deposits more attractive by raising interest rates on saving bank account, permitting tax benefit on deposits, compensating customers for delay in collection of cheques (Committee on Customer Service 1991), interaction between the banks' stall and small scale industry borrowers (Nayak Committee 1994). A Committee on Agricultural Credit (1998) suggested open meetings with farmers to assess their problems and difficulties, tangible incentives to farmers who are prompt in repayment, and rebate to borrowers who repay their dues promptly.

MARKETING ORIENTATION AT PEOPLE-MIX LEVEL

The greater the job satisfaction and organisational commitment of employees, the greater the marketing orientation (Ross 1997; Stanton, Etzel and Walker 1991; Kohli and Jaworski 1990). R.B.I. took initiative in 1969 by opening a College of Agricultural Bank (CAB) in Pune and later on NABARD introduced Bankers' Institute of Rural Development (BIRD), Lucknow in 1983 to meet the training needs of the co-operative banks and RRBs. Beside CAB and

BIRD, many other agencies are also catering to the training requirements of rural banks' like NABARD; RRB Staff Training College; Bolpur Training Centre, Murshidabad; RRB Training Centre, Bangalore and National Institute of Rural Development (NIRD). Dantwala Committee (1977), Steering Committee on RRBs (1981), Kelkar Committee (1986), Agricultural Credit Review Committee (1989) have emphasised the need of skill development of rural bank personnel through training. R.B.I. stressed not only on the RRB offices in unbanked rural areas, but also on personnel with requisite expertise and skills in these branches (*R.B.I. Bulletin* 1990). A Committee on Customers Service (Goiporia 1991) suggested a well planned approach of job enrichment, training to the bank personnel to make them responsive and customer friendly to operate successfully in a competitive environment (Nayak Committee 1994; Rangarajan 1994 and 1996; *R.B.I. Bulletin* 1993 and 1997). Finally a Committee on Agricultural Credit (1998) headed by Sh. R.V. Gupta recommended a package of incentives to bank employees for training in prestigious institutions, educational facilities and corporate recognition of outstanding performances and also to provide weightage to these measures in promotion. It further suggested that training institutions need to design fresh interventions shifting their focus from project-based programmes to borrower appraisal including techniques for assessing the needs of the rural households.

MARKETING ORIENTATION AT PROCESS-MIX LEVEL

This element of marketing-mix requires adequate and timely banking services to the clientele (*R.B.I. Bulletin* 1997; 1994) so as to obtain overall customer satisfaction. All the agriculture-based institutions, mentioned in the aforesaid product mix, have been set up to ensure speedy and smooth flow of bank credit to agricultural sector. Goiporia Committee on Customer Satisfaction (1991) suggested technology upgradation and continuous review of systems and procedures in tune with changing needs of customers to support efficient and effective services viz., immediate encashment of cheques and issuance of drafts, updating of saving bank passbooks and issue of statements of accounts to customers. R.B.I has also directed co-operative, commercial and RRBs to strengthen their appraisal mechanism so that bank loans are properly and effectively disbursed (*R.B.I. Bulletin*, 1992). In this regard R.B.I. had issued various guidelines to banks with the objective of ensuring lending discipline in appraisal, sanction, monitoring and utilization of bank finance (*R.B.I. Bulletin*, 1998).

Though several steps are being taken by both G.O.I. and R.B.I. to implement the recommendations of various committees for the development of rural sector through RRBs, but these steps are inadequate for creating the needed marketing culture in the rural banks. Mere creation of an institution doesn't amount to marketing orientation but it requires continuous understanding and appraising the needs of target people and successfully meeting of the same through interfunctional co-ordination. In this direction, the present study has been undertaken to measure the extent of marketing orientation in RRBs, in general and JRB (J&K) and SKGB (Punjab), in particular and to suggest appropriate strategy for marketing orientation in RRBs.

REFERENCES

1. Agricultural Credit Department (1935), "Role of Reserve Bank in Promoting Rural Development", *R.B.I. Bulletin*, Dec., (Suppl.), 69-70.
2. Agricultural Refinance and Development Corporation (1963), "Role of Reserve Bank in Promoting Rural Development", *R.B.I. Bulletin*, Dec., (Suppl.), 69-70.
3. Bhattacharya, Biswa. N (1989), "Marketing Approach to Promoting Banking Services", *Vikalpa*, Apr.,-June, Vol. 14, No. 2, 35.
4. Budget (1999), Yashwant Sinha Attempts a Please, *Hindustan Times*, Sunday, 28th Feb., 01.

5. College of Agricultural Banking (1969), "Role of Reserve Bank in Promoting Rural Development", *R.B.I. Bulletin*, Dec., (Suppl.), 69-70.

6. Cundiff, Edward W; Richad R. Still and Norman A.P. Govoni (1980), *Fundamentals of Modern Marketing*, Prentice Hall of India, New Delhi, 4th Ed, 137.

7. Enis, Ben. M (1980), Marketing Management, Goodyear Publishing Societies (1971), *Report of National Committee on Agriculture*, G.O.I., New Delhi.

8. Goiporia, M.N. (1991) "Committee on Customer Service", *R.B.I. Bulletin* Jan., 68-69.

9. Gupta, Krishan, Gopal and Rajendra Singh (1985), "A New Look to Regional Rural Banks", *Khadi Gramodyog*, Dec., 461.

10. Gupta, R. V. (1998), "Committee on Agricultural Credit", *R.B.I. Bulletin*, June, 497-503.

11. Hughes, G. David (1980), *Marketing Management*, Addison Wesley Publishing Co., Philippines, 2nd Ed, 4-5.

12. Kanvinde, D.J. (1984), "Bank as a Lever for Rural Development", *Monthly Review*, Jan., 20.

13. Kohli, Ajay K. and Bernard J. Jaworski (1990), Market Orientation: The Construct, Research Propositions and Managerial Implications", *Journal of Marketing*, Apr., Vol. 54.

14. Kotler, Philip (1996), *Marketing Management: Analysis, Planning, Implementation and Control*, Prentice Hall of India, New Delhi, 8th Ed, 472 & 488.

15. Madhukar, R. K. (1992), "Dynamics of Bank Marketing", Reviewed by Prof. Atul Bhatt, *Prajnan*, Vol. XXI, No. 1, 117-118.

16. Maheshwari, S.N. (1991), *Banking: Law and Practice*, Kalyani Publisher, New Delhi, 6th Ed, 259-263.

17. Mark, V.V. (1988), "Deposit Mobilization and Marketing of Bank Services", *Economic Review*, June, Vol. 33, No. 1.

18. McCarthy, E. Jerome; John F. Grashot and Andrew A. Brogowicz (1978), *Reading in Basic Marketing*, Richard D. Irwin, Inc. Revised Ed, 159.

19. Mithani, D.M. (1989), *The Anatomy of Indian Banking*, Himalaya Publishing House, N. Delhi, 1st Ed, 47-48.

20. *Multipurpose Co-operative Societies* (1971), R.B.I. Bombay, Vol. III, Chapter VIII & IX.

21. National Agricultural Credit Fund (1956), "Role of Reserve Bank in Promoting Rural Development", *R.B.I. Bulletin*, Dec., (Suppl.), 69-70.
22. National Bank for Agricultural and Rural Development (1982), "Role of Reserve Bank in Promoting Rural Development", *R.B.I. Bulletin*, Dec., (Suppl) 69-70.
23. Narasimham M. (1992), "Report of the Committee on Financial System," *R.B.I. Bulletin*, Feb., 369-377.
24. Nayak Committee (1994), "Adequacy of Institutional Credit to the Small Scale Industrial Sector", *R.B.I. Bulletin*, Mar., 425-26.
25. Patnaik, U.C. and R.N. Mishra (1993), *Rural Banking in India*, Anmol Publication Pvt. Ltd., New Delhi, 16-17.
26. Rangarajan, C. (1993) "Banking Education and Training", *R.B.I. Bulletin*, Nov., 1365.
27. *R.B.I. Bulletin* (1976), Jan., 62-63.
28. *R.B.I. Bulletin* (1976), June, 61-63.
29. *R.B.I. Bulletin* (1994), Committee for Intensive Use of Technology in Payment Systems, *R.B.I. Bulletin*, Dec., 1598.
30. *R.B.I. Bulletin* (1996), Banking Sector Reforms, *R.B.I. Bulletin*, Mar., 149.
31. Regional Rural Banks (1975), Role of Reserve Bank in Promoting Rural Development, *R.B.I. Bulletin*, Dec. (Suppl.), 69-70.
32. *Report of Agricultural Credit Review Committee* (1998), R.B.I. Bombay.
33. Report of Agricultural Finance Corporation (1989), *Financial Express*, 24th Apr., 05.
34. *Report of the Agricultural Finance Sub-Committee* (1945), G.O.I, New Delhi, 59.
35. *Report of the All India Rural Credit Survey (1954)*, R.B.I. Mumbai, Vol. II, Chapters VIII and IX, 167-174.
36. *Report of the Banking Commission* (1972), G.O.I., New Delhi, 03 & 165-74.
37. *Report of the Committee on Rural Banks* (1975), Working Group, G.O.I., New Delhi, 01.
38. Report of the Committee to Review Arrangements for Institutional Credit for Agriculture and Rural Development (CRAFICARD) (1982), R.B.I. Mumbai.
39. *Report of Kelkar Committee on RRBs* (1986), R.B.I. Mumbai.

40. *Report of the Review Committee on RRBs* (1977), Dantwala Committee, R.B.I. Mumbai.

41. *Report of the Viability of RRBs* (1981), *R.B.I. Bulletin*, Mumbai, 200-41.

42. Report of the Working Group (1975), Regional Rural Banks, G.O.I., New Delhi, 9-10.

43. Ross, Christopher. A (1997), "The Practice of Marketing in Newly Industrialised and Developing Countries—A Survey", *A Questionnaire*, 1-10.

44. *R.B.I. Bulletin* (1998), Banking Development and Policy Perspective, Report on Trend and Progress of Banking in India, Nov., 69.

45. *R.B.I. Bulletin* (1997), Development of Banking Technology in India, Jan., 38.

46. *R.B.I. Bulletin* (1990), "Credit Control and other Measures", Dec., 986.

47. *R.B.I. Bulletin* (1991), "Credit Control and other Measures", Oct., 1007.

48. *R.B.I. Bulletin* (1992), "Credit Control and other Measures", Mar., 521, 796 & 1883.

49. *R.B.I. Bulletin* (1992), "Credit Control and other Measures", July, 1159.

50. *R.B.I. Bulletin* (1993), "Credit Control and other Measures", Apr., 15-17 & 605.

51. *R.B.I. Bulletin* (1994), "Credit Control and other Measures", Mar., 417.

52. *R.B.I. Bulletin* (1994), "Credit Control and other Measures", Aug., 117-118 & 139.

53. *R.B.I. Bulletin* (1995), "Credit Control and other Measures", Jan., 114.

54. *R.B.I. Bulletin* (1995), "Credit Control and other Measures", July, 617-635.

55. *R.B.I. Bulletin* (1995), "Credit Control and other Measures", Sept., 822-24.

56. *R.B.I. Bulletin* (1997), "Credit Control and other Measures", Jan., 88.

57. *R.B.I. Bulletin* (1997), "Credit Control and other Measures", Dec., 50.

58. *R.B.I. Bulletin* (1998), "Credit Control and other Measures", Feb., 201.

59. *R.B.I. Bulletin*, "15-Point Programme", July, 625.

60. *R.B.I. Bulletin* (1996), "On Sound Bank Management", Mar., 153.

61. Sharma, R.D. (1995), "Marketing Effectiveness in American Banks", *Prajnan*, Vol. XXIV, 153.

62. Singh, Harpal, (1976), "Regional Rural Banks", *Yojana*, Vol. XXII, Dec., (16), 167

63. Thingalaya, N.K. (1993), "Role Respponsibilities of Financial Institutions vis-a-vis Programme of Panchayat Raj Institutions", *Economic Review*, Aug.-Oct., Vol. 38, No. 1, 01.

64. Verma, M.L. (1998), *Rural Banking in India*, Rawat Publication, Jaipur, 06.

65. Wadhwa, Charan D. (1980), *Rural Banks and Rural Development*, The Macmillan Co. of India Ltd., Madras, 1-3.

Chapter—2

Review of Related Literature

"Marketing Orientation for RRBs in Northern India" comprising two disciplines viz., Marketing and Rural Banking, require a detailed review of relevant literature on both the aspects of the study. Thus, the relevant literature has been reviewed under the following three broad sections:

RURAL BANKING

Podwal and Bandyopadhya (1973) presented a scientific framework for analysing environmental data to arrive at a meaningful location and branch expansion plan in the rural areas. However, they couldn't pay adequate attention to other components of rural banking such as deposits, advances, rate of interest, bank's staff, promotional tools and processes involved. Similarly Patel (1974) carried out a study to examine the problems and challenges of rural credit and emphasised on the active involvement of nationalised commercial banks in the process of rural development.

Sharda (1980), Patel and Shete (1980), Rao (1980), Reddy and Hussain (1983) appraised the functioning of RRBs; Kumar (1983) examined their performance in eastern U.P., Naidu, Suvarchala and Obulu (1984) attempted to the state of A.P. Lakshminarayana (1984) undertook a case study of Mayurakshi Gramin Bank, W. Bengal. Joshi (1984), Satya (1984), Sangwan (1989), Badne (1990) analysed the performance and progress of RRBs and Kalkundrikar (1990) investigated their role in the economic development with special reference to Gramin Banks in Karnataka. They judged the performance of RRBs' in terms of branch expansion, lending operations, deposit mobilisation, overdues, viability and covered only a few aspects of customers' banking needs. Thus the other important aspects of rural banking like rate of interest, use of promotional techniques and efficient customer services have not been investigated. Wadhwa (1980) reviewed the present working and future prospects of two RRBs viz, Haryana Kshetriya Gramin Bank (HKGB), Bhiwani and Jaipur Nagaur Aanchalik Gramin Bank (JNAGB), Jaipur. He suggested the creation of cell for undertaking research, planning programmes, performance and problems of RRBs, and their inter-relationship with credit plans of other rural credit institutions. No efforts have been made to present the current and future banking requirements of customers.

Main areas of discussion in the RRB Chairmen's conference in 1980 were the role and purpose of RRBs, viability and profitability aspects, appraisal and follow-up business planning and development of human resources. The conference recommended the opening of RRBs' branches in non-banked areas and discouraging of commercial banks to compete with RRBs. It concluded that the involvement of rural people representation is necessary for ensuring rural-oriented banking schemes and finally overall rural development. The main focus was to strengthen the RRBs administration i.e., conference emphasised on the product orientation and completely ignored the customer orientation, which is the main thrust of present marketing strategy in service sector.

Krishnan (1980) highlighted the purpose of RRBs, their capital structure, branch expansion, districts covered, deposit mobilization, loans and problems of overdues. The Study revealed that RRBs have succeeded in taking the banking services to the door steps of rural masses to a great extent. No statistical tools has been used to prove the reliability of the findings. Rao (1981) in a case study of Sri Visakha Gramin Bank analysed the performance of RRBs' in the state of Karnataka. The study examined the impact of rural bank finance in terms of agriculture produce, cropping pattern and the assets of beneficiaries. Varde and Singh (1982) attempted to analyse the overall profitability performance of 40 RRBs over three year (1978-1980). They stressed that for improving profitability, a bank has to aim at increasing the magnitude of burden ratio (manpower expense ratio + other expense ratio - other income ratio) but they have totally ignored personnel and marketing spheres, while emphasising only on the financial requirements of a bank.

Bhatnagar (1983) made the plea that for increasing efficacy of the rural branches, banks need to examine their communication strategies at micro and macro level and rightly pointed out that to be effective, entire communication strategy needs to be designed around the bank customers, their needs, values, way of life etc. But before communicating any information, customers' needs have to be explored so that bank employees are accordingly trained for rural-oriented operations.

Singh (1983) attempted to examine the asset structure and source of financing of RRBs. The main objectives were to examine the extent of earning assets of RRBs, to study the ratio between the cost of borrowings and re-financing and the cost of deposits mobilisation and to find the net earning from investment raised through these sources. However, no statistical tool has been used to test the significance of results. In another study of Singh (1983), an attempt was made to analyse the loan delivery system of four RRBs. The study covered the reasons for delay in the sanction and disbursement of loans, variables considered by bank officials while granting loans and difficulties faced by both the bank officials and customers. He inquired into procedural system but ignored the credit requirements of the customers. Singh and Upadhaya (1984) looked into the question of low recovery of loans by RRBs, and attempted to find out the means to improve the rate of recovery.

In an editorial note Lall (1984) stressed revamping of RRBs by enlarging the definition of target groups, surveys of all the villages served by RRBs' branches and strengthening of professional skills of their staff in project appraisal. He ignored that for improving and maintaining long run profitability, customers' needs and requirements should be given prime importance. Vaishnaw (1984) in his Ph.D thesis laid more stress on opening new branches of RRBs and observed that main problems in setting up of branches are lack of essential infrastructural facilities and lack of trained staff. He also commented upon the working hours of branches, transfer of commercial bank branches to RRBs, poor recovery of loans, credit-deposit ratio and profitability of RRBs. However, he neither pinpointed the optimum utilisation of all promotional media nor incorporated the complexities involved in banking processes.

Savaraiah and Thirupalu (1985) studied the background of RRBs, and their problems like the rising cost of operations and unconducive management-employee relations and suggested to expand the target groups, strategies for proper recruitment, development and deployment of manpower resources. Customers point of view about the functioning of RRBs remained missing in their study. Balishter (1985) attempted to examine the role played by RRBs in financing rural poor in community development in the blocks of Arawan of Mainpuri district, U.P. The study emphasised upon the increasing role of the banks in advancing loans and covering the weaker categories. He totally overpassed the profitability aspect of banks, without which rural development cannot be programmed on a long-term basis. Balaji and Rai (1986) attempted to evaluate the performance of 73 RRBs functioning in 130 districts in the entire country and concluded that advances made by them are greater than the deposits and also probed into the matters of growing overdues, continuous losses and branch licensing. They ignored few other aspects of banking such as rate of interest, banking staff and usage of promotional media.

Singh and Singh (1987) reviewed the financial performance of a RRB branch vis-a-vis rural branch of commercial bank and emphasised on income and expenditure pattern, profit or loss pattern, per employee performance and break even levels for deposits as well as advances. They stressed only on the financial aspect of RRBs while overlooking personnel and marketing spheres of a bank. In another study, Singh (1987) attempted to analyse the process of business planning in RRBs and dealt with the procedure of setting up targets including participation of RRBs, officials, factors considered while determining the targets and facilitating and hindering factors in the achievement of targets. He suggested that RRBs should review their staffing pattern at branch level so that lack of staff may not come in the way of achievement of business targets, except banking personnel he did not give due consideration to any other aspect of rural banking.

Sharma and Tomar (1987) assessed the performance of RRBs in India and concluded that major problems of these banks are the mounting overdues, lack of co-ordination with other rural credit agencies, lack of infrastructure facilities and profitability. They measured the performance only through credit deposit ratio and no other statistical tool was employed by them. Reddy and Rathna Kumari (1987) compared the credit-utilisation pattern of borrowers and association of personal and socio-economic characteristics with credit utilisation pattern of RRBs' borrowers and agricultural development branch of S.B.I. The study revealed that of all the socio-economic variables, education and extension contact were significantly associated with credit-utilisation pattern of both RRBs and ADM borrowers. No efforts have been initiated to outline whether customers banking needs have been fully addressed by RRBs or not, which is infact the main motto behind their establishment.

Khandelwal (1987), Ansari (1987), Khemani and Yerranraju (1987) covered various aspects of RRBs such as their historical development, objective, sponsorship, area of operation, salary structure, manpower planning, recruitment, promotion and training needs. Not even a single aspect of RRBs customer service has been mentioned and as such they have underestimated the significance of customers in running the bank most efficiently and efficaciously. Chabra and Taneja (1988) stressed the progress of RRBs, their viability and need for re-organisation and Savaraiah and Narmalamani (1988) evaluated the performance of Chaitanya Gramin Bank of Gaunter district of A.P., on the following grounds: Branch expansion, internal capital structure, credit deployment, loans outstanding, schematic lending and recovery performance. In order to test the significance of the findings, no statistical tool has been used.

Sanjeevaiah (1988) analysed the performance of co-operative credit societies, farmer's service societies and RRBs, the relevance of their credit policy, procedure and also studied farmers experiences in dealing with these institutions and examined their jurisdiction, management structure, status and concessions. He attempted to make comparisons between the above mentioned three credit institutions from management point of view but ignored the customer-satisfaction facets in their respective performance.

Bapna (1988) laid more emphasis on poor recovery and mounting overdues and suggested that in future RRBs have to mobilise higher deposits and increase adequately their lending business and take care of all current and future cost and that sufficient training should be provided to the RRB staff by various institutions such as BIRD, NABARD and CAB. He covered only financial and personnel sphere of RRBs and bypassed the importance of modern marketing concept in these banks. Hebbar (1989) highlighted various problems being faced by RRBs with respect to low interest on deposits, lack of adequate assistance from state government, inadequate and untimely repayment made by target group, mounting overdues, inadequate training facilites, lack of advertising programmes and difficulties in obtaining branch licences and stressed that RRBs staff should be well-rewarded for their efforts. He has not mentioned anything about the relevance of banking services to local conditions of the target market in rural banking. Balisther (1989), in his Ph.D Thesis, evaluated RRBs' performance in Agra district with respect to deposit mobilisation, advancing credit, growing overdues and their viability. Beside these areas, rate of interest, location of branches, promotional media have been overlooked by him.

Noorbasha and Jyoti (1989) attempted to analyse the financial management pattern of the Chaitanyan Grameen Bank, Tenali, A.P. with an object of assessing its impact on the bank's viability. He covered the financial result, cost structure, interest cost, profit ratios and spread ratios and ignored other major functional areas of management such as personnel and marketing management to evaluate the viability of RRBs. Sankaranarayanan (1990) viewed that losses incurred by many RRBs have been a matter of great concern among both rural bankers and policy makers and suggested that RRBs may be allowed to finance the non-target groups in their service areas. In order to judge the viability, he should have proned to the customers' needs and requirements.

Kalkundrikar (1990) in his abridged version of doctoral thesis, carried the case studies of two RRBs in Karnataka so as to throw light on the role of RRBs in economic development and emphasised upon the need to change the style of RRBs functioning and to adopt more dynamic schemes and policies. He has not specified clearly the policies to be initiated in rural banking. Moreover dynamic schemes must commensurate with the dynamic and everchanging needs and desires of the rural populace and effectively meeting them by suggesting customer-oriented strategies. A detailed analysis of the trend in the mobilisation and deployment of RRBs' funds is attempted by Noorbasha and Jyothi (1990). They opined that present position calls for a more cautious and efficient management of funds by RRBs in general and loss making RRBs in particular. Vijay Kumar and Gurunath (1991) collected the rural mass opinion about

RRBs, and their choice for credit assistance and opinion survey of viability problems in general. Survey was conducted in the state of A.P., Karnataka and Kerala. No statistical tool was employed by them to check the reliability and validity of the results.

Patel and Khankhoje (1991) emphasised the extension of the philosophy of economic liberalisation to financial liberalisation in general and banking sector liberalisation in particular. They focused on the liberalisation of regulatory and procedural framework of commercial banks but they couldn't suggest similar operational pattern for RRBs. Gupta and Singh (1991) investigated the problems of RRBs such as high cost structure, loans to target groups, rising overdues and absence of adequate patronage from state government and suggested that interest of weaker sections can be served only by responding to the changing needs of newly emerging society. They failed to cover few other problems such as inadequate bank staff, lack of funds to employ any promotional tool and greater dependence on sponsor banks.

Bedi (1992) in his doctoral thesis aimed to make a quantitative assessment of deterioration in economic viability of RRBs in Haryana and also looked into their performance, profitability, interest rate structure, credit ceilings and credit insurance etc. He has not worked out customers' requirements with regard to deposit schemes and location of the banks. Niranjan (1992) has taken into consideration important parameters to assess the operational efficiency of RRBs: Credit-deposit ratio, growing overdues and working results. He stressed on a permanent alternative remedy for attainment of RRBs viability and ignored other important areas such as coverage of districts, number of branches, deployment of credit and deposit-mobilisation.

Kothai (1995) pointed out the lack of rural exposure to banking personnel and emphasised on the careful and scientific manpower planning and diligent implementation of the plan, not only to develop business but to face competition in the field of banking. He covered only Human

Resource Development and ignored all other aspects of rural banking.

MARKETING ORIENTATION

Fox and Wheatly (1978) felt than in a marketing oriented organisation, all business activities begin with an attempt to understand the consumer. Enis (1980) said that in a marketing orientation concept, attempts are made to systematically determine customers' wants and to integrate organisational operations for producing products that satisfy these wants. Hughes (1980) opined that in a marketing orientation, all major product and promotional decisions should begin with an understanding of the needs of the consumers and further continued that business activities are organised into profit centres so that all activities are focused toward the market place.

Cundiff, Still and Govoni (1980) commented that in adopting a market orientation, management focuses primarily on the consumers' wants and desires and only incidentally on the product. They emphasised on using market research to remain in touch with market trends and developments. Leader and Kyritsis (1989) pointed out that market orientation starts by analysing what potential customers—who constitute a market-require and at what price and then attempts to systematically direct the organisational efforts towards meeting the customers' requirements.

Kohli and Jaworski (1990) analysed that in a market oriented organisation, three pillars of marketing concept (customer focus, coordination, profitability) are operationally manifest and continued that a market orientation entails:

(1) departments engaged in understanding customers' current and future needs and the factors affecting them; (2) sharing of this understanding across the organisation, and (3) departments engaged in activities designed to meet select customer needs. They concluded that market orientation refers to the organisational wide generation, dissemination and responsiveness to market intelligence. Narver and Slater

(1990) highlighted that market orientation is the organisation culture that most effectively and efficiently creates the necessary behaviour for the creation of superior value for buyers and thus continuous superior performance for the business and stressed that it consists of three behavioural components—customer orientation, competitor orientation and interfunctional coordination- and two decision criteria—long-term focus and profitability.

Stanton, Etzel and Walker (1991) documented that marketing orientation is based on three fundamental beliefs. All planning and operation should be customer oriented, all marketing activities in an organisation should be coordinated, and customer oriented. Coordinated marketing is essential to achieve the organisation's performance and objectives.

Kohli, Jaworski and Kumar (1992) opined that market orientation refers to the organisational generation of market intelligence pertaining to current and future needs of customers, dissemination of intelligence and organisational responsiveness to market intelligence and precised that it comprises three core themes: (1) a customer focus; (2) coordinated marketing, and (3) profitability. Jaworski and Kohli. (1993) reviewed that a market orientation appears to be facilitated by the amount of emphasis top managers place on market orientation through continual reminders to employees that it is critical for them to be sensitive and responsive to market development and concluded that inter-departmental conflict appears to reduce a market orientation, whereas connectedness appears to play a facilitative role.

Schiffman and Kanuk (1995) defined marketing orientation as the key to a company's survival, profitability and growth in a highly competitive marketing environment and its ability to identify and satisfy unfulfilled consumer needs better and sooner than its competitors.

Gupta (1992) in her dissertation estimated the level of overall marketing effectiveness in the public sector banking business and covered deposit portfolio, lending portfolio, miscellaneous services, quality of banking environment, and behavioural appraisal of human resources. She concluded that State Bank of India, Jammu has not created real marketing culture in its functioning, which has been confirmed by the lower overall marketing effectiveness mean value of 2.89 and suggested that a bank should adopt a marketing set up consisting of a complete marketing apparatus, market surveyors, information analysts and marketing consultants. Sharma (1995) reviewed marketing effectiveness (one of the parameters of marketing orientation) in American Banks and worked out that it is the critical evaluation of organisational marketing mix from customers perspective i.e., it measures the degree of managerial success in reading the market, distinguishing the business opportunities, choosing the best market segments and offering them superior goods and/or services at reasonable prices and finally maintained that each controllable variable (marketing mix elements viz. products, place, price and promotion) plays a vital contribution in the overall operational efficiency of a bank.

Kotler (1996) presented that companies are more likely to be hurt by changing customer needs and latent competitors than by their existing competitors and further opined that companies which manage a good balance of consumer and competitor considerations are practising a true market orientation.

Ross (1997) in his questionnaire framed out that a marketing oriented organisation recognises the importance of designing its activities to serve the needs and wants of selected markets; integrate and control the work of marketing management with management in other functional areas such as manufacturing ,purchasing, physical distribution, finance, accounting and personnel; conduct regular marketing research studies on customers, competitors and channels distribution; and finally expect that marketing thinking and orientation at the top is well communicated and implemented down the line.

All the authors and researchers, except Fox and Wheatly(1980), Hughes (1980) and Sharma (1995), didn't recognise the importance of marketing mix variables in a marketing-oriented organisation, in fact they emphasised on market orientation. Gupta (1992) and Sharma (1995) reviewed marketing effectiveness in public sector banks and American banks and all other studies reflected marketing orientation in organisations other than banking business. Thus such an absence of literature on the marketing orientation in rural banking necessitates the present study.

MARKETING ORIENTATION IN RURAL BANKING

Vaghul (1976) while analysing the services provided by commercial banks observed the delays in encashment and collection of cheques, issue of passbooks, chequebooks and drafts, sanction of advances etc. and concluded that customers' expectations remain unfulfilled. He further added that there is cold and impersonal attitude on the part of bank employees and suggested that employees have to be exposed to increasing interaction with clientele so that they develop a market-orientation and that the culture of customer centredness permeate throughout the organisation. Other banking needs pertaining to products, price, place and promotion have been undermined by him. Kshirsagar (1976) reviewed that a bank should have as many of its small size branches as possible in order to better fulfil the customers' needs and expectations and focused on customer centredness by giving few suggestions—timely and complete advice to customers on financial matters, regular execution of standing instructions, timely receipt of updated passbooks and statements, proper calculation of interest etc. Equally important are place, promotion, and employees training which he has not taken into consideration.

Varde (1976) observed that no initiative has been taken by banks in understanding the customers' needs and problems and in giving them advice on how to draw the best possible benefits from the banking schemes and services.

He rightly pointed out that in order to achieve customers satisfaction and long run profitability, banks should probe into the current and future needs of the customers and should devise ways and means to satisfy them. Menezes (1979) reviewed that information about the market is required by the bank on customer needs, benefits and further maintained that new services would have to be introduced after understanding the specific needs of the people that constitute the market and there should be direct involvement of entire staff in the marketing of bank services. He ignored the customers' needs with regard to price, place, promotion and processes involved.

Singh (1980) focused that there is no desire by the banks to look at services from a marketing angle and to experiment with dropping and/or modifying of unneeded and profitable services and concluded that first task of marketer is to find out precisely what is the consumer's need and then to design a suitable service or set of services to fill that need and therefore he should think in terms of pricing, advertising and selling the service. Customers' requirements in terms of location of the branch and the significant contribution of employees in fulfilling all their needs, have been bypassed by him.

Sarkar (1983) stressed that in order to achieve success in selling products, they have to be surrounded with people's expectations and bank should adopt an approach by which the wider expectations of the customers may be met and different means may be employed to meet them. The significance of bank employees in extending the services has been overlooked by him, without their due assistance, a bank cannot incorporate marketing concept in its operation for achieving long run profitability and customer satisfaction. Thingalaya (1984) outlined various steps to be involved in the marketing of bank services, such as: (a) identification of current and future needs of target customers and profile of customers; (b) development of product around those needs; (c) promotion of the product; (d) development of marketing training; and (e) forecasting and researching the future market needs. He pinpointed these steps with reference to the banks in general.

Pai (1987) reviewed various problems faced by the bank's customers such as: lack of courtesy at the counter, counter delays for routine transactions, no upto date passbooks, delay in issue of cheque books and clearance of cheques. Other pressing financial needs in relevance of products, place, price an promotion have been left altogether.

Venkateshwarlu (1987) highlighted that prime function of banks is the creation and delivery of customer-need service in a customer—satisfying manner and concluded that there is a need for personal contact between customers and the bankers in order to promote customer services and suggested on-the-job training for bank staff. But before creating and delivering customer need service, these needs have to be first explored and accordingly require a change in the setting of an organisation in the light of these needs. Mehta (1988) and Rao and Pathak (1990) commented that banker-customer relationship is a contractural relationship but, in actual practice, no written contract is made when a customer opens an account, they concluded that result is widespread ignorance among customers of their bank right and duties with regard to their accounts. Various needs of the customers in relation to four Ps of marketing-mix have not been dealt specifically and they have not clearly presided as to the absence of which needs, customers have become dissatisfied.

Mark (1988) highlighted that the basic bank marketing message is to give people what they want; the right product, at the right price, in the right place, at the right time and promote it instead of simply selling the products/services. The importance of competitors in the market has not been examined. Sometimes products, price, promotional tools have to be moulded in accordance with the competitor' strategies. Hebbar (1988) outlined that banks are the financial leaders of the society and they must learn about the society well enough to anticipate its real needs and meeting them satisfactorily which is the hall mark of successful bank leadership. What sort of needs have to be looked after, whether financial or non-financial has not been apparently mentioned by him. Further to develop bank leadership, employees should be imparted adequate training so as to lead the society and to furnish its needs efficiently and effectively.

Gupta and Torkzadeh (1988) suggested four marketing strategies for banks: (a) personal banking; (b) package banking; (c) market segmentation; (d) advertising. These strategies aim at providing products in accordance with the needs and expectations but do not incorporate consumer meaning before producing the products. These strategies focused on product-orientation instead of providing proper guidelines to marketing-orientation. Bhattacharyay (1989) reviewed that bankers are expected to provide satisfactory benefits through provision of form, place, time and ownership utilities in order to meet their customer needs and further exaggerated that market oriented banking will require a new culture, a disciplined, professional and committed manpower; employees trained for specialised services; strong marketing organisation in different banks; aggressive selling; meeting new customers' expectations; cost effective and efficient services. Customers expectations with respect to the interest rate structure of the bank have not been covered.

Madhukar (1990) stressed that for promoting business the bankers have to evolve the type of services which the customers need at reasonable prices and available to them at places easily accessible, as their interaction with the customers determines the spread of bank marketing and also the feasibility of market penetration. The vitality of the various promotional tools through which these products/ services can be made available to the customers has not been emphasised. Viswanathan and Seth (1991) commented that an understanding of the needs of customers in a dynamic environment is necessary and further expressed that banks should afford a sharper customer-need orientation to products so that a coherent and identifiable group of customers can accept one or more of banking products as being 'tailormade' for their use. Various needs of the customers in terms of products, place, price and promotional tools have not been clearly specified.

Bhatt (1991) in his paper indicated the relevance and application of marketing to Indian banking and market research activities undertaken by Indian banks and continued that marketing functions involve; market research, product development, pricing of the services and developing market-orientation and customer-consciousness through training. Customers' expectations with regard to the location of the bank and various processes involved in opening an account, getting a passbook and chequebook, encashment of cheques, depositing/withdrawal of cash etc. have not been covered by him.

Vyas (1991) in his thesis researched that bank marketing is concerned about taking proper advantage of the opportunities in the market by attempting to meet the needs of the customers as closely as possible by the organisation and this can be achieved by concentrating on four Ps of marketing mix and ignored the significance of bank employees in extending their services. Primary data in this regard has not been collected by him so as to make research more authentic and reliable and consequently applying of statistical tools would have further enhanced its utility. Javalgi (1992) opined that marketing mix and institutional characteristics, reflecting the essence of marketing mix that banks and other financial institutions offer, are the product dimension, pricing strategies and delivery of products to the customers. The necessity of employees training so as to make them well-versed with the banking products/services and thereby achieving all round customer satisfaction has not been emphasised.

Mandanna and Chengappa (1993) reviewed that major thrust of banking industry with respect to market strategy should be to widen the range of products-offered, quality service and to anticipate, identify, reciprocate and satisfy customers' needs efficiently, effectively and profitably. These observations have not been counter checked with first hand information from customers regarding their needs from rural banks.

Balasubramanian (1995) concluded that today 'banking' is a social marketing concept i.e., banking has to create: (1) Customer satisfaction (2) Longrun consumer and public welfare to satisfy the nation's goals and responsibilities and extended that a banker has to do the job of sensing, serving, and satisfying consumer wants, acting in the best long run interest of consumers, institutions and society. Contribution of employees towards the accomplishment of customer satisfaction and public welfare has not been focused. He over emphasised public relations at the expense of banks' profitability.

REFERENCES

1. Ansari, Mohd. Salman (1987), *Working of RRBs in Eastern U.P.*, Unpublished Thesis, Department of Commerce and Business Administration, University of Allahabad, 122-138.
2. Badne, G.C (1990), *The Changing Profile of Banking in India—Structure and Working of RRBs,* Yashwant Mahavidhyalaya, Maharashtra, 52-78.
3. Balaji, N. and H.L. Rai (1986), "RRBs: An Evaluation", *Indian Banking Today and Tomorrow,* March.
4. Balasubramanian, C.S (1995), "Bank Marketing and Public Relations", *IBA Bulletin,* Sept, 11-15.
5. Balishter (1985), "Role of RRBs", *Co-operative Perspective,* Oct.-Dec., Vol. 20, 19-27.
6. Balishter (1989), *An Evaluation of Performance of RRBs in Agra District of U.P.*, Unpublished Thesis, Dept. of Agricultural Economics, R.B.S. College, Bichpuri U.P., 1-35.
7. Bapna, M.S. (1988), "RRBs—Their Working and Growth", *Rural India,* Sept., 180.
8. Bedi, Suresh (1992), *Factors of Deteriorating Economic Viability of RRBs—A Case Study of Haryana,* Unpublished Thesis, Deptt. of Economics, Maharshi Dayanand University, Rohtak, 2-8.

9. Bhatnagar, Deepti (1983), "Diffusion of Banking Innovations and Communication Strategies for Rural Areas", *Prajnan,* July-Sept., Vol. XII, 196-97.
10. Bhatt, Atul (1991), "Bank Marketing, Market Research and Indian Banks", *Prajnan,* Vol. XX, No. 1, 53-54.
11. Bhattacharyay, B.N. (1989), "Marketing Approach to Promoting Banking Services", *Vikalpa,* Apr.-June, Vol. 14, 39.
12. Chabra, Trilok N. and Prem L. Taneja (1988), *Rural Banking in India,* Dhanpat Rai and Sons, Delhi, 130-138.
13. Chairmen's Conference (1980), "RRBs—A Report", *Prajnan,* Jan.-Mar., Vol. IX, No. 2, 195-200.
14. Cundiff, Edward W. Richard R. Still and Norman A. P. Govoni (1980), *Fundamentals of Modern Marketing,* Prentice Hall of India, New Delhi, 3rd ed. 19.
15. Enis, Ben M. (1980), *Marketing Principles,* Goodyear Publishing Co., Inc. California, 3rd ed, 47.
16. Fox, Edward J. and Edward W. Wheatley (1978), *Modern Marketing: Principles and Practice,* Scott, Foresman & Co. Glenview, Illinois, 10-12.
17. Gupta, Krishan, Gopal and Rajendra Singh (1991) "A New Look to Regional Rural Banking", *Khadi Gramodyog,* Sept., 461-464.
18. Gupta, Mamta (1992), *Marketing Effectiveness of Banking Services: A Case Study of S.B.I. in Jammu City,* Unpublished M. Phil. Dissertation, University of Jammu.
19. Gupta, Yashpal and Gholamreza Torkzadeh (1988), "Redesigning Bank Services Systems for Effective Marketing", *Long Range Planning,* Dec., Vol. 21, No. 6, 38-43.
20. Hebbar, A.R.K. (1989), "Problems of RRBs", *Yojana,* April, Vol. 33, 24.
21. Hebbar, C. Kusumakara (1988), "Bank Marketing Strategy in Commercial Banks", *Southern Economist,* Oct., Vol. 27, 17-18.
22. Hughes, David G. (1980), *Marketing Management,* Addison Wesley Publishing Co., 2nd ed., Philippines, 4-5.
23. Javalgi, Rajshekhar. G. (1992), "Marketing Financial Services to Affluent Consumer", *The Journal of Service Marketing,* Spring, Vol. 6, 33-44.
24. Jaworski, Bernard J. and Ajay K. Kohli (1993), "Market Orientation: Antecedents and Consequences", *Journal of Marketing,* Vol. 57 (July), 53-70.

25. Joshi, M.K (1984), "RRBs: Provisions and Review of Progress", *Financing Agriculture,* Apr.-June, Vol. 16, 15-21.

26. Kalkundrikar, A.B (1990), "RRBs: An Analysis", *Southern Economist,* March, Vol. 29, 17.

27. Khandelwal, Anil C. (1987), *Handbook on Personel Management and Industrial Relations for Rural Banks,* Rawat Publications, Jaipur, 61-63.

28. Khemani, C.L and B. Yerranraju (1987), *How and Why of Rural Banking,* Sagar Publications, New Delhi, 16-30.

29. Kohli, Ajay K, and Bernard J. Jaworski (1990), "Market Orientation: The Construct, Research Propositions and Managerial Implications", *Journal of Marketing,* Vol. 54 (April), 1-18.

30. Kohli, Ajay K., Bernard J. Jaworski and Ajith Kumar (1992)," A Measure of Market Orientation", *Journal of Marketing,* (Dec.), 3-4.

31. Kothai, Krishna (1995)," HRD-Rural Banking", *Economic Review,* March, Vol. 35, 11-12.

32. Kolter, Philip (1996), *Marketing Management: Analysis, Planning, Implementation and Control,* Prentice Hall of India, New Delhi, 8th ed., 241-42.

33. Krishnan, C (1980), "RRBs and Rural Development", *Yojana,* Jan., Vol. 33, 32

34. Kshirsagar (1976), "Improving Customer Service of Banks", *Prajnan,* Apr.-June, Vol. IV, 61-63.

35. Kumar, Naresh (1988), "Role of RRBs in Rural Finance—A Case Study of Eastern U.P", *Cooperative Perspective,* July-Sept., Vol. 18.

36. Lakshminarayana, V (1984), "RRBs-Problems and Prospects", *Financing Agriculture,* April-June, Vol. 16, 54-56.

37. Lall, G.S. (1984) "RRBs" Journal of Banking studies, July-Sept., Vol. VII, No. 3, 154-156.

38. Leader, W.G. and N. Kyritsis (1989), *Fundamentals of Marketing,* Hutchinson Education, London, 3-4.

39. Madhukar, R.K. (1990), "Dynamics of Bank Marketing", *Southern Economist,* Nov., Vol. 29, 43-44.

40. Mandanna, P.K. and P.G. Chengappa (1993), "Marketing Approach in Rural Banking", *Economic Review,* June, 6-8.

41. Mark, V.V (1988), "Deposit Mobilisation and Marketing of Bank Services", *Economic Review,* June, Vol. 33, No. 1.

42. Mehta, Ravi R. Singh (1988), "Banking Services; UK Examples", *Prajnan,* Apr.-June, Vol. XVII, No. 2, 235-39.

43. Menezes J.S. William (1979), "Marketing of Bank Service", *Prajnan,* Apr.-June, Vol. VIII, 135-137.

44. Naidu, *et al.* (1984)," RRBs in Andhra Pradesh—A Review", *Khadi Gramodyog,* Sep., Vol. 30, 502-508.

45. Narver, John C. & Stanly F. Slater (1990), "The Effect of a Market Orientation on Business Profitability", *Journal of Marketing,* Oct., 20-35.

46. Niranjana, N. (1992), "Operational Efficiency of RRBs in India", *Rural India,* Apr., 99-101.

47. Noorbasha, Abdul and M. Jyothi (1989), "Viability of RRBs—A Case Study", *Yojana,* May, Vol. 33, 18-21.

48. Noorbasha, Abdul and M. Jyothi (1990), "Funds Management in RRBs—A Case Study", *Yojana,* Oct., 1-15.

49. Pai, M.R (1987), "Customer Service in Banks", *Southern Economist,* Feb., Vol. 25, 21-25.

50. Patel, A. R. (1974), "Problems and Challenges of Rural Credit—A Case for Nationalised Banks". *Prajnan,* July-Sept., 391-409.

51. Patel, K.V. and D.P. Khankhoja (1991), "Liberalisation and Rural Development in India: Role of Banking Sector in the Changing Environment", *Prajnan,* Oct.-Dec., Vol. XX, No. 4, 379-97.

52. Patel, K.V. and N.B. Shete (1980), "RRBs: Performance and Prospects", *Prajnan,* Jan.-Mar., Vol. IX, No. 1, 9-11.

53. Podwal, S. and R. Bandyopadhya (1973), "Bank Branch Location in Rural Areas", *Prajnan,* Apr.-June, 163-186.

54. Roa, B.N. and B.K. Murthy (1981), "Five Years of RRBs—A Case Study," *Kurukshetra,* Jan., Vol. 24, 17-19.

55. Rao, K. D. (1980), "Some Planning Issues for RRBs", *Prajnan,* Apr., 01.

56. Rao, Nageswar and Pramod Pathak (1990), "Customer Service and Banks", *Yojana,* July, Vol. 34, 15-24.

57. Reddy, K. Negi and S. Rathnakumari (1987), "Farm Credit Utilisation—A Comparative Study of RRBs and ADB of SBI", *Southern Economist,* Feb., Vol. 25, 8-9.

58. Reddy, B. Dararadhami and M.Z. Hussain (1983), "Rural Banks in India", *Capital,* Jan., Vol. 189, 31-33.

59. Ross, Christopher A (1997), "The Practice of Marketing in Newly Industrialised and Developing Countries", *A Questionnaire.*

60. Sangwan, S.S. (1989), "Viability of Rural Credit Structure—A Case Study of RRBs", *Prajnan,* Vol. 18, 115-223.

61. Sanjeevaiah, B.C. (1988), "Rural Banking: A Comparative Study of the Performance of Rural Based Credit Institution Co-operative Credit Societies, Farmers' Service Societies and RRBs", Unpublished Thesis, Dept. of Commerce and Management, Banglore University, 01.

62. Sankaranarayanan, V. (1990),"Viability of RRBs", *Economic Review,* Mar., Vol. 35, 03.

63. Sarkar, B.K. (1983), "Bank Marketing for the Target Groups in the Priority Sector", *Prajnan,* July-Sept., Vol. XII, No. 4, 315-25.

64. Satya, Sundarsen (1984), "Strengthening RRBs", *Financing Agriculture,* Apr.-June, 22-24.

65. Savaraiah, G. and N. Narmalamani (1988), "Rural Banking for the Rural Milieu," *Indian Co-operative Review,* Oct., Vol. 26, 204-13.

66. Savaraiah, G. and N. Narmalamani (1985), "RRBs—Marching in Rural Development,", Khadi Gramodyog, Dec., 182.

67. Schiffman, Leon G and Leslie Lazer Kanuk (1995), *Consumer Behaviour,* Prentice Hall of India, New Delhi, 5th ed, 93.

68. Sharda, H.M. (1980), "A Study of RRBs", *Lok Udyog,* June, Vol. 14, 3-5.

69. Sharma, R.D. (1995), "Marketing Effectiveness in American Banks", *Prajnan,* Vol. XXIV, 149-156.

70. Sharma, S.C. and A.K.S. Tomar (1987), "Progress of RRBs in India", *Southern Economist,* Apr., Vol. 25, 15-16.

71. Singh, R.K.P. (1983), "Profitability of RRBs in Bihar",. *Indian Institute of Bankers,* Apr.-June, Vol. 54, 98-107.

72. Singh, R.K.P (1987), "Business Planning in RRBs,", *Khadi Gramodyog,* Jan., 192.

73. Singh, R.K. and K.M. Upadhaya (1984), "A Study of Loan Recovery of RRBs in Bihar", *Financing Agriculture,* Apr.-June.

74. Singh, R.K.P. *et al.* (1986), "Financial Viability of Commercial and RRBs in Bihar—A Case Study", *Indian Institute of Bankers,* Apr.-June, Vol. 58, 83-86.

75. Singh, Sampat P. (1980), "Unbundling Bank Services: A Problem in Bank Marketing", *Prajnan,* Jan.-Mar., Vol. IX, No. 2, 238-252.

76. Stanton, William J., Michael J. Etzel & Bruce J. Walker (1991), *Fundamentals of Marketing,* Mc-Graw Hill, Inc. 9th ed., 8.

77. Thingalaya, N.K. (1984), "Revamping Rural Banks", *Economic Review,* Oct., Vol. 30, 2-6.

78. Vaghul, N. (1976), "Employees Development for Efficient Customers Service", *Prajnan,* Apr.-June, Vol. VI, 172-75.

79. Vaishnaw, Bajranglal (1984), *RRBs in India—An Appraisal with Special Reference to Rajasthan,* Unpublished Thesis, Dept. of Commerce, Univ. of Jodhpur.

80. Varde, S.D. (1976), "Customer Service of Banks," *Prajnan,* Jan.-Mar., Vol. V, No. 1, 134-37.

81. Varde, Varsha, S. and Sampat Singh (1982), "Profitability Performance of RRBs", *Prajnan,* Oct.-Dec., 247-256.

82. Venkateshwarlu, P.K. (1987), "Customer Service in Commercial Banks", *Southern Economist,* Oct., Vol. 26, 5-6.

83. Vijay Kumar, M.N. and H.J. Gurunath (1991), "RRBs: An Analysis", *Southern Economist,* Mar., Vol. 29, 17.

84. Viswanathan, C. V. and Rajeev K. Seth (1991), "Changing Scenario of Bank Marketing: Challenges & Strategies", *Vichar,* Jan., 1-6.

85. Vyas, Vijayshankar (1991), "Marketing Management in Commercial Banks with Special Reference to Customer Service", *Dept. of Commerce and Management Studies,* Univ. of Jodhpur, 23-50.

86. Wadhwa, Charan D. (1980), "Rural Banks for Rural Development", *Prajnan,* Jan.-Mar., Vol. IX, No. 2, 203-209.

Chapter—3

Research Design and Methodology

The study of Marketing Orientation (MKTORIENT) in Regional Rural Bank (RRBs) has been carried out with special reference to Jammu & Kashmir and Punjab States of Northern India by selecting two such areas whose major agricultural activities, cropping pattern and socio-economic profile of the people represent by and large whole of the country covered under 196 RRBs. The various aspects of Research Design and Methodology are discussed as under.

NEED OF THE STUDY

Over a period of about 24 years of operation, RRBs have accumulated huge losses (Table 1.2). Even after the implementation of recommendations of several committees appointed by the government from time to time their operational efficiency and socio-economic impact invariably remained unsatisfactory. Apart from other factors these banks primarily lack adequate marketing culture in their workings (Kaur 1996; Sharma, Bandhu and Kaur 1998).

The extent of marketing culture has never been got evaluated on the basis of the judgement by the customers belonging to different demographic groups of both target and non-target markets of RRBs. Majority of the studies reviewed are conceptual in nature and few of them have been based on secondary information. The nature and extent of marketing orientation in RRBs remained untouched in the existing literature on bank marketing.

Thus, the aforesaid gap in the literature necessitated the present work. This work can prove to be an asset to the bankers, policy makers and the bank customers.

With the introduction of marketing orientation in RRBs, customers' needs would be given top priority which will ultimately enable the RRBs to earn long-term profits (Narver and Slater 1990) and to achieve their socio-economic objective. The greater the marketing orientation the greater the customer satisfaction and repeat business (Kohli and Jaworski 1990) which is necessary for making RRBs, viable.

SCOPE OF THE STUDY

The title of the study viz; "Marketing Orientation for RRBs in Northern India" refers to the extent and nature of marketing orientation in rural banks operating in Northern India. The extent of marketing orientation in these banks has been measured through likert's five-point scale ranging from the minimum of `1' to the maximum of `5' points within the framework of both McCarthy's model of four Ps and additional 2 Ps (Kotler 1996) of marketing mix in rural bank setting. The research findings can be generalised for the whole country where-ever similar conditions within the jurisdiction of RRBs exist. The term marketing orientation has been used interchangeably as marketing status/culture. Similarly product-mix, price-mix, place-mix,promotion-mix, people-mix and process-mix have been used synonymously as `product adequacy and its suitability', `price reasonability', `place effectiveness', `promotion optimality', `personal-selling efforts' and `procedural effectiveness.'

OBJECTIVES

The study aims at achieving the following objectives, beside the primary goal of measuring nature and degree of marketing orientation in RRBs:

1. To determine the level of marketing orientation in Jammu Rural Bank (JRB), Jammu and Shivalik Kshetriya Gramin Bank (SKGB), Hoshiarpur.

2. To measure the degree of marketing orientation in RRBs to be assessed by management and their customers belonging to different geographic and demographic profiles.

3. To know whether the basic rural banking product or service ingredients grouped under four Ps of McCarthy's marketing mix are equally important.

4. To study the customer satisfaction (marketing mix wise) within the framework of marketing orientation.

5. To suggest a suitable strategy for creating and enhancing marketing orientation vis-a-vis profitability in RRBs.

HYPOTHESES

The review of existing literature including the earlier research studies viz, "Marketing Orientation Strategy for Rural Banks" (Sharma, Desh Bandhu and Kaur 1998), "Nature and Extent of Marketing Orientation in Rural Banks" (Sharma, Desh Bandhu and Gurjeet 1998) and "Marketing Strategy to bring Jammu Rural Bank Out of Red" (Kaur 1996) has enabled to reach the following hypotheses for the study.

1. 'Average' level of marketing orientation exists in Jammu Rural Bank (JRB) whereas 'above average' level of marketing orientation prevails in Shivalik Kshetriya Gramin Bank (SKGB). This has been inferred from Kohli and Jaworski (1990) that the greater the marketing orientation, the higher its business performance supported with the fact that inspite of lower deposits and advances with SKGB its profits outshined that of JRB (Tables 3.1 and 3.2).

2. Demographic profiles of the customers effect the extent of marketing orientation (Gupta 1992) in RRBs.

3. All basic banking service ingredients under four Ps of McCarthy's marketing mix have important role in overall marketing orientation (Sharma 1996) in RRBs.

DATA COLLECTION FORMS AND GENERATION OF SCALE ITEMS

The study is primarily based on the primary information collected through systematic random sampling. A schedule for the data from bank customers and two questionnaires for the collection of needed data from top and middle management were developed within the framework of marketing orientation after passing the same through various stages of testing and refinement. Schedule used for the collection of data from customers (Annexure-I) related to demographic profile, 7 queries of general nature, 60 items on marketing orientation in the rural banks and 15 suggestions from the customers. The questionnaire administered to branch managers comprised of 42 items of 6 Ps and 24 suggestions regarding bank marketing mix (Annexure-II). The questionnaire administered to top management consisted of 50 queries of six Ps and 15 queries of general nature (Annexure-III). Apart from primary data, secondary has also been used to substantiate the current investigation.

Items covering all the six Ps of bank marketing mix were generated from the literature and through discussions with knowledgeable people. Some items were kept in negative form so as to have an internal cross checking. A five point likert scale (5 <...> 1) has been used for the questionnaires and schedule. The scale values of negatively worded items were reversed before data processing.

For tabulation, various elements such as income, education, gender profession and landholding have been divided into two parts; customers eligible and not eligible for major loans. Eligibility income limit for major loans was Rs. 11,000 p.a. Thus customers of the bank were primarily divided into two main heads target (having income below Rs. 11000 p.a.) and non-target (having income above Rs. 11,000) groups. On the basis of education, customers were segregated as being literate and illiterate. Landholding was bifurcated among small, medium and large farmers. Small farmers constituted holding of land below 2.5 acrs. Farmers having 2.5 to 5 acrs form medium farmers. Large farmers were those who hold more than 5 acrs. Separate analysis was done for male and female customers of RRBs. Lastly profession variable covered customers associated with agriculture and its allied activities.

PRETESTING

The aforesaid questionnaire and schedule used in the study have passed through several stages of frequent testing and refinement as discussed below-

Stage-I: The original two point scale (Yes/No) draft schedule for the collection of data from bank customers was tested in 1995 by administering it to 25 randomly (first at random and subsequently every 5th house) respondents out of 150 households from a small village viz, Basti Govindpura of Jammu district. The schedule consisted of four items of demographic profile and 25 queries relating to four Ps of bank marketing mix.

Stage-II: After making some alterations as per requirements, the schedule (Annexure-I) was transformed into 5-point scale and it was again tested in 1996 by administering it to 300 randomly selected (1st at random and subsequently every 3rd house) customers out of approximately 950 households from a comparatively larger village viz, Gho Manhasan of Jammu district. The schedule comprised of 9 items of demographic profile, 17 queries of general nature and 30 questions of specific aspects viz, rural banking schemes, interest rates on deposits and advances, branch location, fieldworkers, performance, bank employees behaviour and cash withdrawal/depositing formalities.

The form for the collection of data relating to attitudinal behaviour of management (Annexure-II) within the banking operational domain of marketing was tested in 1996 by administering the draft questionnaire to 20 such managers who had handled majority of rural banking operations of JRB. The questionnaire included 11 queries pertaining to general operation of rural banks (using multiple choice technique) and 11 questions (using 5-point scale) relating to rural banking deposit and advance mix, pricing policy, branch location, promotional aspect, bank expansion/diversification strategy, bank's profitability.

Stage-III: The schedule was again modified and tested in 1997 by disseminating it among 300 randomly selected (every 3rd household) respondents of the same village viz, Gho Manhasan. Beside the number of items in the aforesaid schedule (stage II), the present schedule incorporated 10 more items of specific nature relating to customer awareness about banking products and services.

The refined questionnaire after proper scrutiny was mailed in 1977 to 46 JRB branches operating in Jammu district but couldn't get positive response. Then questionnaire was circulated personally and got 24 completely filled questionnaires. 12 more items were added to initial form to obtain management opinion regarding various R.B.I. policies regulating banking operations.

Stage-IV: The original draft schedule after passing through three stages was finally tested by administering it to 60 randomly selected (every 2nd house) customers; 15 each from Chakroi and Dablehar of Jammu district and 15 each from Bassi Mustafa and Jandoli of Hoshiarpur district. The schedule comprised of 7 items of demographic profile, 15 queries of general nature, 40 questions of MKTORIENT in RRBs and 10 items of similar nature relating to commercial/co-operative/moneylenders pertaining to 6 Ps of marketing mix viz. simple banking procedures, adequate product line, convenient branch location, reasonable and motivating interest rates on advances and deposits, promotion of banking products, courteous and efficient staff.

After the aforesaid phases of testing and refinement both the questionnaire and schedule were administered to the respondents (800 customers and 41 managers) for the research work.

SAMPLE DESIGN

The entire sample of 800 respondents has been drawn from six independent geographical areas comprising three each from Jammu & Kashmir and Punjab States which have been purposely selected on the basis of available information under three groups viz, highly developed, developing and underdeveloped with the help of a draw of chits. Equal number of respondents (400 each) were contacted from both the areas. The villages of Jammu and Hoshiarpur districts have been divided into three heads mentioned above on the basis of the literacy rate, poverty level, per hectare yield and infrastructural facilities such as roads, electricity and schools and where a branch of RRB operates (Exhibit 3.1). From Jammu district; Simbal Camp (Highly developed), Sarore (Developing) and Jakh (Underdeveloped) and from Hoshiarpur district; Baghpur (Highly developed), Pandori Mall (Developing) and Ambala Jattan (Underdeveloped) got selected. The list of customers (Depositors and Loanees) of the RRB branches operating in these areas as on 31-3-97 was obtained from their respective head offices. The customers of Simbal Camp, Sarore and Jakh figured out to be 4645, 3310 and 2200 whereas the total customers of Baghpur, Pandori Mall and Ambala Jattan were 4179, 3275 and 2452. The approximate proportion of JRB customers of every selected branch to were discarded. After recognising the relative importance of each and every item, the factor loadings with less than 0.5 were also ignored.

Items of the schedule were designed in such a manner so as to cover six Ps of bank marketing mix but while analysing the factors, it was observed that many factors of six Ps contain one or two statements only. Thus in order to get more appropriate and relevant factors and to have more reasonable composition of various dimensions having strong perceptual loadings, 6 Ps were converted into McCarthy's four Ps, as such people and process are an extension of main four Ps Only. All the statements in schedule pertaining to rural banks were segregated and factors were computed separately for each 'P'.

In order to avoid duplication, items in the questionnaires, for managers (Annexure-II) and chairmen (Annexure-III), were manually reduced.

MEASUREMENT OF MARKETING ORIENTATION

Extensive pretesting of the schedule (Annexure-III) led to the determination of independent variable extracted from 6 Ps with considerable face validity (Tull & Hawkins 1993; Murray 1991). Thereafter two marketing experts and three specialists in rural banking undertook a careful analysis of the objectives and actual subject matter covered (Hanspal 1998; Beri 1993) which provided sufficient grounds for determining content validity. After the systematic evaluation of the contents of data collection forms, SPSS was used with the help of computer to simplify the data by reducing a large number of variables to a smaller manageable number of variables (factors) through interdependent statistical technique viz; Factor Analysis (Hanspal 1998; Sharma 1996; Tull and Hawinks 1993; Beri 1993; Zimkund 1988; Boyd, Westfall and Stasch 1988; Suprenant and Solomon 1987; Luck and Rubin 1987). The factors finally emerged were put under scree test so as to know which of them are contributing significantly to the total variance in the results obtained (Hanspal 1998). This test examines the graph of eigen values which stop factoring at the point where these values begin to form a straight line with an almost horizontal slope (Cattell 1952). The marketing orientation within its domain determined through the aforesaid procedure for RRBs, has, thus, been measured for each group, every MKTORIENT elements taken and also for the whole of the domain separately for each branch etc. in terms of arithmetic mean which varies from the lowest of one point to the maximum of five points (1....5). Thus the factors which finally emerged as the most important for the study were used to establish a relationship between MKTORIENT (dependent variable) and four Ps of marketing-mix (independent variables) with the help of multiple regression (Kohli and Jaworski 1993; Bellur 1987; Berry 1985) and subsequently the degree/strength of association between dependent and independent variables was worked out through co-efficient of determination (Tull & Hawkins 1993; Zikmund 1988). The reliability and validity of the findings were statistically rested with the help of t-test, F-test and convergent validity. A measure of a theoretical concept has convergent validity when it is highly correlated with different measures of similar construct (Sharma 1996; Chahal 1994; Rasotra 1995, Tull and Hawkins 1993). Convergent validity has been worked out by examining the nature of association between MKTORIENT scores and responses to two statements regarding 'overall performance' and 'service quality'. The ratings obtained on 5-point scale about these two aspects were converted to three points viz. Below Average (>3), Average (=3), Above Average (<3) to make interpretation more meaningful.

BRIEF PROFILE OF TWO RRBS SELECTED FOR THE STUDY

1. Jammu Rural Bank (JRB)

Jammu Rural Bank sponsored by the Jammu and Kashmir Bank Ltd., is operating in Jammu, Kathua, Rajouri and Poonch districts of Jammu and Kashmir State. It was established on 12th March 1976 and is one amongst three RRBs in the State.

1(a). Capital Structure

Authorised and paid up capital of JRB is Rs. 9.40 crores subscribed by the G.O.I., J&K Bank Ltd and Government of Jammu & Kashmir in the ratio of 50:35:15.

1(b). Branch Expansion

JRB has completed 23 years of its services in the field of rural development through the hallowing network of 92 branches in Jammu, Kathua, Rajouri and Poonch districts and 3 area offices at Jammu, Kathua and Rajouri. Two bank branches have been merged viz. Smote and Ghambir Brahmana in the year 1997-98.

Area-wise description of the bank branches-

Area	*Branches*
Rural	78
Semi-urban	12
Urban	2

District-wise position of the branches-

District	*Branches*
Jammu	49
Kathua	14
Rajouri	21
Poonch	08
	92+3 Area Office

1(c). Refinance

JRB has availed refinance to the maximum extent from NABARD, IDBI, SIDBI and in the year 1997-98 from sponsoring bank also. To avail refinance facility in an increasing manner, new schemes have been formulated under Non-Farm Sector (NFS) by the technical cell of the bank. These are:

1. Jammu Carpets
2. Bakers
3. Hand Printing
4. Pashmina Shawls
5. Dhaba Units
6. Bamboo Furniture
7. Denting and Painting
8. Winding of Electric Motors
9. Pottery
10. Electrostat Machines
11. Wheat Grinding and Cotton
12. Carding

The following new schemes were added during the year 1994-95:

1. Two Buffaloes scheme for district Rajouri.
2. Dairy scheme of three animals in district Jammu.
3. Mushroom scheme of 200 and 400 trays.
4. Fishery scheme for Jammu and Kathua district.

Refinance availed of from Apex Institution against sanctioned limit from 1989-90 onwards-

(Amt. in Lakhs)

Year	*NABARD*	*SIDBI*	*IDBI*	*J&K Bank Ltd.*
1989-90	49.50	—	4.00	—
1990-91	189.55	2.00	13.12	—
1991-92	78.21	1.00	—	—
1992-93	61.17	—	—	—
1993-94	111.26	—	—	—
1994-95	181	25.00	—	—
1995-96	234	25.00	—	—
1996-97	288.66	24.03	—	—
1997-98	471	89.00	—	560

Source: Annual Reports of JRB.

1(d). Resource Management

JRB monitors the balances in the current account with sponsoring bank and thus immediately get invested the surplus funds in the short—term deposits with the sponsoring bank with a view to earn maximum return.

Year	*Amount Mobilised (Rs.)*	*Interest Earned (Rs.)*
1989-90	2192	235.15
1990-91	2551	266.38
1991-92	3018	350.82
1992-93	3735	466.72
1993-94	4621.62	565.28
1994-95	5617.67	681.57
1995-96	9116.65	1039.05
1996-97	12717.38	1691.97

Source: Annual Reports of JRB.

1(e). Investment

JRB has started investing its surplus in debentures and bonds of 1995. It had invested Rs. 20 lakhs in 1995-96, Rs. 14 lakhs in 1996-97 and same amount (Rs. 14 lakhs) in 1997-98.

1(f). Deposits and Advances

Financial position of JRB as measured through deposits and advances, reflects an increasing trend (Table 3.1). Deposits have increased from 11.27 (1976) to 370.83 (1980), 1181.50 (1985), 2987.38 (1990-91), 8055.13 (1995) and 18002.72 (1998). Similarly advances have also increased from 2.49 (1976) to 192 (1980), 520.98 (1985), 1014.68 (1990-91) 1940 (1995) and 4026 (1998). But the compound growth rate of deposits and advances has declined from the beginning of JRB. The credit-deposit ratio has exhibited an uneven picture. It increased till 1978 and then started declining. It went up in the year 1983, 1985, 1989-90 and 1998. JRB has earned profits from 1976 to 1979 and 1996 to 1998. In between 1980 to 1995, it has suffered huge losses.

Table 3.1
Financial Position of Jammu Rural Bank

(Rs. in lakhs)

Year	*Deposits (Rs.)*	*Growth rate of deposit (Base-1976)*	*Advances (Rs.)*	*Growth rate of advances (Base-1976)*	*C.D. Ratio*	*Profit/ loss (Rs.)*
1976	11.27	—	2.49	—	22.09	+0.86
1977	72.57	543.82	23.32	836.55	32.13	+1.90
1978	154.07	269.74	90.45	502.70	58.17	+3.93
1979	259.82	184.61	150.70	292.62	58.00	+6.24
1980	370.83	139.50	192.00	196.33	51.77	–1.94
1981	480.90	111.85	228.00	146.80	47.41	–8.83
1982	638.03	95.95	298.01	121.99	46.41	–6.85
1983	766.53	82.73	367.20	104.90	47.90	–14.55
1984	974.58	74.63	381.44	87.57	39.14	—
1985	1181.50	67.69	520.98	81.07	44.09	–21.47
1986	1592.46	63.40	524.79	70.76	34.31	–18.29
1987	2091.06	60.78	633.45	65.46	30.29	–11.14
1988-89	2651.97	57.63	860.13	62.75	32.43	–23.66
1989-90	2987.38	53.61	1006.22	58.67	33.68	–12.57
1990-91	3513.63	50.71	1014.68	53.62	28.88	–25.30
1991-92	4116.25	48.20	1107.99	50.16	26.92	–114.00
1992-93	5017.78	46.40	1219.07	47.27	24.30	–137.52
1993-94	6142.19	44.87	1510.06	45.78	24.59	–410.52
1994-95	8055.13	44.07	1940.00	44.76	24.08	–112.77
1995-96	10211.74	43.10	2408.00	43.59	23.58	+6.30
1996-97	13696.28	42.64	2968.00	42.50	21.67	+25.27
1997-98	18002.72	42.08	4026.00	42.16	22.36	+507.70

Source: Annual Reports of JRB.

Table 3.2
Financial Position of Shivalik Kshetriya Gramin Bank

(Rs. in lakhs)

Year	*Deposits (Rs.)*	*Growth rate of deposit (Base-1983)*	*Advances (Rs.)*	*Growth rate of advances (Base-1983)*	*C.D. Ratio*	*Profit loss (Rs.)*
1983	12.99	—	16.74	—	128.87	+.80
1984	58.79	352.58	54.21	223.84	92.21	-.62
1985	202.31	294.64	168.73	217.48	83.40	-4.95
1986	4ǫ6.35	215.09	297.22	160.88	73.14	-3.57
1987	669.36	167.92	439.45	126.35	65.65	+1.17
1988-89	1082.15	142.18	681.71	109.88	62.99	+13.82
1990	1478.57	120.14	919.96	94.99	62.22	+22.50
1991	1895.60	103.78	11250.50	82.42	59.37	+13.91
1992	2394.72	91.96	1359.42	73.26	56.77	-4.55
1993	2968.72	82.85	1474.46	64.47	49.67	+·1.26
1994	3633.59	75.66	1569.19	57.47	43.19	-16.06
1995	4438.89	69.95	1696.65	52.18	38.22	-78.37
1996	5654.55	65.92	1933.26	48.55	34.19	+78.67
1997	6860.00	61.97	2282.26	45.95	33.27	+59.20
1998	8395.90	58.76	2594.75	43.37	30.90	+261.18

Source: Annual Reports of SKGB.

2. Shivalik Kshetriya Gramin Bank (SKGB)

Shivalik Kshetriya Gramin Bank (SKGB) was set up on 30th Mar., 1983 with its head office at Hoshiarpur and Punjab National Bank (PNB) as its sponsor bank. The bank is providing credit support and banking facilities to the different sections of the society and has completed 16 years to serve Hoshiarpur and Ropar districts of Punjab State. From last 12 years SKGB is also catering to the needs of Nawanshahar district.

2(a). Capital Structure

The authorised capital of SKGB is Rs. 5 crores; the subscribed and paid up capital is Rs. one crore contributed by G.O.I, PNB and Government of Punjab in the proportion of 50. 35. 15.

2(b). Branch Expansion

The total number of branches stood at 41 and one extension counter. Out of these 41; 22 are operating in Hoshiarpur, 17 in Ropar and 2 in Nawanshahar district.

The bank has relocated one loss making branch in the district Hoshiarpur.

Area-wise description of branches as on 31-3-98

Area	*Branches*
Rural	38
Semi-urban	2
Urban	1
	41

2(c). Refinance

SKGB is augmenting its resources by availing refinance from NABARD and PNB under various schemes viz., ST, (SAO), IRDP, SC/ST Action plan, NFS, Dairy development, Animal driven cart and Farm mechanisation.

Year	*Amount Availed (in lakhs)*
1994-95	1936.11
1995-96	2218.23
1996-97	2508.77

Source: Annual Reports of SKGB.

2(d). Investment

SKGB started investing its surplus funds from 1994-95 in government securities, debentures and bonds, Kisan Vikas Patra and C.D. of I.D.B.I.

Year	*Amount Invested (in Lakhs)*
1994-95	1344.50
1995-96	1867.10
1996-97	2821.56
1997-98	4051.75

Source: Annual Reports of SKGB.

2(e). Resource Management

SKGB manages the balance in the current account with sponsoring bank (P.N.B.) and immediately get invested the surplus funds in the short-term deposits with the sponsoring bank with a view to earn maximum return.

Year	*Amount Mobilised (in lakhs)*
1989-90	1173.75
1990-91	1338.75
1991-92	1690.00
1992-93	2136.25
1993-94	2523.55
1994-95	1797.60
1995-96	2461.11
1996-97	2652.91
1997-98	3201.66

Source: Annual Reports of SKGB.

2(f). Deposits and Advances

Growth rate of deposits and advances (Table 3.1) reveals a declining trend from the starting of SKGB. Similarly credit-deposit ratio declined from the beginning i.e., 1983 onwards. SKGB earned profits for nine years viz; 1983, 1987, 1988-89, 1990, 1991, 1993, 1996, 1997 and 1998 whereas it faced losses in the year 1984, 1985, 1986, 1992, 1994 and 1995. On an average financial position of SKGB is better (Table 3.2) as compared to that of JRB (Table 3.1).

CHAPTER SCHEME

The study has been divided into following eleven chapters:

In the first chapter inbuilt marketing orientation in Indian rural banking has been traced out alongwith brief profile of RRBs. The rural banking schemes of R.B.I. and/or G.O.I. addressed to the needs of the different sections of rural communities have not directly focused on marketing orientation in rural banks.

Second chapter included review of related literature, has been divided under three heads viz. rural banking, marketing orientation and marketing orientation in rural banks. Several studies have been conducted pertaining to Indian rural banking, marketing orientation, customer service and bank marketing. Very few studies have focused on rural bank marketing. These studies were not on specific cases and had not undertaken survey or employed any statistical tool i.e., these studies confined to conceptual analysis of rural bank marketing. As per the literature surveyed the absence of any work with regard to rural bank marketing orientation necessitated the conduct of present study.

Third chapter has been devoted to research design and methodology which included need of the study, objectives, hypotheses, sample design, data collection forms, scale purification, measurement of marketing orientation, limitations and brief profile of JRB and SKGB. The present work aimed at providing the required literature in the field to the bankers, policymakers and bank customers. With the introduction of marketing orientation in RRBs, customers needs shall receive top priority which will ultimately lead to long-term profits thereby enabling the institution to achieve its socio-economic objective.

Fourth, fifth and sixth chapters incorporated marketing orientation strategy for JRB in underdeveloped, developing and developed rural sectors of Jammu district.

Customers have been primarily segregated under two heads—target and non-target. Target customers of JRB residing in Jakh, Sarore and Simbal Camp have assigned 3.01, 2.89 and 3.07 scores whereas non-target customers have attributed 2.99,

3.13 and 3.06 values respectively towards marketing orientation in JRB. Thus non-target customers have exhibited higher satisfaction (3.06) as compared to their counterpart (2.99).

Similarly seventh, eighth and ninth chapters suggested marketing orientation strategy for SKGB in underdeveloped, developing and developed rural areas of Hoshiarpur district. Target customers of SKGB residing in Ambala Jattan, Pandori Mall and Baghpur have accorded 3.01, 2.9 and 3.24 scores whereas non-target group scored 3.18, 3.37 and 3.39 values respectively for marketing orientation in SKGB. Thus non-target customers of SKGB have displayed greater satisfaction (3.31) in comparison to target ones (3.05) towards marketing orientation in rural banks.

Tenth chapter worked out marketing orientation through a survey of management opinion. Managers of RRBs are quite optimistic with regard to marketing orientation in their banks as they have assigned 'above average' values to six Ps viz.,'Product adequacy' (3.49), 'Price reasonability' (3.94), 'Place effectiveness' (3.85) 'Promotion optimality' (3.84), 'Customer-personal relation, (4.10) and 'Procedural effectiveness' (3.84). Similarly Chairmen of RRBs have accorded 'above average' points on MKTORIENT scale towards products (3.58), price (4.06), place (3.78), promotion (3.63), people (4.36) and process (3.25) variables of bank marketing. Thus top and middle management of RRBs are quite satisfied with the level of marketing culture in rural banks.

Last chapter entitled, marketing orientation strategy for RRBs included findings, problems and suggestions for enhancing marketing culture in rural banks. Marketing orientation in RRBs is highest in case of developed (3.21) followed by developing (3.12) and underdeveloped areas (3.06).

LIMITATIONS

The present work has been carried out under the following limitations:

(1) Two RRBs whose branches were selected for the study were established on different dates i.e. JRB in 1976 and SKGB in 1983.

(2) Number of large farmers contacted as per research scheme was negligible and therefore they were ignored from the study.

(3) Due to the exclusion of some very significant items in the process of data reduction i.e., the items that should have been in the construct are neglected (Berry and Feldman 1985; Sancheti and Kapoor 1991), co-efficient of determination worked out was very less in almost all the cases.

(4) Since the number of target customers contacted figured out was very less in all the villages surveyed, multiple regression has been computed for total respondents and not separately for target and non-target customers.

(5) The level of development in a particular rural area where the extent of MKTORIENT has been worked out is not based upon empirical work. The status of an area has been considered on the basis of some parameters like poverty, literacy, per hectare yield and infrastructural facilities.

To some extent the aforesaid limitations have affected the findings of the study viz; had there been inclusion of those important items which have been otherwise neglected, higher co-efficient of determination would have been achieved and degree of association between MKTORIENT and four Ps of marketing mix would further have been strengthened. However, inspite of these unmanageable lacunae at individual level an effort has been made to maintain the validity and reliability of the research work. Therefore research in future ought to be initiated carefully in the light of the aforesaid limitations.

Exhibit 3.1
Brief Profile of the Areas Taken for the Study

Name of the rural banks and villages	*Jammu*	*Rural*	*Bank*		*Shivalik Kshetriya Gramin Bank*	
Brief Profile ↓	*Jakh*	*Sarore*	*Simbal Camp*	*Ambala Jattan*	*Pandori Mall*	*Baghpur*
Population	962	3472	6697	1486	536	3128
Households	228	604	880	282	98	309
Target Group	64%	33%	31%	38%	22%	16%
Literacy Rate	58%	71%	74%	68%	78%	82%
Per Hectare Yield	32qtl/hec	38qtl/hec	41qtl/hec	35 qtl/hec	51 qtl/hec	69 qtl/hec
Status of an area	**Underdeveloped**	**Developing**	**Developed**	**Underdeveloped**	**Developing**	**Developed**

Exhibit 3.2
Sample Design and Data Collection

Name of the village surveyed	*Name of the branches surveyed*	*Status of the branch*	*Total Houses in villages selected*	*Number of customers as on 31.3.97*	*Number of respondents contacted*	*Selection of the houses at random*
(1)	(2)	(3)	(4)	(5)	(6)	(7)
1. Simbal Camp	Simbal Camp	Health	880	4645	180 (9:21)	Every 4th
2. Sarore	Sarore	Average	604	3310	135 (7:21)	Every 4th
3. Jakh and Dhamore	Jakh	Sick	228 & 113	2200	85 (5:21)	Every 3rd
4. Baghpur and Sataur	Baghpur	Healthy	309 & 375	4179	175 (17:41)	Every 3rd
5. Pandori Mall, Dhalewal and Mirzapur	Pandori Mall	Average	98 86 & 106	3275	125 (13:41)	Every 2nd
6. Ambala Jattan	Ambala Jattan	Sick	282	2452	100 (11:41)	Every 2nd

REFERENCES

1. Bellur, V.V. (1987), *Marketing Research: Theory and Practice,* Himalaya Publishing House, Bombay, 33.
2. Beri, G.C. (1994), *Marketing Research,* Tata McGraw Hill, N. Delhi, 2nd ed, 312-316 & 139-140.
3. Berry, William D. and Stanley, Feldman (1985), *Multiple Regression in Practice,* Sage Publications, Inc. 1-2 & 25-26.
4. Boyd, Harper W; Ralph Westfall and Stanley F. Stasch (1988), *Marketing Research—Test and Cases,* Richard D. Irwin Inc. Illinois, 6th ed, 596.
5. Cattell, R.B. (1952), *Factor Analysis: An Introduction and Manual for the Psychological and Social Scientist,* New York, Harper.
6. Chahal, Hardeep (1994), *Cstomer Satisfaction in Public Health System—A Case Study of Jammu District,* Unpublished Thesis, Department of Commerce, University of Jammu, 46-47.
7. Hanspal, Savita (1998), *Lifestyles of the Middle-Class in Delhi-Implications for Marketing Strategies,* Unpublished Thesis, Department of Commerce, Delhi School of Economics, University of Delhi, 74.
8. Hotelling, H. (1983), "Analysis of a Complex of Statistical Variable into Principal Components", *Journal of Education Psychology,* Vol. 24, 417-441 & 498-520.
9. Kaiser, H.F. (1958), "The Varimax Criterion for Analytic Rotation in Factor Analysis", *Psychology,* Vol. 23, 187-2000.
10. Kohli, Ajay K and Bernard J. Jaworski (1993), "Marketing Orientation: Antecedents and Consequences", *Journal of Marketing,* July, Vol. 57, 53-58.
11. Kotler, Philip (1998), *Marketing Management: Analysis, Planning, Implementation and Control,* Prentice Hall of India, N. Delhi, 272.
12. Luck, David J. and Ronald S. Rubin (1987), *Marketing Research,* Prentice Hall of India, New Delhi, 542-43.
13. Rasotra, Poonam (1995), *Consumer Satisfaction in Insurance Service —A Case Study of LIC in Jammu Division,* Unpublished Thesis, Department of Commerce, University of Jammu, 31-32.
14. Sancheti, D.C. and V.K. Kapoor (1993), *Statistics—Theory, Method and Applications,* Sultan Chand and Sons, N. Delhi, 93-94.

15. Sharma, R.D. (1996), "MKTEFFECT: A Multiple Item Scale for Measuring Marketing Effectiveness in American Consumer Banking Through Customers Judgement", *Vikalpa,* Jan-Mar., Vol. 21, No. 1, 61-62.

16. Surprenant, Carol F. and Micheal R. Soloman (1987), "Predictability and Personalisation in the Service Encounter," *Journal of Marketing,* Apr., Vol. 51, 86-96.

17. Zikmund, William GG. (1988), *Business Research Methods,* College Publishing, Oriando, Dryden Press, 575-78.

Chapter—4

Measurement of Marketing Orientation in JRB with Reference to Underdeveloped Rural Area

BACKGROUND

This chapter has been designed to work out the nature and extent of Marketing Orientation in a RRB branch situated in an underdeveloped rural sector and the information has been collected from 85 randomly selected respondents belonging to the villages viz., Jakh and Dhamore of Jammu district falling within the operational paradigm of Jammu Rural Bank (JAKH). As on 31-03-97 Jakh had 962 population, 228 households, 64% households living below poverty line, 58% illiterate population, poor infrastructural facilities such as broken roads, frequent power cuts, no dispensary and Dhamore had 544 population with 113 households, 57% level of poverty, 69% literacy rate and just one government (middle) school (Exhibit 4.1). The branch Jakh had accumulated loss of Rs. 2.35 lakhs as on 31-03-97 (Exhibit 4.2).

As compared to other two branches of JRB under study, this bank has disbursed highest loan (Rs. 6.90 lakhs) as on 31-03-97 but since majority of the people are illiterate and live below poverty line, their intention before taking loan is to use it for private purposes instead of channelising into productive resources and not to repay it. Beside this still others are in a hope that government will waive off their loan, as a result of which this branch has accumulated huge non-performing assets finally making it a sick branch.

The research findings have been drawn from the data gathered from 85 randomly selected customers of JRB from the aforesaid area with as many as 60 statements within the domain of marketing orientation purified through factor analysis which finally resulted into 34 items, grouped under 15 dimensions (4 product, 2 price, 4 place and 5 promotion) of MKTORIENT (Table 4.0). The reliability of major factors contributing to the marketing orientation in rural banks has been counter checked through scree tests.

STATUS OF MARKETING ORIENTATION

Status of marketing orientation has been worked out on the basis of the responses extracted from the aforesaid sample customers (comprising 57 male and 28 female) of JRB living in the village JAKH. The level of marketing orientation has varied significantly among different sections of the bank's clientele falling in both target and non-target groups. Therefore the degree of marketing orientation in the given RRB branch has been studied separately under the following broad two headings:-

1. Target Group

It has already been stated that RRBs were established to meet the banking needs of rural masses particularly living below poverty line (Working Group 1975) but surprisingly the proportion of such beneficiaries of the given RRB branch has arrived at just 15% i.e., majority of the people are not availing of the bank services despite the fact that nearly 64% of the village population is living below poverty line.

Literate male small farmers belonging to target group engaged in agricultural activities have accorded highest score to 'place effectiveness'(3.78) (Table 4.1) followed by 'product adequacy'(3.33), 'price reasonability' (3.0) and lowest mean value went to the various aspects of 'promotion optimality'

(1.73) viz., 'frequent and effective promotional communication', 'fieldworkers promotional skill', 'promotion for high interest deposit and low interest need based loan schemes' 'adequate and educative advertisement for favourable changes' and 'personal involvement'.

Both literate and illiterate male non-farmers engaged in agricultural allied activities have given highest response to 'place effectiveness' (3.95 & 4.0), followed by 'product adequacy' (3.85 & 3.11), 'price reasonability' (3.09 & 2.0) and least score obtained by 'promotion mix variables' (1.94 & 1.27) i.e. 'prompt and result-oriented promotional communication', 'fieldworkers performance', 'promotion for interest focused and need based new schemes', 'sufficient and informative advertisements for frequent changes' and 'personal selling efforts'.

Literate female customers having income below Rs. 11,000 p.a. under agricultural allied activities, have assigned highest mean score to 'price reasonability' (4.0), followed by 'product adequacy' (3.93), 'place effectiveness' (3.78) and lowest score responded to 'promotional elements' (1.77) such as 'timely and efficacious promotional communication', 'fieldworkers promotional competence', 'result oriented advertisements' and 'face to face communication'.

Illiterate female non-farmers belonging to target group, have ranked 'place effectiveness' at the top (4.06), second rank accorded to 'price reasonability' (3.25), followed by 'product adequacy' (3.22) and last rank went to 'promotion-mix' items (1.5) viz., 'speedy and compelling promotional communication', 'fieldworkers promotional ability', 'promotion for new schemes,' 'educative and effective advertisements' and 'personal involvement in selling banking services.'

Fifteen dimensions of MKTORIENT grouped under four Ps of marketing mix variables segregated into three orientation regions of customer satisfaction within the framework of marketing orientation revealing the extent of MKTORIENT (Table 4.2) reflects that target customers of JRB are highly satisfied with regard to 'time efficient and hasslefree procedure', 'efficient and adequate bank services', 'accurate and timely passbook entries', 'timely information on new interest rates', 'convenient and nearest branch location', co-operative and informative employees', 'competent and efficient personnel' and 'adequate staff'. These customers have expressed average level of satisfaction with 'reasonable and attractive interest rates' and are least satisfied due to 'inconvenient purchase schemes', 'infrequent and ineffective promotional communication', 'absence of fieldworkers promotional skills', 'inadequate promotion for high interest and innovative new schemes', 'lack of adequate and educative advertisements for favourable changes' and 'lack of personal involvement'. Thus there is a need to maintain the present level of effectiveness with regard to all those rural banking services which have generated above average score and also more attention has to be given to those which obtained just average response or below average mean values on 5-point likert scale.

The proportion of the target market of the group under reference falling in different scales of marketing orientation (Table 4.3) reveals that two dimensions viz., accurate and timely passbook entries and convenient branch location have fallen in the highest range of MKTORIENT with as high as 92.31% and 100% of the sample respondents. Similarly the majority of respondents have given their ratings in the "3-4" range of MKTORIENT with regards to `adequate staff' (92.31%), "competence and efficiency of bank personnel' (84.62%), `co-operative and informative employees' (69.23%), and `timely information on new interest rates' (53.85%). Among the dimensions obtaining `below average' score, about 62% of sample respondents have valued the `responsibility and attractiveness of the deposit interest rates' between "2-3" region of MKTORIENT. The Table 4.3 has again confirmed the lack of marketing orientation in the said RRB branch with regard to the promotion of banking schemes. The majority of respondents have given poor values just between "1-2" scale of MKTORIENT to the `frequency and effectiveness of promotional communication' (92.31%), promotional skill of fieldworkers' (84.62%), 'adequate and educative advertisements for attractive changes in banking schemes' (69.23%), 'promotion for high interest deposits and need based loans' (69.22%) and personal involvement in the banking operations' (69.22%).

Similarly the 'time efficient and hasslefree procedure' and 'efficient and adequate bank services' have received more than average assessment score from respectively 53.85% and 69.23% of respondents but about 50% of respondents have rated one of the dimensions viz., 'convenient purchase schemes' as extremely poorly handled in terms of marketing orientation.

Overall marketing orientation in JRB branch as obtained from the level of satisfaction pertaining to four Ps of bank marketing mix among target customers arrived at 3.01 (Table-4.1). The highest mean score given to 'place effectiveness' (3.95), followed by 'product adequacy' (3.58), 'price reasonability' (3.0) and 'promotion optimality' (1.65). Thus among all the four Ps, promotion mix is the most critical one which demands greater attention in order to strengthen the overall marketing orientation in rural banks.

2. Non-Target Group

With the recommendation of Narasimham Committee (1991) to extend the rural banking services to non-target group i.e. the rural people living above poverty line, the number of non-target customers today has far exceeded the number of target customers. From the village under reference out of total sample of 85 customers, 85% of customers belong to non-target group, which implies that the target customers are either hesitant to avail of the RRB services or they are yet not properly educated to come forward for improving their socio-economic conditions through RRB system.

Male literate and illiterate small farmers having income above Rs. 11,000 p.a. associated with agricultural activities, have given highest score of MKTORIENT to 'place effectiveness' (3.94 & 3.83) ((Table 4.1) followed by 'product adequacy' (3.0 & 3.17), 'price reasonability' (2.88 & 2.75) and 'promotion optimality' scored less than average mean values (1.86 & 1.55) for the items such as 'frequent and effective promotional communication', 'fieldworkers promotional aptitude', 'promotion for interest emphasising new schemes', 'efficacious and informative advertisements' and 'interaction with customers'.

Male literate and illiterate non-farmers belonging to non-target group engaged in activities allied to agriculture have assigned higher mean values to 'place effectiveness' (4.04 & 4.07), followed by 'product adequacy' (3.66 & 3.63), 'price reasonability' (3.01 & 3.25), and lowest mean score awarded to the 'promotional variables' (1.76 & 1.64) viz., 'recurrent and effective promotional communication', 'fieldworkers promotional expertise', 'high interest deposit and need based loan schemes', 'competent and productive advertisements' and 'face to face communication'.

Female literate and illiterate non-farmers who have taken loan for various activities allied to agriculture have shown their highest satisfaction with regard to 'place mix' (3.98 & 3.98), followed by 'product mix' (3.81 & 2.52), 'price mix' (3.11 & 2.25) and less than average value obtained by the elements of 'promotion mix' (1.75 & 1.80) viz., 'continual and operative promotional communication', fieldworkers promotional proficiency', 'promotion for interest exhibiting new schemes', 'adequate and informative advertisements' and 'personal involvement in banking services'.

Literate male medium farmers belonging to non-target group engaged in agricultural business have shown highest satisfaction with respect to 'place effectiveness' (3.56), less than average score obtained by 'product adequacy' (2.67), 'price reasonability' (2.50) and 'promotion optimality' (1.82), whereas its illiterate counterpart have accorded highest mean value to 'place mix' (4.44), followed by 'price mix' (4.25), 'product mix' (4.11) and less than 3 point on MKTORIENT scale to 'promotion mix' (2.18). Thus both categories of customers have assigned less than average mean score to 'promotional aspects' of rural banking which include 'convincing promotional communication.' 'fieldworkers promotional efficiency', 'promotion for new schemes', 'requisite and instructive advertisements' and 'personal participation in banking services.'

Literate male landless customers under agricultural allied activities have reflected their highest satisfaction with regard to 'place mix' (3.94), followed by 'product mix' (3.59), 'price mix' (2.84) and 'promotion mix' (1.75), whereas illiterate respondents of this category have assigned equal mean values (3.67) to 'product and place mix', average mean score to 'price mix' (3.0) and the lower mean value to 'promotion mix' (1.91).

Thus both type of customers have given less than average score to the 'promotion mix' variables which incorporate 'result-oriented promotional communication', 'fieldworkers promotional intelligence', 'promotion for new schemes', 'sufficient and 'informative advertisements' and 'field selling efforts.'

Illiterate female non-farmers belonging to non-target group have reflected above average satisfaction so far as 'place and product variables' (3.63 & 3.21) are concerned, where as 'price variable' has generated below average (2.78) score on MKTORIENT scale and they feel highly dissatisfied with respect to 'promotional variables' (1.64) viz., 'persistent and effective promotional communication', 'fieldworkers promotional ability', 'interest focused and motivating new schemes', 'competent and effective advertisements' and 'personal selling banking schemes'.

Marketing orientation dimensions grouped under 4 Ps of marketing mix elements divided into two orientation regions of customer satisfaction within the paradigm of MKTORIENT (Table 4.4) exhibits that non-target customers of JRB have given 'above average' response to the eight dimensions, viz., 'time efficient and hasslefree procedure', 'efficient and adequate bank services', 'accurate and timely passbook entries', timely information on new interest rates,' 'convenient and nearest branch location', 'co-operative and informative employees', 'competent and efficient personnel' and 'adequate staff. These customers are least satisfied due to 'inconvenient purchase schemes,', 'unreasonable and unattractive interest rates', in 'frequent and ineffective promotional communication', 'absence of fieldworkers promotional calibre', 'inadequate promotion for interest oriented new schemes', 'lack of adequate and educative advertisements' and 'impersonal selling of banking schemes.' Thus there is a need to suggest two types of strategies—one, maintenance strategy for dimensions which scored 'above average' and second, improvement strategy for dimensions falling 'below average' on 5-point likert scale.

The number of non-target customers falling in different regions of MKTORIENT (Table 4.5) reflects that three dimensions viz., 'accurate and timely entries of passbook', 'convenient and nearest branch location' and 'co-operative and informative employees' have fallen in the highest range of marketing orientation with 73.61%, 98.61% and 58.33% of the sample customers. Alike the majority of respondents have given their high scores falling in the "3-4" range of MKTORIENT with respect to 'competent and efficient personal' (79.17%), 'adequacy of staff' (66.67%), 'timely information on new interest rates' (61.12%), 'efficiency and adequacy of banking services' (52.78%). 50% of this category of customers have fallen in the aforesaid range with regard to 'time efficient and hasslefree procedure'. Further among the dimensions generating below average score, about 75% of samples respondents have valued the 'convenient purchase schemes' and 68.66% have scored the 'reasonability and attractiveness of the deposit interest rates' between "2-3" region of MKTORIENT. Lastly, like target customers, non-target ones have also shown their dissatisfaction regarding all the dimensions of 'promotion mix' i.e., 'frequent and effective promotional communication' (97.22), 'personal involvement' (95.83%), 'fieldworkers promotional competence' (91.66%), 'adequate and educative advertisements' (77.78%) and 'promotion for interest centred new schemes' (65.28%). This indicates that strong strategic action is most desirable for 'promotion-mix' aspect of bank marketing mix.

Overall marketing orientation, as worked out on the basis of responses obtained from non-target customers towards 4 Ps of 'bank marketing mix' came out to be 2.99 which is below average on MKTORIENT scale. This category of customers have given highest mean value to 'place effectiveness' (3.89), followed by 'product adequacy' (3.35), 'price reasonability' (2.95) and 'promotion optimality' (1.77) (Table 4.1).

On the basis of the responses gathered from both 'target and non-target customers' towards various rural banking services of JRB residing in the village JAKH, the overall MKTORIENT worked out to be 2.996. They have accorded highest mean score to 'place mix' (3.92), followed by 'product mix' (3.38), 'price mix' (2.96) and 'promotion mix' (1.73). Thus both price and promotion mix have generated below average mean value on the likert scale which requires careful attention of both management and policy-makers towards these two aspects of rural banking in order to enhance the overall marketing orientation in these banks.

The relationship between rural banks marketing orientation and fifteen dimensions in the construct grouped under four Ps of marketing mix established with a statistical technique of multiple regression is as under:

$$\begin{aligned}\text{MKTORIENT} = {} & 3.142 - .057(\text{PRDMEAN1}) + .032(\text{PLAMEAN4}) \\ & + .307(\text{PRMMEAN1}) - .031(\text{PRMMEAN2}) - \\ & .031(\text{PRMMEAN3}) - .135(\text{PRMMEAN4}) - \\ & .029(\text{PRMMEAN5}) + .021(\text{PRDMEAN2}) - \\ & .959(\text{PRDMEAN3}) + .217(\text{PRDMEAN4}) + \\ & .074(\text{PRIMEAN1}) + .131(\text{PRIMEAN2}) + \\ & .572(\text{PLAMEAN1}) - .205(\text{PLAMEAN2}) - \\ & .111(\text{PLAMEAN3}).\end{aligned}$$

The regression equation indicates that marketing orientation is both positively and negatively associated to different dimensions of 4 Ps. The result in terms of the relative importance of fifteen dimensions in predicting the overall marketing orientation indicates that first dimension of place mix is the most critical one. Next two ranks in order of merit have gone to first dimension of promotion mix and fourth dimension of product mix. Third dimension of product mix appears to be least important (-.959). Steps have got to be initiated in a manner that not only ensuring the present level of marketing orientation with regards to such dimensions which have obtained positive values but also to revert the negative situations regarding such variables which have obtained negative level of marketing orientation into positive one.

VALIDITY AND RELIABILITY OF DATA

'Service quality' and 'overall performance' have been converged with the other important aspects of marketing orientation (Table 4.12). Marketing Orientation, which arrived at 2.996 (Table 4.1), has been proved convergently valid as majority of JRB customers have fallen under 'average' region of service quality (79%) and overall performance (78%) by assigning 2.89 and 2.91 values respectively.

Multiple correlation (R) between independent and dependent variables worked out to be .57 which implies high degree of association between marketing orientation and four Ps of bank marketing mix. The value of coefficient of determination (R^2) figured out to be .32 which indicates that 32% of the variation in marketing orientation can be explained by four variables in the linear equation. Residual being the result of two reasons: first is the non-linearity between dependent and independent variables (Berry & Feldman 1985; Myer 1990); it may be stated that linear model applied here cannot give due cognizance to the curvilinear relationship; and/or second is the exclusion of some very important variables i.e., one or more variables that should have been in the model are omitted (Berry & Feldman 1985; Sancheti Kapoor 1991), which lays down the scope for further research in future. Moreover it is difficult to answer (in social sciences) as to what is an acceptable values of R^2 (Myer 1990).

Since the calculated value (2.14) of 'F' is smaller than the tabulated value (2.42) at 1% level of significance (df_{v1v2} 13,84) so the hypothesis of equality of 15 dimensions is accepted. Thus these dimensions have equal impact on overall marketing orientation.

Further the values of 't' were tested both at 1% and 5% level of significance (df_{v1} 13). Except for the fourth dimension of product mix, second dimension of price mix and first dimension of place mix; all other 12 dimensions have not fallen in the ejection region at 1% level of significance (3.012) whereas all the 15 dimensions have fallen in the acceptance region at 5% level of significance (2.160). This reflects that all the factors of four Ps have their significant contribution in the computation of bank marketing orientation at 5% level of significance.

STRATEGIC ACTION

The extent of marketing orientation in JRB branch, under reference, worked out here (Table 4.1) indicates three types of strategies for creating marketing culture in the working of RRBs.

The first type of strategic action emerging from the findings is such a marketing plan which not only retains the present level of MKTORIENT regarding those aspects where target and non-target customers of JRB enjoy 'above average' score of orientation but also to take it to the highest possible level on MKTORIENT scale. Accordingly strategies have been suggested for target and non-target groups on the basis of their responses towards four Ps of marketing mix.

54.01% customers contacted have shown their satisfaction towards 'time efficient and hasslefree procedure' but the ramaining customers feel some complicacies while withdrawing cash and availing loan schemes. Thus R.B.I. should reduce the number of formalities involved in obtaining loans so that the hesitant customers would also think of getting loan services from RRBs (Bhatnagar 1983).

Majority of JRB customers (74.21%) find rural banks' services quite efficient and adequate but in order to attain greater satisfaction, the present number of deposit schemes should be increased and thus few more deposit schemes tailored to the requirements of rural masses should be introduced (Mandanna & Chegappa 1993).

More than 95% customers opine accurate and timely passbook entries, which indicate good moral relationship between rural customers and banker. In future as well bank employees should try to maintain their customers faith by passing accurate and upto date entries at the time of deposit or withdrawal of cash (Kshirsagar 1976).

Majority of the customers (64.59%) responded that bank employees provide quick information regarding new interest rates. Further efforts should be made to increase their number by extending this type of services (Hebbar 1988) to those who have given 'below average' response toward it.

All the customers contacted (85) have given 'above average' response to 'convenient branch location.' Thus it may be concluded that there is no need of shifting these branches to any other places as these are always located within accessible limits of the people residing in the villages where branches are situated.

More than 90% sample customers have shown favourable attitude towards bank employees personal behaviour. Thus employees should keep on extending their wholehearted co-operation by also providing effective non-monetary services.

82% of the customers contacted opine that reasonable market operates around branch location and bank employees are quite competent in handling their services. Requisite training should be imparted to bank staff, so as to make themselves capable of rendering banking services more efficiently and effectively (Bapna 1988).

Maximum customers (82.96%) find adequate and satisfactory bank staff and thus they are of the view that present number of employees can successfully undertake the operations of rural banks. Suitable rewards should be given for the outstanding performance of employees (Hebbar 1989).

The second type of marketing strategy requires improvement in the present level of marketing orientation about all those items where JRB obtained 'average level' of orientation. Only one factor viz., 'reasonable and attractive interest rates' falling in the average region (Table 4.2) necessitates rectification in the present working of rural banks. Thus there is a need to revise the present interest rate structure in accordance with the socio-economic status of rural masses. Moreover in order to face growing competition (Menezes 1979), RRBs should provide more interest on deposits and charges less on advance than other banks operating in rural areas.

The third type of strategic action arising from the main result is the immediate attention of the policy-makers and administrators towards all those aspects of marketing mix which scored 'below average' level of orientation. One aspect of product mix viz., 'convenient purchase of assets through bank finance and all items of promotion mix require special care to achieve better customer satisfaction and long run profitability'.

75% samples customers observed inconvenient purchase of assets through rural banks and thus found some difficulties in procuring assets through bank finance. So far as possible rural illiterate customers should be provided with full co-operation in getting products through rural banks.

Almost all the customers have shown their dissatisfaction towards ever employment of any advertising media for the promotion of rural banking services. Thus there is an urgent desire to promote banking schemes and interest rates through television, radio, newspapers and magazines, in order to attract majority of rural people to avail rural banking services. Sponsoring banks should undertake joint advertising programme in order to make RRBs and their services more prominent and well known in the rural areas (Hebbar 1989).

More than 90% sample customers have exhibited their dissonance towards 'fieldworkers performance'. According to them fieldworkers never motivated them to avail banking services. Thus fieldworkers should be provided with adequate field training and be equipped with requisite information in order to promote banking schemes (Mandanna & Chengappa 1993).

Approximately 70% of customers contacted viewed that employees of rural bank had never co-operated in educating them about new schemes and interest rates unless they ask themselves. Thus better tools, equipments, manpower and incentives should be provided to motivate the employees for such a co-operation (Vijaykumar & Gurunath 1991).

92.68% JRB customers residing in the village, under reference, have strongly disagreed towards the conduct of any customer awareness meet, thus in order to create consciousness among rural masses, customer banker meeting would be an appropriate step (Pai 1987) and would prove to be quite productive for both the parties.

REFERENCES

1. Bapna, M.S. (1988), "RRBs: Their Working and Growth", *Rural India,* Sept., 180.
2. Berry William. D and Stanley. Feldman (1985), *Multiple Regression in Practice,* Sage Publication, Inc., 1-2 & 25-26.
3. Bhatnagar, Deepti (1983), "Diffusion of Banking Innovations and Communications Strategies for Rural Areas", *Prajnan,* July-Sept., Vol. XII, 205.
4. Hebbar, C. Kusumakara (1988), "Bank Marketing Strategy in Commercial Banks", *Southern Economist,* Oct., Vol. 27, 18.
5. Hebbar, A.R.K (1989), "Problems of RRBs", *Yojana,* April, Vol. 33, 24.

6. Hundekar, S.G (1991), "Rural Banking Scenario", *Khadi Gramodyog,* June, 341.

7. Kshirsagar (1976), "Improving Customers Services of Banks", "*Prajnan,* Apr.-June, Vol. VI, 155.

8. Manadanna, P.K and P.G. Chengappa (1993), "Marketing Approach in Rural Banking", *Economic Review,* June, 6.

9. Menezes, J.S. William (1979), "Marketing of Bank Services System Approach to Business Planning and Performance Evaluation", *Prajnan,* Apr.,-June, Vol. VIII, 135.

10. Myer, Raymond H. (1990), *Classical and Modern Regression with Applications,* PWS-Kent Publishing Co., Boston, 2nd ed., 37.

11. Pai, M.R. (1987), "Customer Services in Banks", *Southern Economist,* Feb., Vol. 25, 21.

12. Sancheti, D. C and V. K. Kapoor (1993), *Statistics—Theory, Methods and Applications,* Sultan Chand and Sons, N. Delhi, 93-94.

13. Vijaykumar, M.N and H.J. Gurunath (1991), "R.R.Bs: An Analysis", *Southern Economist,* Mar., Vol. 22, 17.

14. Working Group, *Report of the Committee on Rural Banks,* (1975), G.O.I.

Exhibit 4.1
Brief Profile of the Villages viz., Jakh and Dhamore of Jammu District as on 31-03-97

	Jakh	*Dhamore*
(1) Total Population	962	544
(2) Male; Female	57:43	61:39
(3) Total Households	228	113
(4) Poverty	64%	57%
(5) Literacy	58%	69%
(6) Infrastructural facilities:		
(a) Roads	Broken	Muddy
(b) Electricity	Frequent power cuts	Low voltage
(c) Govt. School	Two	One
(d) Private School	Three	
(7) Land soil suitable for growing wheat and maize.		
(8) Per Hectare Yield		
	Irrigated	*Non-Irrigated*
Wheat	32 qtl/hec	18 qtl/hec
Maize	—	18 qtl/hec.

Exhibit 4.2
Brief Profile of the Branch Jakh of JRB

(Rs. in '000)

Year	*Deposits*		*Advances*		*Profit*	*C.D. Ratio*
	A/C	*Rs*	*A/C*	*Rs*	*(Rs.)*	
1992-93	2413	7102	245	4021	-351.83	57
1993-94	2559	8354	275	4511	-445.87	54
1994-95	2671	10289	301	5359	-158.10	52
1995-96	2402	12042	304	5793	-115.89	48
1996-97	2821	16114	328	6646	-235.78	41
1997-98	3158	23013	351	7957	-218.14	35
1998-99	3239	25744	353	8753	+80.17	34

(a) Four branches of other banks at a distance of 6 kms.

(b) Number of Projects financed;

	1996-97	*1997-98*
(i) Retail Trade	19	6
(ii) Dairy	10	9
(iii) Mules & Ponies	2	2

Table 4.0
Summary of Results from Scale Purification—Loading and Variance Explained

Bank Marketing Mix	*Factor-Wise Dimension*	*Factor Loadings*	*% of Variance Explained*
1	2	3	4
Product	**Factor First-**		**32.9**
	Loan procedure easy even to a layman.	.86	
	Simple loan formalities.	.86	
	Comfortable loan security and guarantee.	.84	
	Quick withdrawal facilities.	.49	
	Factor Second-		**18.4**
	Sufficient number of deposit scheme.	.92	
	Bank proves to be a good prime bank.	.90	
	Factor Third-		**16.0**
	Easy repayment of instalments.	.93	
	Convenient purchase of assets through bank finance.	.92	
	Factor Fourth-		**11.1**
	Timely updating of pass-books.	.90	
	Accurate pass-book entries.	.87	
	Total variance explained = 78.4%.		
Price	**Factor First-**		**53.1**
	Motivating deposit interest rates.	.94	
	Attractive & adequate interest rates.	.94	
	Reasonable loan interest rates.	.52	
	Factor Second-		**25.5**
	Quick information regarding new interest rates.	.94	
	Total variance explained = 78.6%		
Place	**First Factor**		**27.2**
	Convenient branch location.	-.92	
	Nearest location.	.86	

Contd. . .

1	2	3	4
	Branch location of hitherto unbanked areas.	.83	
	Factor Second-		**18.4**
	Co-operative and friendly employees.	.87	
	Reasonable market around the location.	.74	
	Factor Third-		**14.3**
	Competent and efficient employees.	.73	
	Reasonable market around the location.	.65	
	Factor Fourth-		**11.2**
	Adequate bank's staff.	.83	
	Satisfactory present bank's staff.	.72	
	Total variance explained = 71.1%.		
Promotion	**Factor First-**		**25.7**
	Frequent advertisements.	-.82	
	Effective T.V. & Radio ads.	.75	
	Heavy promotion through newspapers and magazines.	.64	
	Promotion of schemes through attractive posters.	-.63	
	Factor Second-		**17.7**
	Fieldworkers convincing skills.	.93	
	Promotion through fieldworkers.	.91	
	Factor Third-		**13.9**
	Employees co-operation in educating clients about new interest rates.	.94	
	Employees co-operation in educating clients about new schemes.	.93	
	Factor Fourth-		**12.7**
	Customer awareness meets.	.82	
	Heavy ads of new interest rates.	.74	
	Factor Fifth-		**9.4**
	Promotion through personal involvement.	.87	
	Total variance explained = 79.4%		

Table 4.1
Overall Marketing Orientation—Customers Assessment

				Education										Overall Mean				
				LITERATE					ILLITERATE									
Income	*Land Holding*	*Gender*	*Occupation*	*A*	*B*	*C*	*D*	*M*	*A*	*B*	*C*	*D*	*M*	*A*	*B*	*C*	*D*	*M*
	Small Farmers	Male	Agriculture	3.33	3.0	3.78	1.73	2.96	-	-	-	-	-	3.33	3.0	3.78	1.73	2.96
Target Group	Male		Allied to Agriculture	3.85	3.09	3.95	1.94	3.21	3.11	2.0	4.0	1.27	2.60	3.48	2.55	3.98	1.61	2.91
	Female		Allied to Agriculture	3.93	4.0	3.78	1.77	3.37	3.22	3.25	4.06	1.50	3.01	3.58	3.63	3.92	1.64	3.19
	Target Group Mean			3.70	3.36	3.84	1.81	3.18	3.17	2.63	4.03	1.39	2.81	3.44	3.0	3.95	1.65	3.01
	Small Farmers	Male	Agriculture	3.0	2.88	3.94	1.86	2.92	3.17	2.75	3.83	1.55	2.83	3.08	2.81	3.89	1.70	2.87
Non-Target Group	Male		Allied to Agriculture	3.66	3.01	4.04	1.76	3.12	3.63	3.25	4.07	1.64	3.15	3.64	3.13	3.05	1.70	3.13
	Female		Allied to Agriculture	3.81	3.11	3.98	1.75	3.16	2.52	2.25	3.98	1.80	2.64	3.16	2.68	3.98	1.77	2.90

continued. . .

Table 4.1 (Continued)

				Education										Overall Mean				
				LITERATE					ILLITERATE									
In-come	*Land Holding*	*Gender*	*Occupa-tion*	*A*	*B*	*C*	*D*	*M*	*A*	*B*	*C*	*D*	*M*	*A*	*B*	*C*	*D*	*M*
	Mean			3.49	3.0	3.99	1.79	3.07	3.11	2.75	3.96	1.66	2.87	3.29	2.87	3.97	1.72	2.97
	Medium Farmers	Male	Agricul-ture	2.67	2.50	3.56	1.82	2.64	4.11	4.25	4.4	2.18	3.75	3.39	3.37	4.0	2.0	3.19
Non Target	Male		Allied to Agricul-ture	3.59	2.84	3.94	1.75	3.03	3.67	3.0	3.67	1.91	3.06	3.63	2.92	3.80	1.83	3.05
Group	Female		Allied to Agricul-ture	-	-	-	-	-	3.21	2.78	3.63	1.64	2.82	3.21	2.78	3.63	1.64	2.82
	Mean			3.13	3.67	3.75	1.79	2.84	3.66	3.34	3.91	1.91	3.21	3.41	3.02	3.81	1.82	3.01
	Non-Target Group Mean			3.31	2.84	3.87	1.79	2.95	3.39	3.05	3.94	1.79	3.04	3.35	2.95	3.89	1.77	2.99
	Overall Mean			3.44	3.01	3.86	1.80	3.03	3.31	2.91	3.97	1.65	2.96	3.38	2.96	3.92	1.73	2.99

Abbreviations used-
A=Product B=Price C=Place D=Promotion M=Mean of four Ps.

Table 4.2
Fourteen Dimensions of the Construct Falling under Two Orientation Regions of Target Customers' Satisfaction and the Respective Mean Values Revealing the Extent of MKTORIENT

Below Average *(-3 points)*			*Above Average* *(+3 points)*		
F_3	=	'Convenient purchase schemes' (2.75).	F_1	=	'Time efficient and hasslefree procedure' (3.26).
F_{11}	=	'Frequent and effective promotional communication' (1.54).	F_2	=	'Efficient and adequate bank services' (3.81).
F_{12}	=	'Fieldworkers promotional skill' (1.65).	F_4	=	'Accurate and timely passbook entries' (4.81).
F_{13}	=	'Promotion for interest oriented and innovative new schemes' (2.19).	F_6	=	'Timely information on new interest rates' (3.69).
F_{14}	=	'Adequate and educative advertisements for favourable changes' (1.85).	F_7	=	'Convenient and nearest branch location' (4.49).
F_{15}	=	'Personal involvement' (1.88).	F_8	=	'Cooperative and informative employees' (3.88).
		Average (3 points)	F_9	=	'Competent and efficient personnel' (3.54).
F_5	=	'Reasonable and attractive interest rates' (3.0).	F_{10}	=	'Adequate staff and satisfactory performance' (3.54).

Table 4.3
Number of Target Customers under Dimension-wise MKTORIENT Regions

Responses →	*1-2*		*2-3*		*3-4*		*4-5*	
Dimensions ↓	*No*	*(%)*	*No*	*(%)*	*No.*	*(%)*	*No.*	*(%)*
F_1 (13)	01	7.69	05	38.46	05	38.46	02	15.39
F_2 (13)	01	7.69	03	23.08	06	46.15	03	23.08
F_3 (13)	10	50	–	–	01	50	–	–
F_4 (13)	–	–	–	–	01	7.69	12	92.31
F_5 (13)	01	7.69	08	61.54	03	23.08	01	7.69
F_6 (13)	–	–	05	38.46	07	53.85	01	7.69
F_7 (13)	–	–	–	–	–	–	13	100
F_8 (13)	–	–	01	7.69	09	69.23	03	23.08
F_9 (13)	–	–	02	15.38	11	84.62	–	–
F_{10} (13)	–	–	01	7.69	12	92.31	–	–
F_{11} (13)	12	92.31	01	7.69	–	–	–	–
F_{12} (13)	11	84.62	01	7.69	01	7.69	–	–
F_{13} (13)	09	69.22	02	15.39	02	15.39	–	–
F_{14} (13)	09	69.23	04	30.77	–	–	–	–
F_{15} (13)	09	69.22	02	15.39	02	15.39	–	–

Table 4.4
Fourteen Dimensions of the Construct Falling under Two Orientation Regions of Non-Target Customers' Satisfaction and the Respective Mean Values Revealing the Extent of MKTORIENT

Below Average (-3 points)			*Above Average* (+3 points)		
F_3	=	'Convenient purchase schemes' (2.31).	F_1	=	'Time efficient and hasslefree procedure' (3.11).
F_5	=	'Reasonable and attractive interest rates' (2.80).	F_2	=	'Efficient and adequate bank services' (3.81).
F_{11}	=	'Frequent and effective promotional communication' (1.62).	F_4	=	'Accurate and timely passbook entries' (4.58).
F_{12}	=	'Fieldworkers promotional skill' (1.51).	F_6	=	'Timely information on new interest rates' (3.68).
F_{13}	=	'Promotion for interest oriented and innovative new schemes' (2.22).	F_7	=	'Convenient and nearest branch location' (4.49).
F_{14}	=	'Adequate and educative advertisements for favourable changes' (1.86).	F_8	=	'Cooperative and informative employees' (4.19).
F_{15}	=	'Personal involvement' (1.13).	F_9	=	'Competent and efficient personnel' (3.52).
			F_{10}	=	'Adequate staff and satisfactory performance' (3.51).

Table 4.5
Number of Non-Target Customers under Dimension-wise MKTORIENT Regions

Responses →	*1-2*		*2-3*		*3-4*		*4-5*	
Dimensions ↓	*No*	*(%)*	*No*	*(%)*	*No.*	*(%)*	*No.*	*(%)*
F_1 (72)	07	9.72	26	36.11	36	50	03	4.17
F_2 (72)	06	8.33	09	12.50	38	52.78	19	26.39
F_3 (8)	02	25	06	75	–	–	–	–
F_4 (72)	–	–	02	2.78	17	23.61	53	73.61
F_5 (67)	02	17.91	46	68.66	07	10.45	02	2.98
F_6 (72)	06	8.33	16	22.22	44	61.12	06	8.33
F_7 (72)	–	–	–	–	01	1.39	71	98.61
F_8 (72)	–	–	03	4.17	27	37.5	42	58.33
F_9 (72)	–	–	14	19.44	57	79.17	01	1.39
F_{10} (72)	–	–	19	26.39	48	66.67	05	6.94
F_{11} (72)	70	97.22	02	2.78	–	–	–	–
F_{12} (72)	66	91.66	03	4.17	03	4.17	–	–
F_{13} (72)	47	65.28	16	22.22	09	12.5	–	–
F_{14} (72)	56	77.78	16	22.22	–	–	–	–
F_{15} (72)	69	95.83	03	4.17	–	–	–	–

Table 4.6
Marketing-Mix Variables Obtaining Less than Average Score—Target Group

Product (A)	*Price (B)*	*Place (C)*	*Promotion (D)*
F_1 = (46.15%) (1) Simple loan formalities. (2) Loan procedure easy even to a layman. (3) Quick withdrawal facilities. (4) Timely purchase through bank	F_5 = (15.38%) (1) Attractictive and adequate interest rates. (2) Reasonable loan interest rates. (3) Motivating deposit interest rates.		F_{11} = (100%) (1) Frequent advertisements (2) Effective T. V. and Radio ads. (3) Heavy promotion through newspapers & magazines. (4) Promotion of schemes through attractive posters.
F_2 = (15.38%) (1) Sufficient number of deposit schemes. (2) Bank proves to be a good prime bank	F_6 = (30.77%) (1) Quick information regarding. new interest rates.		F_{12} = (92.31%) (1) Promotion through fieldworkers (2) Fieldworkers convincing skill.
F_3 = (50%) (1) Convenient purchase of assets through bank finance. (2) Easy repayment of instal-ments.			F_{13} = (76.93). (1) Employees co-operation in educating clients about new schemes. (2) Employees co-operation in educating clients about new interest rates.
			F_{14} = (92.31%). (1) Heavy ads of new interest rates. (2) Customer awareness meets.
			F_{15} = (76.93%). (1) Promotion through personal involvement.

Table 4.7
Marketing-Mix Variables Obtaining Average Score—Target Group

Product (A)	*Price (B)*	*Place (C)*	*Promotion (D)*
F_2 = (15.38%) (1) Sufficient number of deposit schemes. (2) Bank prove to be a good prime bank.	F_5 = (53.85%) (1) Attractive and adequate interest rates. (2) Reasonable loan interest rates. (3) Motivating deposit interest rates. F_6 = (7.69%) (1) Quick information regarding new interest rates.	F_8 = (7.69%) (1) Co-operation and friendly employees. (2) Employees have sufficient information. F_9 = (15.38%) (1) Competent and efficicent employees. (2) Reasonable market around branch location. F_{10} = (7.69%) (1) Adequate bank staff. (2) Satisfactory present bank's staff	F_{13} = (7.69%) (1) Employees co-operation in educating clients about new schemes. (2) Employees co-operation in educating clients about new interest rates. F_{14} = (7.69%) (1) Heavy ads. of new rates. (2) Customer awareness meets F_{15} = (7.69%) (1) Promotion through personal involvement.

Table 4.8
Marketing-Mix Variables Obtaining More than Average Score—Target Group

Product (A)	*Price (B)*	*Place (C)*	*Promotion (D)*
F_1= (53.85%) (1) Simple loan formalities (2) Loan procedure easy even to a layman. (3) Quick withdrawal facilities. (4) Timely purchase through bank. F_2 = (69.24%) (1) Sufficient number of deposit schemes. (2) Bank proves to be a good prime bank. F_3 = (50%) (1) Convenient purchase of assets through bank finance. (2) Easy repayment of instalments. F_4 = (100%) (1) Accurate passbook entries. (2) Timely updating of passbooks.	F_5 = (30.77%) (1) Attractive and adequate interest rates. (2) Reasonable loan interest rates. (3) Motivating deposit interest rates. F_6 = (61.54%) (1) Quick information regarding new interest rates.	F_7 = (100%) (1) Convenient branch location (2) Branch location at hitherto unbanked area. (3) Nearest location. F_8 = (92.31%) (1) Co-operate and friendly employees. (2) Employees have sufficient information. F_9 = (84.62%). (1) Competent and efficient employees. (2) Reasonable market around bank location. F_{10} = (92.31%) (1) Adequate bank staff. (2) Satisfactory present bank's staff.	F_{12} = (100%) (1) Promotion through fieldworkers. (2) Fieldworkers convincing skills. F_{13} = (15.38%) (1) Employees co-operation in educating clients about new schemes. (2) Employees co-operation in educating clients about new interest rates. F_{15} = (15.38%) (1) Promotion through personal involve ment.

Table 4.9
Marketing-Mix Variables Obtaining Less than Average Score—Non-Target Group

Product (A)	*Price (B)*	*Place (C)*	*Promotion (D)*
F_1 = (31.94%) (1) Simple loan formalities. (2) Loan procedure easy even to a layman. (3) Quick withdrawal facilities. (4) Timely purchase through bank. F_2 = (9.27%) (1) Sufficient number of deposit schemes. (2) Bank proves to be a good prime bank. F_3 = (100%) (1) Convenient purchase of assets through bank finance. (2) Easy repayment of instalments.	F_5 = (47.76%) (1) Attractive and adequate interest rates. (2) Reasonable loan interest rates. (3) Motivating deposit interest rates. F_6 = (4.17%) (1) Quick information regarding new interest rates.	F_9 = (5.56%) (1) Competent and efficient employees. (2) Reasonable market around branch location. F_{10} = (1.39%) (1) Adequate bank staff. (2) Satisfactory present bank's staff.	F_{11} = (100%) (1) Frequent advertisements. (2) Effective T.V. and Radio ads. (3) Heavy promotion through newspaper & magazines. (4) Promotion of schemes through attractive posters. F_{12} = (91.66%) (1) Promotion through fieldworkers. (2) Fieldworkers convincing skill. F_{13}= (69.44%). (1) Employees co-operation in educating clients about new schemes.

Table 4.9 (Contd.)

Product (A)	*Price (B)*	*Place (C)*	*Promotion (D)*
			(2) Employees co-operation in educating clients about new interest rates. F_{14} = (93.06%) (1) Heavy ads. of new interest rates. (2) Customer awareness meets. F_{15} = (97.22%). (1) Promotion through personal involvement.

Table 4.10
Marketing-Mix Variables Obtaining Average Score—Non-Target Group

Product (A)	*Price (B)*	*Place (C)*	*Promotion (D)*
F_1 = (13.89%) (1) Simple loan formalities. (2) Loan procedure easy even to a layman. (3) Quick withdrawal facilities. (4) Timely purchase through bank. F_2 = (11.11%) (1) Sufficient number of deposit schemes. (2) Bank proves to be a good prime bank. F_4 = (2.78%) (1) Accurate passbook entries. (2) Timely updating of pass-books.	F_5 = (38.81%) (1) Attractive and adequate interest rates. (2) Reasonable loan interest rates. (3) Motivating deposit interest rates. F_6 = (26.39%) (1) Quick information regading new interest rates.	F_8 = (4.17%) (1) Co-operative & friendly employees. (2) Employees have suffi-cient information. F_9 = (13.89%) (1) Competent and effi-cient employees. (2) Reasonable market around branch location. F_{10} = (25%) (1) Adequate bank's staff. (2) Satisfactory present bank's staff.	F_{12} = (4.17%) (1) Promotion through fieldworkers. (2) Fieldworkers convi-ncing skill. F_{13} = (18.06%) (1) Employees co-operation in educa-ting clients about new schemes. (2) Employees co-opera-tion in educating clients about new interest rates. F_{14} = (6.91%) (1) Heavy ads. of new interest rates. (2) Customer awareness meets. F_{15} = (2.78%) (1) Promotion through personal involvement.

Table 4.11
Marketing-Mix Variables Obtaining More than Average Score = Non-Target Group

Product (A)	*Price (B)*	*Place (C)*	*Promotion (D)*
F_1 = (54.17%) (1) Simple loan formalities. (2) Loan procedure easy even to a layman. (3) Quick withdrawal facilities. (4) Timely purchase through bank.	F_5 = (13.43%) (1) Attractive and adequate interest rates. (2) Reasonable loan interest rates. (3) Motivating deposit interest rates.	F_7 = (100%) (1) Convenient branch location. (2) Branch location at hitherto unbanked area. (3) Nearest location.	F_{12} = (4.17%) (1) Promotion through fieldworkers. (2) Fieldworkers convincing skill.
F_2 = (79.17%) (1) Sufficient number of deposit schemes. (2) Bank proves to be a good prime bank.	F_6 = (69.44%) (1) Quick information regading new interest rates.	F_8 = (95.83%) (1) Co-operative and friendly employees. (2) Employees have sufficient information.	F_{13} = (12.50%) (1) Employees co-operation in educating clients about new schemes. (2) Employees co-operation in educating clients about new
F_4 = (97.22%) interest rates. (1) Accurate passbook entries. (2) Timely updating of passbooks.		F_9 = (80.55%) (1) Competent and efficient employees. (2) Reasonable market around branch location.	
		F_{10} = (73.61%) (1) Adequate bank staff. (2) Satisfactory present bank's staff.	

Table 4.12
Service Quality and Overall Performance-wise Marketing Orientation

Marketing	*Service*	*Quality*		*Overall*	*Performance*	
Mix Factors ↓	*BA*	*A*	*AA*	*BA*	*A*	*AA*
PRDMEAN 1	2.44	1.87	2.53	—	2.38	2.42
PRDMEAN 2	2.06	3.12	4.21	—	3.75	2.81
PRDMEAN 3	2.50	2.61	3.02	—	2.25	2.75
PRDMEAN 4	4.28	4.05	4.68	—	4.45	4.63
GRPRDMEAN	2.82	3.03	3.61	—	3.21	3.41
PRIMEAN 1	2.37	1.79	2.33	—	2.2	2.26
PRIMEAN 2	3.22	3.92	3.70	—	3.4	3.72
GRPRIMEAN	2.80	2.86	3.02	—	2.8	2.99
PLAMEAN 1	4.56	4.41	4.50	—	4.33	4.52
PLAMEAN 2	3.39	3.62	3.52	—	3.6	3.51
PLAMEAN 3	3.33	3.54	3.54	—	3.4	3.53
PLAMEAN 4	3.56	3.96	4.14	—	4.05	4.05
GRPLAMEAN	3.71	3.88	3.93	—	3.85	3.90
PRMMEAN 1	1.47	1.65	1.62	—	1.55	1.62
PRMMEAN 2	1.39	1.42	1.57	—	1.7	1.51
PRMMEAN 3	1.78	2.05	2.21	—	2.2	2.21
PRMMEAN 4	1.72	2.12	1.83	—	1.85	1.86
PRMMEAN 5	1.67	1.31	1.73	—	1.5	1.68
GRPRMMEAN	1.61	1.80	1.79	—	1.76	1.78
MKTORIENT	**2.74**	**2.89**	**3.09**	—	**2.91**	**3.02**
No. & %age of Respondents	8(9%)	67(79%)	10(12%)	—	66(78%)	19(22%)

Chapter—5

Measurement of Marketing Orientation in JRB with Reference to Developing Rural Area

BACKGROUND

The marketing orientation in a RRB operating in developing area has been worked out by selecting a village viz; Sarore where total population was 3472, with 604 households, 33% poverty level, 70% literacy rate, good infrastructural facilities like pacca roads, few power cuts, two government, 3 private schools (Exhibit-5.1) and a branch of JRB Sarore operates at a break even point with just Rs. 2000 profits as on 31.3.97 (Exhibit 5.2). Amount of deposits and advances has increased year after year but credit-deposit ratio exhibited a declining trend (Exhibit 5.2).

The findings of the study have been drawn from the responses generated from 135 randomly selected customers of the aforesaid JRB branch with 60 statements falling within the jurisdiction of MKTORIENT, which through factor analysis finally resulted into 30 items grouped under 12 dimensions (5 product, 1 price, 2 place and 4 promotion) of MKTORIENT (Table 5.0).

The scree tests (Figures 5.1, 5.2, 5.3 and 5.4) reveal that twelve factors are major contributors and rest of them are not significantly contributing to the total variance in the results obtained. Thus, further analysis would be restricted to these twelve factors.

STATUS OF MARKETING ORIENTATION

The extent of MKTORIENT has been determined on the basis of the opinion gathered from sample customers (comprising 81 males and 54 females) of JRB residing in the village Sarore. The status of MKTORIENT has differed significantly among various groups of respondents falling in both target and non-target sections. Therefore the level of marketing orientation in the given RRB branch has been worked out separately under target and non-target groups.

1. Target Group

As mentioned earlier, RRBs were set up primarily to cater the banking requirements of the weaker sections of the society (Working Group 1975) but the percentage of such customers in the given JRB branch has arrived at 18.52 which means that still large number of target people are not enjoying the banking services despite the fact that 33% of the village population belongs to such as category.

Male literate and illiterate non-farmers belonging to target group engaged in activities allied to agriculture have assigned highest mean score to 'place effectiveness' (3.86 & 3.97) (Table 5.1), followed by 'product adequacy' (3.28 & 3.50), 'price reasonability' (3.10 & 3.36) and lowest mean value accorded to various aspects of 'promotion optimality' (1.61 & 1.55) viz; 'fieldworkers promotional skill', 'frequent and educative advertisements', 'promotion for high interest deposit and low interest need based loan schemes' and 'customer-bank relations'.

Both literate and illiterate female customers having income below Rs. 11,000 p.a. under agricultural allied activities, have given highest response to 'place mix' (3.70 & 3.99), followed by 'product mix' (3.29 & 3.12), 'less than average' score obtained by 'price mix' variables (2.25 & 2.80) viz; 'attractive deposit interest rates,' 'reasonable loan interest rates and accurate interest calculations' and 'promotion mix' elements (1.42 & 1.41) viz; 'fieldworkers performance', 'sufficient and informative advertisements', 'promotion for interest focusing new schemes' and 'personal selling efforts.'

Marketing orientation dimensions grouped under four Ps of marketing mix, divided into two orientation regions of customer satisfaction within the jurisdiction of MKTORIENT (Table 5.2) reveals that target customers of JRB are highly satisfied with regard to six dimensions viz; 'adequate and need based deposit schemes,' 'simple and quick banking operations', 'efficient deposit and withdrawal services,' 'easy access to branch location', adequate staff and satisfactory performance' and 'promotion for interest oriented new schemes'. These customers have shown their dissatisfaction due to 'complicated loan obtaining procedure', 'inconvenient loan repayment policy', 'unreasonable and unattractive interest rates, 'absence of fieldworkres promotional skills,' 'lack of educative advertisements' and 'impersonal selling of banking services.'

The number of target customers under reference falling in four marketing orientation regions (Table 5.3) reveals that one dimension viz; 'convenient branch location' has fallen in the highest range of MKTORIENT with about 88% of the sample customers. Majority of the respondents have given their ranking in the "3-4" range of MKTORIENT to 'adequate and need based deposit schemes' (64%) & 'reasonable interest rates and accurate calculations' (56%). Beside these, other dimensions securing 'above average' score are 'simple and quick banking operations' (84%), 'quick deposit and withdrawal facilities' (60%) and 'adequate staff and satisfactory performance' (52%).

Maximum of the respondents have given their responses between "2-3" range of MKTORIENT with respect to `loan procurement formalities' (56%). Among the dimensions generating `below average' score 100% of sample respondents have valued `simple loan repayment policy' and 56% have scored `promotion for interest oriented and innovative new schemes' between "1-2" and "2-3" regions of MKTORIENT. The Table 5.3 has again reflected the lack of marketing culture in the said JRB branch with respect to the promotion of banking services. The majority of respondents have given their ratings in the "1-2" range at MKTORIENT to `fieldworkers promotional skill' (92%), `frequent and educative advertisements' (92%) and `personal involvement in selling banking service' (88%).

Overall marketing orientation in given JRB branch obtain from the level of satisfaction among target customers, pertaining to four Ps of marketing mix arrived at 2.89 (Table 5.1). The highest mean value has been given to 'place effectiveness' (3.89), followed by 'product adequacy' (3.30), 'price reasonability' (2.88) and 'promotion optimality' (1.50). Thus among all the four Ps, price and promotion mix have obtained less than 3-point on MKTORIENT scale, which require special attention in order to increase overall marketing orientation in rural banks.

2. Non-Target Group

After the recommendations of Narasimham Committee (1991), the number of non-target customer in RRBs has far exceeded to that of target ones. From the given village out of total sample customers of 135, 81.48% of respondents belong to non-target group, which indicates that there is a need to motivate target customers to avail rural banking services, which is basically meant for the people with small earnings and for the purpose of which, RRBs have been named as 'small man's bank.'

Literate male small farmers having income above Rs. 11,000 p.a. have given highest score to 'place mix' (3.80), followed by 'price mix' (3.38), 'product mix' (3.33) and less than 2-point on MKTORIENT scale to 'promotion mix' (1.72) for the items such as, 'fieldworkers promotional competence,' 'promotion for interest emphasising new schemes,' 'efficacious and educative advertisements' and 'interaction with customers.'

Male literate and illiterate non-farmers belonging to non-target group engaged in activities allied to agriculture have assigned higher mean values to 'place effectiveness' (4.0 & 3.94), followed by 'product adequacy' (3.47 & 3.26), 'price reasonability' (3.44 & 3.06) and lower mean score awarded to 'promotional mix variables' (1.75 & 1.87) viz; 'fieldworkers promotional expertise,' 'promotion for high interest deposit and need based loan schemes,' 'competent and productive advertisements' and 'personal involvement in banking services.'

Female literate customers who have taken loan for various activities allied to agriculture have shown their highest satisfaction with regard to 'place-mix' (4.06), followed by 'product mix' (3.74), 'price mix' (3.60) and less than average value obtained by 'promotion mix' (1.81). Whereas its illiterate counterpart has accorded highest mean value to 'place effectiveness' (3.96), followed by 'price reasonability' (3.31), 'product adequacy' (3.25) and 'promotion optimality, (1.82). Thus both categories of customers have given less than 3-point to promotional aspects of rural banking which involve 'fieldworkers promotional proficiency', 'promotion for interest exhibiting new schemes', 'adequate and informative advertisements' and 'face to face communication'.

Literate male customers having income above Rs. 11,000 p.a. engaged in both agriculture and its allied activities have reflected their highest satisfaction with respect to 'place mix' (3.90 & 4.0) followed by 'product mix' (3.45 & 3.47), 'price mix' (3.29 & 3.30) but they feel highly dissatisfied with respect to 'promotional elements' (1.78 & 1.97) viz., 'fieldworkers promotional ability', 'competent and effective advertisement,' 'interest focused and motivating new schemes,' and 'personal selling efforts.'

Literate female customers belonging to non-target group under agricultural allied activities have highlighted their maximum satisfaction with regard to 'place effectiveness' (4.0), followed by 'product adequacy' (3.56), 'price reasonability' (3.42) and 'promotion optimality' (1.78) whereas illiterate respondents of this category have assigned highest mean value to 'place mix' (4.07), followed by 'price mix' (3.17), 'product mix' (3.15) and lowest mean score being accorded to 'promotion mix' (1.89). Thus both literate and illiterate female respondents of non-target group have given less than 2-point score on MKTORIENT scale to the promotion mix variables which incorporate 'fieldworkers promotional ability,' 'promotion for interest oriented and innovative new schemes,' 'frequent and result oriented advertisements' and 'selling efforts in the field.'

The level of non-target customers falling in different regions of MKTORIENT (Table 5.5) highlights that two dimensions viz; 'simple and quick banking operations' and 'convenient branch location' have secured highest range of MKTORIENT (4-5) with 64% and 99% of the sample customers. Further the majority of respondents have given their high ratings in the "3-4" range of MKTORIENT with respect to 'adequate and need based deposit schemes' (54%), 'reasonable interest rates and accurate interest calculations' (54%), 'efficient deposit and withdrawal facilities' (53%) and only 50% respondents have fallen in the said range for 'adequate staff and satisfactory performance'.

Similarly 'simple loan repayment policy' and 'easy loan obtaining formalities' have received 'less than average' score from respectively 71.5% and 61% of sample respondents. Like target group, non-target customers have also shown their dissonance towards all the 'promotional aspects' and therefore majority of them have given responses between "1-2" range of MKTORIENT to the 'fieldworkers promotional skill" (95%), 'frequent and effective advertisement' (94%), 'customer personal relations' (72%) and 'promotion for interest focused and innovative new schemes' (51%). Thus there is an urgent need to divert considerable amount of time, money and energy towards 'promotional aspect' of bank marketing mix.

Twelve dimensions of MKTORIENT combined under four Ps of marketing mix separated into two orientation regions of customer satisfaction within the framework of MKTORIENT (Table 5.4) reveals that non-target customers of JRB have given 'above average' response with regard to six dimensions viz; 'adequate and need satisfying deposit schemes', 'simple and quick banking operations', 'efficient deposit and withdrawal facilities', 'reasonable interest rates and accurate calculations', 'convenient branch location' and 'adequate staff and satisfactory performance'. These customers have given 'below average' score to the remaining six dimensions due to 'complicated loan formalities', 'inconvenient loan recovery policy', 'absence of fieldworkers promotional skill' and 'sales promotional tools', 'inadequate promotion for high interest on deposit and low on loan schemes', 'lack of frequent and educative advertisements' and 'lack of personal selling efforts'. Thus two dimensions of 'product mix' and all the dimensions of 'promotion mix' require special attention of the JRB management as these dimensions have obtained less than 3-point on MKTORIENT scale.

Overall marketing orientation in the JRB branch, under reference, as assessed by non-target customers on the basis of their responses towards four Ps of rural bank marketing (Table 5.1) came at 3.13. They have accorded highest mean score to 'place mix' (3.96) followed by 'product mix' (3.42), 'price mix' (3.33) and lowest value assigned to 'promotion mix' (1.82). Thus promotional element has secured the mean value below 2-point on MKTORIENT scale. In order to strengthen overall marketing orientation in JRB, promotional variable has to be geared up by effective utilisation of its various aspects.

The association between rural bank marketing orientation and twelve factor dimensions in the scale clubbed under four Ps of marketing mix formulated with a statistical tool of Multiple Regression is as under:

MKTORIENT = 3.13 + .105 (PRDMEAN1) - .041 (PRMMEAN2) - .129 (PRMMEAN3) + .122 (PRMMEAN4) + .090 (PRDMEAN2) + .223 (PRDMEAN3) - .056

(PRDMEAN 4) - .051 (PRDMEAN5) + .020 (PRIMEAN1) - .221 (PLAMEAN1) + .189 (PLAMEAN2) - .023 (PRMMEAN1).

The regression equation highlights that marketing orientation in JRB is both positively and negatively related to 12 dimensions of four Ps. The findings in terms of relative significance of these dimensions in estimating the overall marketing orientation reflects that third dimensions of product mix is the most important one and next rank in order of merit has gone to second dimension of place mix. First dimension of place mix seems to be least significant (-.221). Efforts have to be made not only to retain the present status of marketing orientation with respect to such dimensions which have obtained positive values but also to reverse the negative position of such dimensions which appear to have been ignored in the present marketing efforts by the RRB branch office.

VALIDITY AND RELIABILITY OF DATA

Two aspects viz; 'service quality' and 'overall performance' have been converged with other important items of marketing orientation (Table5.12). Marketing orientation with regard to four Ps of marketing mix of 3.03 (Table 5.1) has been proved convergently valid as majority of JRB customers falling under 'above average' region of 'service quality' (70%) and 'overall performance' (91%) have accorded 3.16 and 3.14 values of MKTORIENT respectively.

Multiple correlation (R) between overall marketing orientation and four Ps of marketing mix arrived at .52 which implies fairly good degree of association between these variables. The value of co-efficient of determination (R_2) figured out to be .27 which indicates that 27% of the variation in marketing orientation can be explained by four variables in the linear equation.

As the calculated value (3.51) of 'F' is greater than the tabulated value (3.60) at 1% level of significance (d.f v_1 v_2 11,134) so the hypothesis of equality of 12 dimensions is accepted. Thus these dimensions have equal effect on overall MKTORIENT.

The value of 't' were tested both a 1% and 5% level of significance (d.f_{v1} 10). Except for the third dimension of product mix, all the 11 dimensions have not fallen in the rejection region at 5% level of significance (2.228) whereas all the 12 dimensions have fallen in the acceptance region at 1% level of significance (3.169). This highlights that all the factors at four Ps have their important contribution in the computation of bank marketing orientation at 1% level of significance.

STRATEGIC ACTION

The level of marketing orientation, in said JRB branch, worked out here (Table 5.1) necessitates two types of strategies for creating and enhancing the extent of marketing orientation in the functioning of RRBs.

The first type of strategy resulting from the findings is such an action plan which will not only retain the present status of MKTORIENT with regard to those aspects where JRB customers enjoy 'above average' response of orientation but also to take it to the top level on MKTORIENT scale.

75% sample customers feel satisfied with present number of need based deposit schemes, but in order to increase this number new deposit schemes would have to be introduced or existing schemes have to be revised after giving due 'consideration to customers' needs and wants (Menezes 1979).

About 90% respondents opined that rural bank has simple account opening formalities and immediate issuance and updating of passbooks (Kshirsagar 1976) in order to obtain 100% customer satisfaction in this regard.

Majority of the customers (71.5%) contacted have exhibited their positive opinion towards quick deposit and withdrawal facilities of rural banks. For remaining 29% customers this type of service should be provided in a more efficient and effective manner (Bhattacharyay 1989).

Approximately 61% customers, residing in the village under reference, have shown their satisfaction with respect to interest rates in rural banks and their accurate calculations but services should be offered at more attractive interest rates (Menezes 1979) to increase clientele of the bank. 54.5% sample respondents are of the opinion that present rural bank staff is adequate. However there is a need to recruit more professionally well equipped people so that better expansion and diversification of banking schemes suitable to local conditions are formulated.

The second type of strategic action emerging from the main findings require considerable care towards all those dimensions of marketing mix which scored 'below average' level of orientation. Two aspects of product mix and all dimensions of promotion mix need special attention so as to increase present level of marketing orientation in rural banks.

44% sample customers have shown their dissatisfaction towards loan procurement from rural banks due to cumbersome formalities. Thus atleast advance managers should be given instructions to help illiterate masses in getting loans by way of completing as many formalities as they can (Bhattacharyay 1989).

50% of loanees contacted have expressed their negative opinion towards loan recovery policy and find difficulty in making repayment of even the principal amount during adverse circumstances. State government should assist rural banks in providing concessions to the agriculturists during the unfavourable weather conditions.

Out of total sample size, 94.5% respondents opined that fieldworkers of rural banks have neither promoted any scheme nor motivated them to avail banking facilities. Special rewards should be announced for the fieldworkers for attracting the maximum customers (Hebbar 1989). Moreover some promotional gifts, like pen, diary, calendar should also be distributed to the customers.

Almost half of the respondents have highlighted their dissonance with regard to employees co-operation in extending information regarding new schemes and interest rates. Non-monetary counter services should also be provided by employees (Kshirsagar 1976) and at least in case of new schemes and/or variation in interest rates, adequate information should be given to the customers (Hebbar 1988).

Approximately all the sample customers are of the view that JRB has never used any advertising media for promoting its services. If not frequently, atleast the new schemes, interest rates, financial position of the bank should be advertised once in a month in all local newspapers.

85.5% respondents contacted have reflected their unhappiness towards employees indifferent behaviour and reported that they never take any interest in helping customers to fill deposit/withdrawal forms. Thus some arrangements should be made to help rural masses in filling their forms (Bhatnagar 1983). This will save time of both customer and bankers and will help building sound rapport between them.

REFERENCES

1. Bhatnagar, Deepti (1983), "Diffusion of Banking Innovations and Communication Strategies for Rural Areas", *Prajnan*, July-Sept., Vol. XII, 196-197.
2. Bhattacharyay, Biswa N. (1989), "Marketing Approach to Promoting Banking Services for Rural Areas", *Prajnan*, July-Sept, Vol XIII, 205.
3. Hebbar, C. Kusumakara (1988), "Bank Marketing Strategy in Commercial Banks", Southern Economist, Oct., Vol. 27, 18.
4. Hebbar, A.R.K. (1989), "Problems of RRBs", *Yojana*, April, Vol. 33, 24.
5. Kshirsagar (1976), "Improving Customer Service of Banks", *Prajnan*, Apr-June, Vol. VI, 155.
6. Menezes, J.S. William (1979), "Marketing and Bank Services: System Approach to Business Planning and Performance Evaluation", *Prajnan*, Apr-June, Vol. VIII, 135.
7. Sing, R.K.P (1987), "Business Planning in RRBs" Khadi Gramodyog, Jan., 192.
8. Working Group (1975), Report of the Committee on Rural Banks, G.O.I., 16.

Exhibit 5.1
Brief Profile of the Village Sarore of Jammu District as on 31.3.97

1. Total Population : 3472
2. Male: Female : 2037 : 1435
3. Total Households : 604
4. Tentative Economic Status
   (a) Below poverty line-33%
   (b) Above poverty line-67%
5. Literacy Rate-
   (a) Literate-70%
   (b) Illiterate-30%
6. Infrastructural Facilities-
   (a) Roads—Pacca
   (b) Electricity—Rare power cuts
   (c) Two Govt. (middle & high) School
   (d) Three private middle school.
7. Land soil suitable for growing paddy, wheat, maize and vegetables.
8. Per Hectare yield

	Irrigated	*Non-irrigated*
Wheat	30qtl/hec	20qtl/hec
Paddy	46qtl/hec	—
Maize	—	19 qtl/hec

Exhibit 5.2
Brief Profile of the Branch Sarore of JRB

(Rs in '000)

Year	*Deposits*		*Advances*		*Profit*	*C.D. Ratio*
	A/C	*Rs*	*A/C*	*Rs*	*(Rs.)*	
1992-93	1852	5629	202	1046	-276.23	19
1993-94	1935	6288	274	1475	-328.49	23
1994-95	2044	8423	275	2104	-29.15	25
1995-96	1602	9103	240	2081	-5.68	23
1996-97	1798	13549	221	2716	+2.00	20
1997-98	1968	18595	260	3347	+249.63	18
1998-99	2073	21123	273	3591	+348.55	17

(a) Five branches of other banks at a distance of 6 kms

(b) Number of Projects financed;

		1996-97	*1997-98*
(i)	Tractor	2	8
(ii)	Dairy	10	13
(iii)	Sheep	01	8
(iv)	Horsecart	4	7
(v)	Retail Trade	9	17

Table 5.0
Summary of Results from Scale Purification—Loading and Variance Explained

Bank Marketing Mix	*Factor-Wise Dimension*	*Factor Loadings*	*% of Variance Explained*
1	2	3	4
Product	**Factor First-**		**34.0**
	Simple loan formalities.	.73	
	No switching intentions for loans.	.63	
	Loan procedure easy even to a layman.	.72	
	Timely purchase of assets through bank.	.77	
	Factor Second-		**12.8**
	Need meeting deposit schemes.	.69	
	Sufficient number of deposit schemes.	.82	
	Bank proves to be a good prime bank.	.87	
	Factor Third-		**10.2**
	Simple account opening formalities.	.73	
	Immediate issuance of new cheque/ passbooks.	.82	
	Timely updating of passbooks.	.61	
	Factor Fourth-		**8.5**
	Comfortable loan recovery policy.	.93	
	Easy repayment of instalments.	.93	
	Factor Fifth-		7.2
	Quick withdrawal facilities.	.80	

1	2	3	4
	No delay in depositing money.	.88	
	Total variance explained = 72.7%		
Price	**Factor First-**		**54.7**
	Attractive and adequate interest rates.	.86	
	Reasonable loan interest rates.	.50	
	Motivating deposit interest rates.	.74	
	Authentic interest calculations.	.55	
	Total variance explained = 54.7%		
Place	**Factor First-**		**33.4**
	Convenient branch location.	-.88	
	Branch location in hitherto unbanked area.	.55	
	Nearest location.	.75	
	Factor Second-		**26.2**
	Adequate bank's staff.	.78	
	Satisfactory present bank's staff.	.76	
	Total variance explained = 59.6%		
Promotion	**Factor First-**		**23.3**
	Promotion through fieldworkers.	.91	
	Fieldworkers convincing skills.	.87	
	Attractive promotional gifts.	-.62	
	Factor Second-		**22.2**
	Employees co-operation in educating clients about new schemes.	.93	
	Employees co-operation in educating clients about new interest rates.	.92	
	Factor Third-		**15.6**
	Frequent advertisements	-71	
	Effective T.V. and radio ads.	.83	
	Factor Fourth-		**11.5**
	Heavy ads of new interest rates.	.86	
	Promotion through personal involvement.	.54	
	Total variance explained = 72.6%		

Table 5.1
Overall Marketing Orientation—Customers Assessment

				Education										Overall Mean				
				LITERATE					ILLITERATE									
Income	*Land Holding*	*Gender*	*Occupation*	*A*	*B*	*C*	*D*	*M*	*A*	*B*	*C*	*D*	*M*	*A*	*B*	*C*	*D*	*M*
	Small Farmers	Male	Agriculture	-	-	-	-	-	-	-	-	-	-	-	-	-	-	-
Target Group	Male		Allied to Agriculture	3.28	3.10	3.86	1.61	3.03	3.50	3.36	3.97	1.55	3.15	3.39	3.23	3.92	1.58	3.09
	Female		Allied to Agriculture	3.29	2.25	3.70	1.42	2.82	3.12	2.80	3.99	1.41	2.86	3.21	2.53	3.85	1.42	2.84
	Target Group Mean			3.29	2.68	3.78	1.52	2.93	3.31	3.08	3.98	1.48	3.01	3.30	2.88	3.89	1.50	2.89
	Small Farmers	Male	Agriculture	3.33	3.38	3.80	1.72	3.06	-	-	-	-	-	3.33	3.38	3.80	1.72	3.06
Non Target Group	Male		Allied to Agriculture	3.47	3.44	4.0	1.75	3.17	3.26	3.06	3.94	1.87	3.03	3.37	3.25	3.97	1.81	3.10
	Female		Allied to Agriculture	3.74	3.60	4.06	1.81	3.30	3.25	3.31	3.96	1.82	3.09	3.50	3.46	4.01	1.82	3.20

Table 5.1 *(Continued)*

				Education										*Overall Mean*				
				LITERATE					*ILLITERATE*									
In-come	*Land Holding*	*Gender*	*Occupa-tion*	*A*	*B*	*C*	*D*	*M*	*A*	*B*	*C*	*D*	*M*	*A*	*B*	*C*	*D*	*M*
	Mean			3.51	3.47	3.95	1.76	3.18	3.26	3.19	3.95	1.85	3.06	3.40	3.36	3.93	1.78	3.12
	Medium Farmers	Male	Agricul-ture	3.45	3.29	3.90	1.78	3.11	-	-	-	-	-	3.45	3.29	3.90	1.78	3.11
Non Target Group	Male		Allied to Agricul-ture	3.47	3.30	4.0	1.97	3.19	-	-	-	-	-	3.47	3.30	4.0	1.97	3.19
	Female		Allied to Agricul-ture	3.56	3.42	4.0	1.78	3.19	3.15	3.17	4.07	1.89	3.07	3.36	3.30	4.04	1.84	3.13
	Mean			3.49	3.34	3.97	1.84	3.16	3.15	3.17	4.07	1.89	3.07	3.43	3.30	3.98	1.86	3.14
	Non-Target Group Mean			3.50	3.41	3.96	1.80	3.17	3.21	3.17	4.01	1.87	3.07	3.42	3.33	3.96	1.82	3.13
	Overall Mean			3.43	3.16	3.90	1.85	3.09	3.24	3.15	4.0	1.79	3.05	3.34	3.16	3.95	1.66	3.03

Abbreviations used-

A=Product B=Price C=Place D=Promotion M=Mean of four Ps.

Table 5.2
Twelve Dimensions of the Construct Falling under Two Orientation Regions of Target Customers Satisfaction and the Respective Mean Values Revealing the Extent of MKTORIENT:

Below Average (-3 points)	*Above Average (+3 points)*
F_1 = "Easy loan formalities" (2.93).	F_2 = "Adequate and need-based deposit schemes" (3.44).
F_4 = "Simple loan repayment policy" (2.25).	F_3 = "Simple and quick banking operations" (3.89).
F_6 = "Reasonable interest rates & accurate calculations" (2.96).	F_5 = "Efficient deposit & withdrawal facilities" (3.58).
F_9 = "Fieldworkers promotional skill and sales promotional tools" (1.6).	F_7 = "Easy access to branch location" (4.28).
F_{11} = "Frequent and educative advertisements" (1.6).	F_8 = "Adequate staff and satisfactory performance" (3.28).
F_{12} = "Customer-bank relation" (1.72).	F_{10} = "Promotion for interest oriented and innovative new schemes" (3.26).

Table 5.3
Number of Target Customers under Dimension-wise MKTORIENT Regions

Responses →	1-2		2-3		3-4		4-5	
Dimensions ↓	*No.*	*(%)*	*No.*	*(%)*	*No.*	*(%)*	*No.*	*(%)*
F_1 (25)	2	(8)	14	(56)	8	(32)	1	(4)
F_2 (25)	2	(8)	4	(16)	16	(64)	3	(12)
F_3 (25)	—	—	4	(16)	11	(44)	10	(40)
F_4 (4)	2	(50)	2	(50)	—	—	—	—
F_5 (25)	4	(16)	6	(24)	11	(44)	(56)	—
F_6 (25)	4	(16)	7	(28)	14	(56)	4	(16)
F_7 (25)	—	—	—	—	3	(12)	22	(88)
F_8 (25)	—	—	12	(48)	12	(48)	1	(4)
F_9 (25)	23	(92)	—	—	2	(8)	—	—
F_{10} (25)	8	(32)	6	(24)	8	(32)	3	(12)
F_{11} (25)	23	(92)	2	(8)	—	—	—	—
F_{12} (25)	22	(88)	1	(4)	2	(8)	—	—

Table 5.4
Twelve Dimensions of the Construct Falling under Two Orientation Regions of Non-Target Customers Satisfaction and the Respective Mean Values Revealing the Extent of MKTORIENT:

Below Average (-3 points)	*Above Average (+3 points)*
F_1 = "Easy loan formalities" (2.96).	F_2 = "Adequate and need-based deposit schemes" (3.48).
F_4 = "Simple loan repayment policy" (2.82).	F_3 = "Simple and quick banking operations" (4.25).
F_9 = "Fieldworkers promotional skill and sales promotional tools" (1.5).	F_5 = "Efficient deposit & withdrawal facilities" (3.92).
F_{10} = "Promotion for interest oriented and innovative new schemes" (2.5).	F_6 = "Reasonable interest rates "and accurate calculations (3.30).
F_{11} = "Frequent and educative advertisements" (1.61)	F_7 = "Easy access to branch location" (4.43).
F_{12} = "Customer-bank relation" (2.0).	F_8 = "Adequate staff and satisfactory performance" (3.35).

Table 5.5
Number of Non-Target Customers under Dimension-wise MKTORIENT Regions

Responses →	*1-2*		*2-3*		*3-4*		*4-5*	
Dimensions ↓	*No.*	*(%)*	*No.*	*(%)*	*No.*	*(%)*	*No.*	*(%)*
F_1 (110)	16	(15)	15	(46)	37	(34)	6	(5)
F_2 (110)	5	(4)	24	(22)	59	(54)	22	(20)
F_3 (110)	—	—	4	(3)	36	(33)	70	(64)
F_4 (110)	4	(2.85)	6	(43)	4	(28.5)	—	—
F_5 (110)	7	(6)	12	(11)	58	(53)	33	(30)
F_6 (110)	3	(3)	33	(30)	60	(54)	14	(13)
F_7 (110)	—	—	—	—	1	(1)	109	(99)
F_8 (110)	—	—	47	(43)	55	(50)	8	(7)
F_9 (110)	105	(95)	4	(4)	1	(1)	—	—
F_{10} (110)	56	(51)	35	(32)	19	(17)	—	—
F_{11} (110)	103	(94)	6	(6)	—	—	—	—
F_{12} (110)	79	(72)	23	(21)	8	(7)	—	—

Table 5.6
Marketing-Mix Variables Obtaining Less than Average Score—Target Group

Product (A)	*Price (B)*	*Place (C)*	*Promotion (D)*
F_1 = (44)	F_6 = (36)	F_8 = (8%)	F_9 = (92%)
(1) Simple loan formalities.	(1) Attractive and adequate interest rates.	(1) Adequate bank staff.	(1) Promotion through fieldworkers.
(2) No switching intentions for loan.	(2) Reasonable loan interest rates.	(2) Satisfactory present bank's staff.	(2) Fieldworkers convincing skill.
(3) Loan procedure easy even to a layman	(3) Motivating deposit interest rates		(3) Attractive promotional gifts.
(4) Timely purchase of assets through bank	(4) Authentic interest calculations.		F_{10} = (36%)
F_2 = (16%)			(1) Employees co-operation in educating clients about new schemes.
(1) Need meeting deposit schemes.			(2) Employees co-operation in educating clients about new interest rates.
(2) Sufficient number of deposit schemes.			F_{11} = (100%)
(3) Bank proves to be a good prime bank.			(1) Frequent advertisements.
(4) Simple loan formalities.			
(5) No switching intentions for loans.			

Continued. . .

Table 5.6 (Contd.)

Product (A)	*Price (B)*	*Place (C)*	*Promotion (D)*
F_3 = (16%) (1) Simple account opening formalities. (2) Immediate issuance of new cheque/passbooks. (3) Timely updating of pass-books. F_4 = (50%) (1) Comfortable loan recovery policy. (2) Easy repayment of install-ments. F_5 = (16%) (1) Quick withdrawal facili-ties. (2) No delay in depositing money.			(2) Effective T.V. and Radio advertise-ments. F_{12} = (92%) (1) Heavy ads. of new interest rates. (2) Promotion through personal involve-ment.

Table 5.7
Marketing-Mix Variables Obtaining Average Score—Target Group

Product (A)	*Price (B)*	*Place (C)*	*Promotion (D)*
F_1 = (20%)	F_6 = (8%)	F_8 = (40%)	F_9 = (20%)
(1) Simple loan formalities. (2) No switching intentions for loan. about	(1) Attractive and adequate interest rates. (2) Reasonable loan	(1) Adequate bank staff. (2) Satisfactory present bank's staff.	(1) Employees co-operation in educa- ting clients
(3) Loan procedure easy schemes.	interest rates.		new
even to a layman. Timely purchase of assets in educa-	(3) Motivating deposit interest rates.		(2) Employees co- (4) operation
through bank. about	(4) Authentic interest		ting clients
F_2 = (8%)	calculations.		new interest rates.
(1) Need meeting deposit scheme.			
(2) Sufficient number of deposit schemes.			
(3) Bank proves to be a good prime bank.			
F_4 = (50%)			
(1) Comfortable loan recovery policy.			
(2) Easy repayment of instalments.			
F_5 = (24%)			
(1) Quick withdrawal facilities.			
(2) No delay in depositing money.			

Table 5.8
Marketing-Mix Variables Obtaining More than Average Score—Target Group

Product (A)	*Price (B)*	*Place (C)*	*Promotion (D)*
F_1 = (36%) (1) Simple loan formalities. (2) No switching intentions for loan. (3) Loan procedure easy even to a layman. (4) Timely purchase of assets through bank. F_2 = (76%) (1) Need meeting deposit schemes. (2) Sufficient number of deposit schemes. (3) Bank proves to be a good prime bank. F_4 = (84%) (1) Simple account opening formalities. (2) Immediate issuance of new cheque/passbooks. (3) Timely updating of passbooks. F_5 = (60%) (1) Quick withdrawal facilities. (2) No delay in depositing money.	F_6 = (56%) (1) Attractive and adequate interest rates. (2) Reasonable loan interest rates. (3) Motivating deposit interest rates. (4) Authentic interest calculations.	F_7 = (100%) (1) Convenient branch location. (2) Branch location at hitherto unbanked area. (3) Nearest location. F_8 = (52%) (1) Adequate bank staff. (2) Satisfactory present bank's staff.	F_9 = (8%) (1) Promotion through fieldworkers. (2) Fieldworkers convincing skill. (3) Attractive promotional gifts. F_{10} = (44%) (1) Employees co-operation in educating clients about new schemes. (2) Employees co-operation in educating clients about new interest rates. F_{12} = (8%) (1) Heavy ads. of new interest rates. (2) Promotion through personal involvement.

Table 5.9
Marketing-Mix Variables Obtaining Less Average than Score—Non-Target Group

Product (A)	*Price (B)*	*Place (C)*	*Promotion (D)*
F_1 = (44%)	F_6 = (25%)	F_8 = (8%)	F_9 = (97%)
(1) Simple loan formalities.	(1) Attractive and adequate interest rates.	(1) Adequate bank staff.	(1) Promotion through
(2) No switching intentions fieldworkers. for loan.	(2) Reasonable loan interest rates.	(2) Satisfactory present bank's staff.	(2) Fieldworkers convincing skill.
(3) Loan procedure easy even to a layman.	(3) Motivating deposit interest rates.		(3) Attractive promotional gifts.
(4) Timely purchase of assets through bank.	(4) Authentic interest calculations.		F_{10} = (64%)
F_2 = (22%)			(1) Employees co- (1) operation in educating
Need meeting deposit scheme. clients			about new schemes.
(2) Sufficient number deposit schemes.			(2) Employees cooperation in educating clients about new interest rates.
(3) Bank proves to be a good prime bank.			
F_3 = (4%)			

(Contd.)

Table 5.9 *(Contd.)*

Product (A)	*Price (B)*	*Place (C)*	*Promotion (D)*
(1) Simple account opening formalities.			F_{11} = (99%)
(2) Immediate issuance of new cheque/passbooks.			(1) Frequent advertisements.
(3) Timely updating of passbooks.			(2) Effective T.V. and Radio advertisements.
F_4 = (50%)			F_{12} = (85%)
(1) Comfortable loan recovery policy.			(1) Heavy ads. of new interest rates.
(2) Easy repayment of instalments.			(2) Promotion through personal involvement.
F_5 = (8%)			
(1) Quick withdrawal facilities.			
(2) No delay in depositing money.			

Table 5.10
Marketing-Mix Variables Obtaining Average Score—Non-Target Group

Product (A)	*Price (B)*	*Place (C)*	*Promotion (D)*
F_1 = (17%) (1) Simple loan formalities. (2) No switching intentions for loan. (3) Loan procedure easy even to a layman. (4) Timely purchase of assets through bank.	F_6 = (8%) (1) Attractive and adequate interest rates. (2) Reasonable loan interest rates. (3) Motivating deposit interest rates. (4) Authentic interest calculations.	F_8 = (35%) (1) Adequate bank staff. (2) Satisfactory present bank's staff.	F_9 = (2%) (1) Promotion through field-workers. (2) Fieldworkers convincing skill. (3) Attractive promotional gifts.
F_2 = (22%) (1) Need meeting deposit schemes. (2) Sufficient number deposit schemes. (3) Bank proves to be a good prime bank.			F_{10} = (19%) (1) Employees co-operation in educating clients about new schemes. (2) Employees co-operation in educating clients about new interest rates.
F_4 = (21%) (1) Comfortable loan recovery policy. (2) Easy repayment of instalments.			F_{11} = (1%) (1) Frequent advertisements. (2) Effective T.V. and Radio advertisements..
F_5 = (9%) (1) Quick withdrawal facilities. (2) No delay in depositing money.			F_{12} = (8%) (1) Heavy ads. of new interest rates. (2) Promotion through personal involvement.

Table 5.11
Marketing-Mix Variables Obtaining More than Average Score—Non-Target Group

Product (A)	*Price (B)*	*Place (C)*	*Promotion (D)*
F_1 = (39%)	F_6 = (67%)	F_8 = (100%)	F_9 = (1%)
(1) Simple loan formalities.	(1) Attractive and adequate interest rates.	(1) Convenient branch location.	(1) Promotion through field-workers.
(2) No switching intentions for loan.	(2) Reasonable loan interest rates.	(2) Branch location at hitherto unbanked area.	(2) Fieldworkers convincing skill.
(3) Loan procedure easy even to a layman.	(3) Motivating deposit interest rates.	F_8 = (57%)	(3) Attractive promotional gifts.
(4) Timely purchase of assets through bank.	(4) Authentic interest calculations.	(1) Adequate bank staff.	F_{10} = (17%)
F_2 = (74%)		(2) Satisfactory present bank's staff.	(1) Employees co-operation in educating client about new schemes.
(1) Need meeting deposit schemes.			(2) Employees co-operation in educating clients about new interest rates.
(2) Sufficient number deposit schemes.			F_{12} = (7%).
(3) Bank proves to be a good prime bank.			(1) Heavy ads. of new interest rates.
F_3 = (96%)			(2) Promotion through personal involvement.
(1) Simple account opening formalities.			
(2) Immediate issuance of new cheque/passbooks.			
(3) Timely updating of passbooks..			

Table 5.11 *(Contd.)*

Product (A)	*Price (B)*	*Place (C)*	*Promotion (D)*
(3) Timely updating of pass-books.			
F_4 = (29%)			
(1) Comfortable loan recovery policy.			
(2) Easy repayment of instalments.			
F_9 = (83%)			
(1) Quick withdrawal facilities.			
(2) No delay in depositing money.			

Table 5.12
Service Quality and Overall Performance—wise Marketing Orientation

Marketing Mix Factors ↓	*Service Quality*			*Overall Performance*		
	BA	*A*	*AA*	*BA*	*A*	*AA*
PRDMEAN 1	1.93	2.63	3.19	1.84	1.63	3.07
PRDMEAN 2	2.07	2.83	2.85	2.5	3.17	3.55
PRDMEAN 3	3.71	3.92	4.33	3.3	3.67	4.27
PRDMEAN 4	3.0	2.42	2.82	—	3.0	2.68
PRDMEAN 5	3.29	3.73	3.98	3.1	4.5	3.91
GRPRDMEAN	2.8	3.11	3.43	2.69	3.19	3.50
PRIMEAN 1	2.75	2.96	3.39	2.66	2.75	3.29
GRPRIMEAN	2.75	2.96	3.39	2.66	2.75	3.29
PLAMEAN 1	4.45	4.32	4.42	4.47	4.67	4.39
PLAMEAN 2	2.93	3.33	3.41	2.9	3.0	3.38
GRPLAMEAN	3.69	3.83	3.92	3.69	3.84	3.89
PRMMEAN 1	1.52	1.51	1.52	1.5	1.5	1.52
PRMMEAN 2	1.79	2.21	2.44	1.95	2.5	2.36
PRMMEAN 3	1.68	1.52	1.63	1.6	1.25	1.62
PRMMEAN 4	1.46	1.90	2.03	1.55	1.5	1.99
GRPRMMEAN	1.61	1.79	1.91	1.65	1.69	1.87
MKTORIENT	**2.71**	**2.92**	**3.16**	**2.67**	**2.87**	**3.14**
No. & Percentage of Respondents	**14(10%)**	**26(19%)**	**95(70%)**	**2(2%)**	**10(7%)**	**123(91%)**

4.76
1.79
1.42
1.19
1
0.83
0.6
0.54
0.5
0.36
0.33
0.27

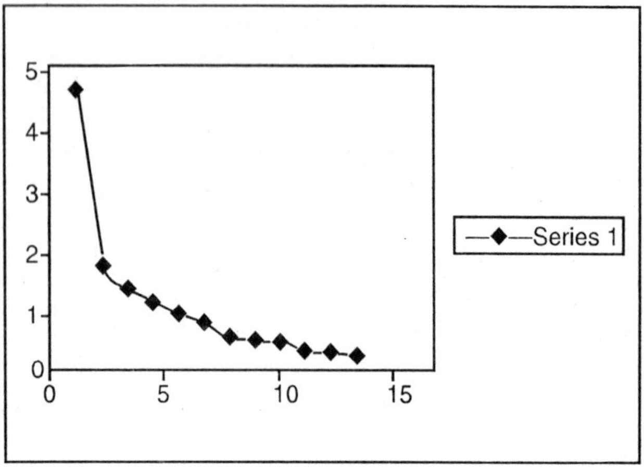

Fig. 5.1: Scree Plot (Product)

2.74
0.96
0.64
0.53
0.14

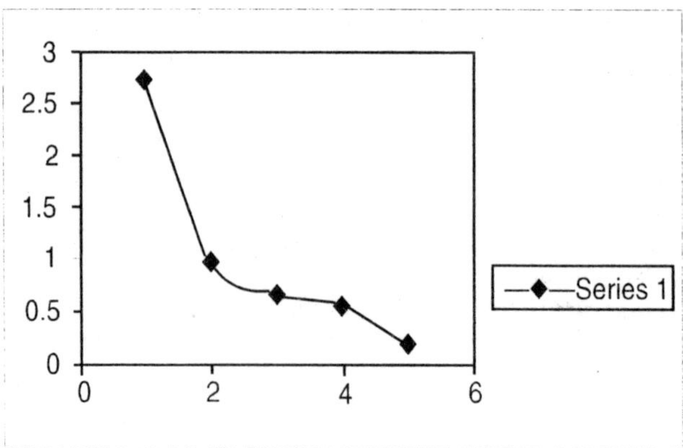

Fig. 5.2: Scree Plot (Price)

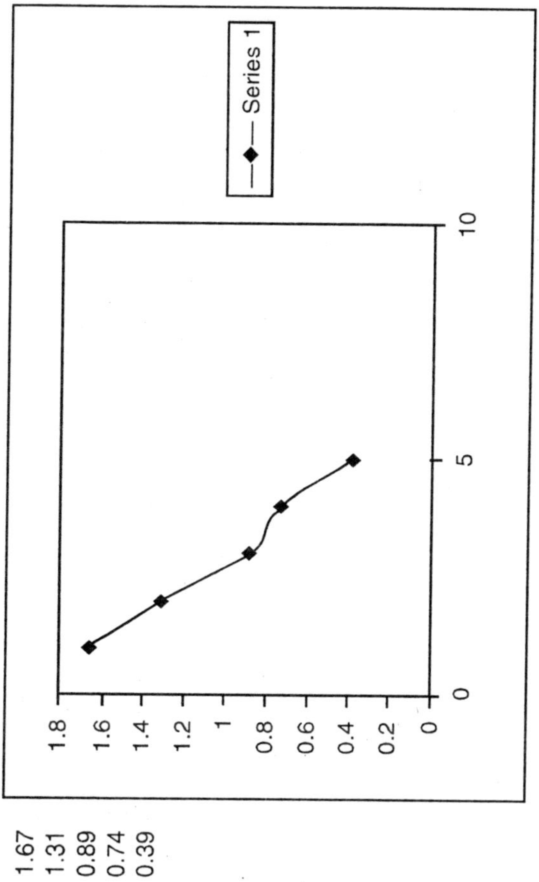

Fig. 5.3: Scree Plot (Place)

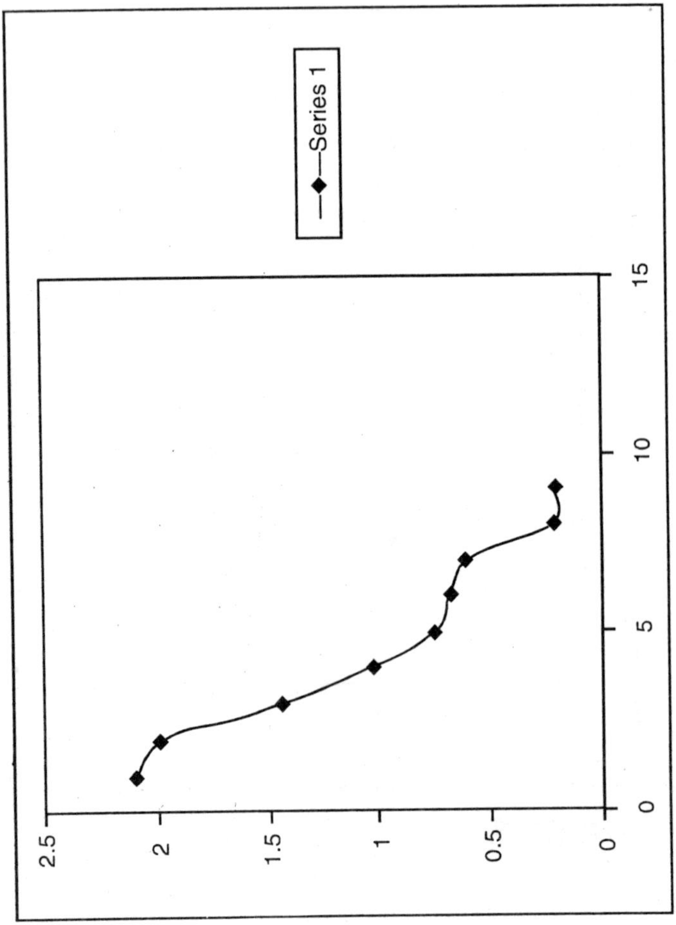

Fig. - 5.4: (Scree plot (Promotion)

Chapter—6

Measurement of Marketing Orientation in JRB with Reference to Developed Rural Area

BACKGROUND

Marketing orientation in RRBs for developed area has been examined by selecting Simbal Camp as a case study (Exhibit 6.1), which is comparatively developed area with 6697 population, 880 households, 30% households living below poverty line, 72% literacy rate, quite good infrastructural facilities such as good condition of roads, very few power cuts, 2 government and 5 private schools and the branch of JRB had accumulated profit of Rs. 96,000 as on 31-03-97 (Exhibit 6.2).

The date for the study has been collected from 185 randomly selected customers of the JRB with 60 statements within the operations of MKTORIENT. After reduction and purification through factor analysis, 43 statements got grouped under 14 dimensions (5 product, 2 price, 3 place and 4 promotion) of MKTORIENT. Further the scree tests (Figs. 6.1, 6.2, 6.3 & 6.4) also provided sound basis for the selection of 14 factors.

STATUS OF MARKETING ORIENTATION

Status of Marketing Orientation has been determined on the basis of the judgement by 80 male and 105 female customers of JRB from the village Simbal Camp of Jammu district separately under the following two broad categories-

1. Target Group

Out of the total customers contacted from the village under reference, 20% belong to target group. Inspite of the fact that 30% population lives below poverty line (Exhibit 6.1), all of them are not availing rural banking services for whom the RRBs were set up (Working Group 1975).

Literate male small farmers having income below Rs. 11,000 p.a. have accorded highest mean value to 'place effectiveness' (3.71) (Table 4.1) followed by 'product adequacy' (2.83), viz., 'time efficient and hasslefree loan procedure', 'adequate and need satisfying deposit schemes,' 'convenient purchase schemes,' 'accurate and timely passbook entries,' 'efficient and satisfactory bank services,' 'price reasonability' (2.67) viz., 'attractive deposit interest rates and accurate calculations' 'reasonable loan interest rates' and lowest mean score assigned to 'promotion optimality' (1.89) for the items such as 'frequent and effective promotional communication,' 'fieldworkers promotional efficiency', 'promotion for interest oriented and motivating new schemes,' 'requisite and instructive advertisements' and 'personal selling efforts.'

Literate male customers belonging to target group under agricultural allied activities have attributed highest value to 'place mix' (3.9) followed by 'product mix' (3.31), 'price mix' (3.22) and lowest score responded to 'promotional elements' (1.86) such as 'persistent and effective promotional communication,' 'fieldworkers promotional intelligence,' 'promotion for new scheme,' 'sufficient and informative advertisements' and 'employees' efforts in selling banking services. Whereas its illiterate counterpart has shown highest satisfaction towards 'product adequacy' (3.94) followed by 'place effectiveness' (3.88), 'price reasonability' (3.6) and exhibited lowest satisfaction with regard to 'promotion optimality' (1.82).

Both literate and illiterate female customers engaged in agricultural allied activities, have highlighted their highest satisfaction with regard to 'place mix effectiveness' (3.99 & 3.93), followed by 'product mix effectiveness' (3.70 & 3.54), 'price mix effectiveness' (3.28 & 3.25) and least score obtained by 'promotion mix variables' (1.84 & 1.85) i.e., 'frequent and effective promotional communication', 'fieldworkers promotional skill', 'promotion for high interest deposit and low interest loan schemes', 'adequate and educative advertisements for favourable changes' and 'field selling efforts.'

Fourteen dimensions of MKTORIENT clubbed under four Ps of marketing mix variables segregated into two orientation regions of customers satisfaction within the paradigm of marketing orientation revealing the extent of MKTORIENT (Table 6.2) reflects that target customers of SKGB are highly satisfied with regard to 'sufficient and need satisfying deposit schemes', 'efficient and adequate bank services', 'attractive deposit interest rates and authentic calculations,' 'correct and timely passbook entries,' 'nearest branch location' and 'co-operative, informative and efficient employees.' These customers are least satisfied due to 'time inefficient and hassleful loan procedure', 'inconvenient purchase schemes,' 'unreasonable loan interest rates,' 'inadequate bank staff, 'lack of fieldworkers promotional skill', 'inadequate and ineffective advertisements,' 'insufficient promotion for interest oriented and innovative new schemes' and 'infrequent and ineffective promotional communication'.

The proportion of target customers falling in different marketing orientation regions (Table 6.3) reveals that two dimensions viz., 'correct and timely passbook entries' and 'competent and co-operative employees' have fallen in the highest range ("4-5") of MKTORIENT with as high as 81.08% of the sample respondents. Similarly the majority of respondents have given their high ratings in "3-4" range of MKTORIENT, with regard to 'time efficient and hasslefree procedure' (57.14%), 'nearest branch location and satisfactory staff (72.97%), 'motivating deposit interest rates and accurate calculations' (59.46%), and 'sufficient and need based deposit schemes' (51.35%). One more dimension has secured 'more than average' response from majority of the customers (89.19%) towards'efficient and satisfactory bank services'.

Maximum of the sample customers have given their responses between "2-3" range of orientation with respect to `adequate bank staff' (54.05%). Further majority of respondents have given poor values just between "1-2" scale of MKTORIENT to the `reasonable loan interest rates' (64.87%), `adequate and educative advertisements' (91.89%), `fieldworkers promotional skill' (94.59%), `frequent and effective promotional communication' (97.30%), `promotion through personal selling efforts' (97.30%). Finally 70% sample customers have responded between "1-2" and "2-3" range for third dimension of `product mix' viz., `convenient purchase schemes.'

Overall marketing orientation in JRB branch as worked out from the extent of satisfaction pertaining to four Ps of bank marketing mix among target customers figured out to be 3.07 (Table 6.1). The highest mean score given to 'place effectiveness' (3.85), followed by 'product adequacy and its suitability' (3.36),'price reasonability' (3.12) and 'promotion optimality' (1.86). Thus among all the four Ps promotion mix is the critical one, which implies that promotional tools have not been optimally employed by rural banks to propagate their schemes and services.

2. Non-Target Group

Number of beneficiaries in non-target group, in the village under reference, has arrived at 148 (80% of sample customers), exceeding target group by four times. Thus it can be concluded that still all target people in rural areas have not been covered by RRBs whereas non-target ones have taken full advantage of the rural banking facilities.

Male literate small farmers having income above Rs 11000 p.a. have given highest score to 'place effectiveness'

(3.50) (Table 6.1) followed by 'price reasonability' (3.0), 'product adequacy' (2.72), just average mean value to 'promotional optimality' (3.0) for the items such as 'reasonable and attractive interest rates,' and 'timely information on new interest rates.'

Illiterate male small farmers belonging to non-target group have awarded higher mean value to 'place mix' (4.13) followed by 'product mix' (4.11) 'price mix' (3.67) and lower mean score assigned to the 'promotion mix variables' (1.67) viz., 'prompt and result oriented promotional communication,' 'fieldworkers performance,' 'promotion for interest focused and need based new schemes,' 'sufficient and informative advertisements' and 'field selling efforts.'

Both male literate and illiterate customers belonging to non-target group engaged in activities allied to agriculture have shown their highest satisfaction with regard to 'place effectiveness' (3.84 & 3.81) followed by 'product adequacy' (3.52 & 3.21) 'price reasonability' (3.32 & 2.5) and 'promotion optimality' scored lowest mean score (1.78 & 1.54) for the items such as 'recurrent and effective promotional communication,' 'fieldworkers promotional expertise,' 'high interest on deposit and need satisfying loan schemes,' 'competent and productive advertisements' and 'face to face communication.'

Female literate and illiterate non-target customers who have taken loan for various activities allied to agriculture have attributed highest mean score to 'place effectiveness' (3.96 & 3.88), followed by 'product adequacy' (3.76 & 3.81), 'price reasonability' (3.15 & 3.37) and lowest mean values accorded to 'promotion mix' (1.73 & 1.63) which incorporates 'fieldworkers promotional proficiency', 'convincing promotional communication,' 'efficacious and informative advertisements', and 'face to face communication.'

Male literate medium farmers engaged in agricultural business have exhibited highest satisfaction with respect to 'place mix' (3.88) followed by 'product mix' (3.28) 'price mix'

(3.1) and less than average value obtained by the elements of 'promotion mix' (1.86) viz., 'speedy and compelling promotional communication', 'fieldworkers promotional ability', 'promotion for new schemes,' 'adequate and result oriented advertisements' and 'personal participation in selling banking schemes'.

Literate male non-farmers who have taken loan for various activities allied to agriculture have shown highest satisfaction with regard to 'place mix effectiveness' (3.82) followed by 'price mix effectiveness' (3.05), 'product mix effectiveness' (3.04) and feel highly dissatisfied towards 'promotion mix variables' (1.84) viz., 'frequent and effective promotional communication,' 'fieldworkers promotional aptitude', 'promotion for interest emphasising new schemes,' 'efficacious and informative advertisements' and 'interaction with customers.'

Literate and illiterate female non-farmers having income above Rs. 11,000 p.a engaged in allied agricultural activities have reflected their highest satisfaction towards 'place effectiveness' (3.88 & 4.14) followed by 'product adequacy' (3.81 & 4.33), 'price reasonability' (3.28 & 3.75) and lower mean value to 'promotion optimality' (1.61 & 1.58). Thus both categories of customers have assigned lowest mean score to promotional aspect of rural banking which include 'convincing and operative promotional communication', 'fieldworkers promotional proficiency', 'promotion for interest oriented new schemes,' 'adequate and informative advertisements' and 'field selling efforts.'

MKTORIENT dimensions grouped under four Ps of marketing mix segregated into two orientation regions of customer satisfaction within the parameters of MKTORIENT (Table 6.4) highlights that non-target customers of JRB have given 'above average' response to the six dimensions viz., 'adequate and need based deposit schemes,' 'efficient and adequate bank services,' 'accurate and timely passbook entries,' 'motivating deposit interest rates and authentic calculations,' 'nearest branch location' and 'co-operative, information and efficient employees.' However these customers are least satisfied due to 'unreasonable interest rates,' 'time ineffective and hassleful loan procedure,' 'inconvenient purchase schemes',' 'inadequate bank staff, 'fieldworkers ineffective promotional skill', 'inadequate and uneducative advertisements,' 'inadequate promotion for interest oriented and innovative new schemes.'

The number of non-target customers falling in different regions of MKTORIENT (Table 6.5) exhibits that two dimensions viz., 'accurate and timely passbook entries' and 'competent and co-operative employees' have secured highest score on MKTORIENT with 78.77% and 77.55% of the sample customers. Similarly majority of respondents have given their high scores falling between "3-4" range of MKTORIENT with respect to 'nearest branch location and satisfactory staff' (76.19%), 'attractive deposit interest rates and correct calculations' (63.70%), 'efficient and satisfactory bank services' (57.83%) and 'sufficient and need satisfying deposit schemes' (51.02%). Further one dimension viz., 'adequate bank staff' has obtained responses between "2-3" range from maximum respondents (57.43%).

Like target customers, non-target ones have also expressed their dissatisfaction regarding various dimensions of "promotion mix" i.e., `fieldworkers promotional skill' (84.36%), `adequate and educative advertisements' (89.66%),' frequent and effective promotional communication' (97.26%) and `promotion through personal involvement' (76.87%). Beside these, other dimensions which have scored `below average' mean value ("1-2" and "2-3") are `convenient purchase schemes' (72.73%), `time efficient and hasslefree loan procedure' (66.67%) and `reasonable loan interest rates' (63.64%).

Overall marketing orientation as worked out on the basis of responses extracted from non-target customers towards four Ps of marketing mix, arrived at 3.06. This category of customers have given highest mean value to 'place mix'

(3.88), followed by 'product mix' (3.50), 'price mix' (3.20) and 'promotion mix' (1.70).

On the basis of responses obtained from both 'target and non-target customers' towards various banking service of JRB residing in the aforesaid village the overall marketing orientation worked out to be 3.07. They have assigned highest mean score to 'place effectiveness' (3.87), followed by 'product adequate, (3.45), 'price reasonability' (3.17) and 'promotion optimality' (1.78). All the techniques adopted to determine marketing orientation in JRB have indicated one major lacunae in the operation of rural banking which is non-utilisation of promotional tools, as this aspect has secured below 2-point on MKTORIENT scale from both target and non-target customers. This implies a sound strategic action to be initiated for effective employment of promotional media so that a balanced growth in the four Ps of marketing mix can be ensured. Beside promotion mix, other variables have got to be geared up so as to take up MKTORIENT to the highest point on the orientation construct thereby strengthening overall marketing orientation in Rural Banks.

The relationship between rural banks' marketing orientation and fourteen dimensions in the scale combined under four Ps of marketing mix formulated with a statistical techniques of Multiple Regression is as under:-

MKTORIENT = -2.046 + .254 (PRDMEAN 1) + .109 (PLAMEAN3) .088 (PRMMEAN1) + .012 (PRMMEAN2) + .093 (PRMMEAN3) - .037 (PRMMEAN4) + .033 (PRDMEAN3) +.030 (PRDMEAN4) + .098 PRDMEAN5) -034 (PRIMEAN1) - .158 (PRIMEAN2) + .708 (PLAMEAN 1) + .296 (PLAMEAN 2)

The relative importance of 14 dimensions estimating the overall marketing orientation highlights that first dimension of place mix is the most critical one. Next two ranks in order of merit have gone to second and third dimensions of place mix. Second dimension of price mix appears to be least important (-.158).

VALIDITY AND RELIABILITY

'Service Quality' and 'Overall Performance' have been converged with other important aspects of marketing orientation (Table 6.12). Marketing Orientation, which worked out to be 3.07 (Table 6.1), has been proved convergently valid because majority of JRB customers have fallen under 'above average' region of 'service quality' (83%) and 'overall performance' (86%) by attributing 3.04 and 3.03 values respectively.

Multiple correlation (R) between independent and dependent variables figured out to be .46 which reflects 46% association between marketing orientation and four Ps of marketing mix. The value of co-efficient of determination (R^2) arrived at .22 which implies that 22% of the variation in the marketing orientation can be explained by four variables in the linear equation.

As the calculated value (2.03) of 'F' is smaller than the tabulated value (2.18) at 1% level of significance ($d.f_{v1v2}$ 12, 184) so the hypothesis of equality of 14 dimensions is accepted. Thus these dimensions have equal impact on overall marketing orientation.

The values of 't' were tested both at 1% and 5% level of significance (df_{v1}, 12). Except for first dimension of place mix, all the ramaining dimensions have fallen in the acceptance region both at 1% (3.055) and 5% (2.179) level of significance. This highlights that except for the first dimension of place mix, others have contributed significantly in the calculation of overall MKTORIENT.

STRATEGIC ACTION

There is an immediate need of such a marketing plan which requires greater attention of RRBs administration and the government towards all those banking aspects which have generated 'below average' score on orientation scale.

54.77% sample customers opined that the purchase of assets through rural bank finance is very complicated. One assistant to every advance manager should be appointed who would help rural people to avail loan schemes and procure assets very conveniently.

Majority of the JRB customers (55.16%) feel that loan procurement is quite cumbersome. Patel and Khankhoja's (1991) recommendations for the simplification of banking operations would prove to be a right step in the light of day-to-day complicacies in banking operations. With this relaxation a bank can reduce number of formalities involved in getting loan in accordance with educational level of the target customers.

About 60% respondents are of the opinion that loan interest rates are unreasonable with the deregulation of interest rates (Narasimham Committee 1992), R.B.I. has allowed RRBs to freely determine their lending rates. Thus rural banks should charge minimum loan interest rates owing to poor socio-economic status of the people residing in the villages.

57.10% customers contacted felt that there is a shortage of staff in rural banks from the branch manager to peon every person is busy with the daily operations of the bank and no employee ever get time to inform customers about new schemes. Thus R.B.I. should remove ban on the recruitment of staff in rural banks, so that proper co-operation, guidance and assistance may be extended to customers.

Maximum customers contacted (94.91%) have regretted that fieldworkers have never organised public meet in the rural areas. Every required information should be imparted to the field staff so that customers meet can be organised in order to spread banking habits and to achieve rapid expansion in banking network (Pai 1987).

96.27% sample customers have highlighted their dissatisfaction due to the absence of promotion through personal involvement. In every rural bank one day need to be fixed exclusively for disseminating information regarding new schemes or interest rates.

Approximately all the customers contacted have responded that JRB had never given any advertisement on television, newspapers, magazines etc. In order to make an advertisement more effective, regional language should be used, this would attract customers from far flung areas as well.

Second type of marketing strategy needs attention of all the concerned towards those rural banking operations which have acquired 'above average' mean values on MKTORIENT construct.

89.16% sample customers have shown their satisfaction towards number and nature of deposit schemes in rural banks, but still there is a need to introduce more innovative and need satisfying deposit schemes (Mandanna & Chengappa 1993).

About 89% respondents have exhibited their positive attitude with respect to efficient banking services, yet there is a desire of remaining customers to introduce new procedures so that old ones may be dispensed with on an ongoing basis (Goiporia Committee 1996).

67.35% sample customers opined that deposit interest rates are motivating and interest calculations are authentic. Thus 38% respondents have shown their dissatisfaction towards this aspect of rural banking which requires alteration in present interest rate structure after going through the economic status of the rural clientele.

Almost all the customers contacted (99%) are of the opinion that branch is located within the accessible limits and in the area where no other bank branch is operating. Further bank employees are quite cooperative and friendly, which implies that bank should provide more training programmes to them which should be in line with customer service orientation (Goiporia Committee 1996) so that present level of customer satisfaction may be retained.

REFERENCES

1. Goiporia Committee (1996), "Customer Service in Banks", *Planning Bulletin*, June-July, 289 & 295.
2. Mandanna, P.K and P.G. Chengappa (1993), "Marketing Approach in Rural Banking", *Economic Review*, June, 6.
3. Narasimham Committee (1992), "Report of the Committee on Financial System," *RBI Bulletin*, Feb., 371.
4. Pai, M.R. (1987), "Customer Service in Banks", *Southern Economist*, Feb., Vol. 25, 21.
5. Patel, K.V. and D.P. Khankhoja (1991), "Liberalisation and Rural Development in India: Role of Banking Sector in Changing Environment", *Prajnan*, Oct.-Dec.., Vol. XX, No. 4, 379-97.
6. Working Group (1986), "RRBs—A Resume", G.O.I. Dept. of Economic Affairs, New Delhi, 19-22.

Exhibit 6.1
Brief Profile of the Village Simbal Camp of Jammu District as on 31.3.97

1. Total Population : 6697
2. Male : Female : 3377 : 3320
3. Total Households : 880
4. Tentative Economic Status-
   (a) Target Group=30%
   (b) Non-Target Group=70%
5. Literacy Rate-
   (a) Literate=72%
   (b) Illiterate=28%
6. Infrastructural Facilities-
   (a) Roads—Good condition
   (b) Electricity—not frequent cuts
   (c) Two government schools (middle & higher)
   (d) Five private middle schools.
7. Land soil suitable for growing paddy and wheat.
8. Per hectare yield-

	Irrigated	*Non-irrigated*
Paddy	42qtl/hec	—
Wheat	40qtl/hec	20qtl/hec

Exhibit 6.2
Brief Profile of the Branch Simble Camp of JRB

(Rs in '000)

Year	*Deposits*		*Advances*		*Profit*	*C.D. Ratio*
	A/C	*Rs*	*A/C*	*Rs*	*(Rs.)*	
1992-93	3516	8325	271	1665	+429.24	20
1993-94	3841	11477	303	2483	+503.24	22
1994-95	4468	16799	293	3528	+94.21	21
1995-96	4811	22374	295	4542	+140.21	20
1996-97	4228	29801	336	5690	+95.94	19
1997-98	4660	40846	354	7503	+291.27	18
1998-99	4655	52383	335	9061	+813.06	17

		1996-97	1997-98
(a)	Two branches of other banks at a distance of 4 kms		
(b)	Number of Projects finaned;		
(i)	Transport	9	10
(ii)	Retail Trade	51	107
(iii)	Dairing	66	80

Table 6.0
Summary of Results from Scale Purification—Loading and Variance Explained

Bank Marketing Mix	*Factor-Wise Dimension*	*Factor Loadings*	*% of Variance Explained*
1	2	3	4
Product	**Factor First-**		**31.4**
	Comfortable loan security and guarantee.	.96	
	Comfortable loan recovery policy.	.93	
	Easy repayment of instalments.	.93	
	Sufficient number of loan schemes.	.92	
	Convenient purchase of assets through bank finance.	.90	
	Need meeting loan schemes.	.87	
	Standard product purchase through bank finance	.84	
	Factor Second-		**18.5**
	Sufficient number of deposit schemes.	.84	
	Bank proves to be a good prime bank.	.90	
	Need meeting deposit schemes.	.83	
	Factor Third-		**11.0**
	Loan procedure easy even to a layman.	.87	
	Simple loan formalities.	.83	

Contd. . .

1	2	3	4
	Timely purchase of assets through rural bank.	.65	
	Factor Fourth-		8.3
	Accurate passbook entries.	.80	
	Timely updating of passbook.	.85	
	Factor Fifth-		5.8
	Quick withdrawal facilities.	.69	
	No delay in depositing cash.	.75	
	Timely encashment of cheques.	-.71	
	Total Variance explained = 74.9%		
Price	**Factor First-**		49.5
	Attractive and adequate interest rates.	.89	
	Motivating deposit interest rates.	.87	
	Authentic interest calculations.	.71	
	Quick information regarding new interest rates.	.59	
	Factor Second-		20.2
	Reasonable loan interest rates.	.89	
	Total variance explained = 69.7%		
Place	**Factor First-**		31.7
	Branch location at hitherto unbanked area.	.66	
	Reasonable market around branch location.	.64	
	Satisfactory present bank's staff.	.60	
	Nearest location.	.58	
	Factor Second-		15.6
	Competent and efficient employees.	.79	
	Co-operative and friendly employees.	.76	
	Convenient branch location.	.58	

Contd. . .

1	2	3	4
	Factor Third-		**13.1**
	Adequate bank's staff.	.87	
	Total variance explained = 60.4%		
Promotion	**Factor First-**		**29.7**
	Fieldworkers convincing skill.	.91	
	Promotion through fieldworkers.	.90	
	Customers awareness meets.	.62	
	Factor Second-		**17.2**
	Promotion through personnel involvement.	.76	
	Employees co-operation in educating client about new interest rates.	.72	
	Employees co-operation in educating client about new schemes.	.72	
	Attractive promotional gifts.	.58	
	Factor Third-		**12.7**
	Frequent advertisements.	.77	
	Promotion of schemes through posters.	.70	
	Heavy ads. of new interest rates.	.63	
	Factor Fourth-		**11.0**
	Effective T.V. and Radio ads.	.78	
	Heavy promotion through newspaper and magazines.	.72	
	Total variance explained =70.7%		

Table 6.1
Overall Marketing Orientation-Customers Assessment

In-come	*Land Holding*	*Gender*	*Occupa-tion*	*Education*										*Overall Mean*				
				LITERATE					*ILLITERATE*									
				A	*B*	*C*	*D*	*M*	*A*	*B*	*C*	*D*	*M*	*A*	*B*	*C*	*D*	*M*
	Small Farmers	Male	Agricul ture	2.83	2.67	3.71	1.89	2.78	-	-	-	-	-	2.83	2.67	3.71	1.89	2.78
Target Group	Male		Allied to Agricul-ture	3.31	3.22	3.90	1.86	3.3	3.94	3.60	3.88	1.82	3.23	3.63	3.41	3.89	1.84	3.12
	Female		Allied to Agricul-ture	3.70	3.28	3.99	1.84	3.15	3.54	3.25	3.93	1.85	3.06	3.62	3.27	3.96	1.85	3.11
	Target Group Mean			3.28	3.06	3.87	1.86	2.98	3.74	3.43	3.91	1.84	3.15	3.36	3.12	3.85	1.86	3.07
	Small Farmers	Male	Agricul-ture	2.72	3.0	3.50	1.42	2.66	4.11	3.67	4.13	1.67	3.40	3.42	3.34	3.82	1.55	3.03
Non-Target Group	Male		Allied to Agricul-ture	3.52	3.32	3.84	1.78	3.12	3.21	2.50	3.81	1.54	2.77	3.37	2.91	3.83	1.66	2.94
	Female		Allied to Agricul-ture	3.76	3.15	3.96	1.73	3.15	3.81	3.37	3.88	1.63	3.17	3.79	3.26	3.92	1.68	3.16

Table 6.1 *(Contd.)*

In-come	*Land Holding*	*Gender*	*Occupa-tion*	*Education*										*Overall Mean*				
				LITERATE					*ILLITERATE*									
				A	*B*	*C*	*D*	*M*	*A*	*B*	*C*	*D*	*M*	*A*	*B*	*C*	*D*	*M*
	Mean			3.33	3.16	3.77	1.64	2.98	3.71	3.18	3.94	1.61	3.11	3.53	3.17	3.86	1.63	3.04
	Medium Farmers	Male	Agricul-ture	3.28	3.10	3.88	1.86	3.01	-	-	-	-	-	3.28	3.10	3.88	1.86	3.01
Non-Target Group	Male		Allied to Agricul-ture	3.04	3.05	3.82	1.84	2.94						3.04	3.05	3.82	1.84	2.94
	Female		Allied to Agricul-ture	3.81	3.28	3.88	1.61	3.15	4.33	3.75	4.14	1.58	3.45	4.07	3.52	4.01	1.60	3.30
	Mean			3.38	3.14	3.86	1.77	3.03	4.33	3.75	4.14	1.58	3.45	3.46	3.22	3.90	1.77	3.08
	Non-Target Group Mean			3.36	3.15	3.82	1.71	3.01	4.02	3.47	4.04	1.60	3.28	3.50	3.20	3.88	1.70	3.06
	Overall Mean			3.33	3.12	3.38	1.70	3.0	3.93	3.45	4.0	1.57	3.24	3.45	3.17	3.87	1.78	3.07

Abbreviations used-
A=Product B=Price C=Place D=Promotion M=Mean of four Ps.

Table 6.2
Fourteen Dimensions of the Construct Falling under Two Orientation Regions of Target Customers' Satisfaction and the Respective Mean Values Revealing the Extent of MKTORIENT

Below Average (-3 points)	*Above Average (+3 points)*
F_1 = "Time efficient and hassle-free loan procedure" (2.77).	F_2 = "Adequate and need satisfying deposit schemes" (3.83.)
F_3 = "Convenient purchase schemes" (2.82).	F_4 = "Accurate and timely pass-book entries" (4.62).
F_7 = "Reasonable loan interest rates" (1.35).	F_5 = "Efficient and satisfactory bank services" (4.15).
F_{10} = "Adequate bank staff" (2.62).	F_6 = "Atractive deposit interest rates and authentic calculations" (3.33).
F_{11} = "Fieldworkers promotional skill" (1.56).	F_8 = "Nearest branch location and satisfactory staff" (3.98).
F_{12} = "Promotion through personal involvement" (1.69).	F_9 = "Efficient and co-operative employees" (4.36).
F_{13} = "Frequent promotional communication" (1.63).	
F_{14} = "Adequate and effective advertisements" (1.61).	

Table 6.3
Number of Target Customers under Dimension-wise MKTORIENT Regions

Responses → / *Dimensions* ↓	1-2		2-3		3-4		4-5	
	No.	*(%)*	*No*	*(%)*	*No.*	*(%)*	*No.*	*(%)*
F_1 (7)	02	28.57	01	14.29	04	57.14	—	—
F_2 (37)	—	—	04	10.81	19	51.35	14	37.84
F_3 (30)	09	30	12	40	07	23.33	02	6.67
F_4 (37)	—	—	—	—	07	18.92	30	81.08
F_5 (37)	01	2.70	03	8.11	18	48.65	15	40.54
F_6 (37)	—	—	12	32.43	22	59.46	03	8.11

Contd. . .

Table 6.3 *(Contd.)*

Responses → *Dimensions* ↓	1-2		2-3		3-4		4-5	
	No.	*(%)*	*No*	*(%)*	*No.*	*(%)*	*No.*	*(%)*
F_7 (37)	24	64.87	8	21.62	05	13.51	—	—
F_8 (37)	—	—	—	—	27	72.97	10	27.03
F_9 (37)	—	—	—	—	07	18.92	30	81.08
F_{10} (37)	14	37.84	20	54.05	03	8.11	—	—
F_{11} (37)	35	94.59	02	5.41	—	—	—	—
F_{12} (37)	36	97.30	01	2.70	—	—	—	—
F_{13} (37)	36	97.30	01	2.70	—	—	—	—
F_{14} (37)	34	91.89	03	8.11	—	—	—	—

Table 6.4

Fourteen Dimensions of the Construct Falling under Two Orientation Regions of Non-Target Customers' Satisfaction and the Respective Mean Values Revealing the Extent of MKTORIENT

Below Average *(-3 points)*	*Above Average* *(+3 points)*
F_1 = "Time efficient and hasslefree loan procedure" (2.78).	F_2 = "Adequate and need satisfying deposit schemes" (3.80).
F_3 = "Convenient purchase schemes" (2.76).	F_4 = "Accurate and timely passbook entries" (4.63).
F_7 = "Reasonable loan interest rates" (2.75).	F_5 = "Efficient and satisfactory bank services" (4.04).
F_{10} = "Adequate bank staff" (2.66).	F_6 = "Attractive deposit interest rates and authentic calculations" (3.34).
F_{11} = "Fieldworkers promotional skill" (1.71).	F_8 = "Nearest branch location and satisfactory staff" (3.90).
F_{12} = "Promotion through personal involvement" (1.92).	F_9 = "Efficient and co-operative employees" (4.29).
F_{13} = "Frequent promotional communication" (1.58).	
F_{14} = "Adequate and effective advertisements" (1.68).	

Table 6.5
Number of Non-Target Customers under Dimension-wise MKTORIENT Regions

Responses →	*1-2*		*2-3*		*3-4*		*4-5*	
Dimensions ↓	*No.*	*(%)*	*No*	*(%)*	*No.*	*(%)*	*No.*	*(%)*
F_1 (15)	03	20	07	46.67	05	33.33	—	—
F_2 (147)	03	2.04	13	8.84	75	51.02	56	38.10
F_3 (121)	41	33.89	47	38.84	28	23.14	05	4.13
F_4 (146)	—	—	—	—	31	21.23	115	78.77
F_5 (147)	08	5.44	09	6.12	85	57.83	45	30.61
F_6 (146)	—	—	48	32.88	93	63.70	05	3.42
F_7 (44)	16	36.37	12	27.27	15	34.09	01	2.27
F_8 (147)	—	—	02	1.36	112	76.19	33	22.45
F_9 (147)	—	—	02	1.36	31	21.09	114	77.55
F_{10} (148)	55	37.16	85	57.43	08	5.41	—	—
F_{11} (147)	124	84.36	12	8.16	10	6.80	01	0.68
F_{12} (147)	113	76.87	28	19.05	06	4.08	—	—
F_{13} (146)	142	97.26	03	2.06	01	0.68	—	—
F_{14} (145)	130	89.66	14	9.66	01	0.68	—	—

Table 6.6

Marketing-Mix Variables Obtaining Less than Average Score—Target Group

Product (A)	*Price (B)*	*Place (C)*	*Promotion (D)*
F_1 = (42.86%) (1) Comfortable loan security and guarantee. (2) Comfortable loan recovery policy. (3) Easy repayment of instalments. (4) Sufficient number of loan schemes. (5) Convenient purchase of assets through bank finance. (6) Need meeting loans schemes. (7) Standard product purchase through bank finance. F_2 (10.81%) (1) Sufficient number of deposit schemes.	F_6 = (33.51%) (1) Attractive and adequate interest rates. (2) Motivating deposit interest. (3) Authentic interest calculations. (4) Quick information regarding new interest rates. F_7 (64.86%) (1) Reasonable loan interest rates.	F_{10} = (37.84%) (1) Adequate bank's staff.	F_{11} = (97.30%) (1) Fieldworkers convincing skill. (2) Promotion through fieldworkers. (3) Customer awareness meets. F_{13} (97.30%) (1) Promotion through personal involvement. (2) Employees cooperation in educating clients about new interest rates. (3) Employees cooperation in educating clients about new schemes.

Contd. . .

Table 6.6 *(Contd.)*

Product (A)	*Price (B)*	*Place (C)*	*Promotion (D)*
(2) Bank proves to be a good prime bank.			(4) Attractive Promotional gifts.
(3) Need meeting deposit schemes.			F_{13} (100%)
F_{13} (46.67%)			(1) Frequent advertisements.
(1) Loan procedure easy even to a layman.			(2) Promotion of schemes through posters.
(2) Simple loan formalities.			(3) Heavy ads. of new interest rates.
(3) Timely purchase of assets through rural bank.			F_{14} (100%)
F_5 (5.41%)			(1) Effective T. V. & Radio ads.
(1) Quick withdrawal facilities.			(2) Heavy promotion through newspaper & magazines.
(2) No delay in depositing cash.			
(3) Timely encashment of cheques.			

Table 6.7
Marketing-Mix Variables Obtaining Average Score—Target Group

Product (A)	*Price (B)*	*Place (C)*	*Promotion (D)*
F_3 = (18.92%) (1) Loan procedure easy even to a layman. (2) Simple loan formalities. (3) Timely purchase of assets through rural banks. F_5 = (5.41%) (1) Quick withdrawal facilities. (2) No delay in depositing cash. (3) Timely encashment of cheques.	F_6 = (18.92%) (1) Attractive and adequate interest rates. (2) Motivating deposit interest rates. (3) Authentic interest calculations. (4) Quick information regarding new interest rates. F_7 (21.62%). (1) Reasonable loan interest rates.	F_{10} = (54.05%) (1) Adequate bank's staff.	F_{11} = (2.70%) (1) Fieldworkers convincing skill. (2) Promotion through fieldworkers. (3) Customer awareness meets. F_{12} (2.70%) (1) Promotion through personal involvement. (2) Employees cooperation in educating clients about new interest rates. (3) Employees cooperation in educating clients about new schemes. (4) Attractive promotional gifts.

Table 6.8
Marketing-Mix Variables Obtaining More than Average Score—Target Grop

Product (A)	Price (B)	Place (C)	Promotion (D)
F_1 = (57.14%)	F_6 = (67.57%)	F_8 = (100%)	
(1) Comfortable loan security and guarantee.	(1) Attractive and adequate interest rates.	(1) Branch location at hitherto unbanked area.	
(2) Comfortable loan recovery policy.	(2) Motivating deposit interest.	(2) Reasonable market around branch location.	
(3) Easy repayment of instalments.	(3) Authentic interest calculations.	(3) Satisfactory present bank's staff.	
(4) Sufficient number of loan schemes.	(4) Quick information regarding new interest rates.	(4) Nearest location.	
(5) Convenient purchase of assets through bank finance.	F_7(13.51%)	F_9(100%)	
(6) Need meeting loans finance.	(1) Reasonable loan interest rates.	(1) Competent & efficient employees.	
(7) Standard product purchase through bank finance.		(2) Co-operative & friendly employees.	
F_2(89.19%)		(3) Convenient branch location.	
(1) Sufficient number of deposit schemes.		F_{10}(8.11%)	
(2) Bank proves to be a good prime bank.		(4) Adequate bank's staff.	
(3) Need meeting deposit scheme.			

Table 6.8 *(Contd.)*

Product (A)	*Price (B)*	*Place (C)*	*Promotion (D)*
F_3(30%)			
(1) Loan procedure easy even to a layman.			
(2) Simple loan formalities.			
(3) Timely purchase of assets through bank finance.			
F_4(100%)			
(1) Accurate passbook entries.			
(2) Timely updating of pass-books.			
F_5(89.19%)			
(1) Quick withdrawal facilities.			
(2) No delay in depositing cash.			
(3) Timely encashment of cheques.			

Table 6.9
Marketing-Mix Variables Obtaining Less than Average Score—Non-Target Group

Product (A)	*Price (B)*	*Place (C)*	*Promotion (D)*
F_1 = (66.67%) (1) Comfortable loan security and guarantee. (2) Easy loan recovery policy. (3) Easy repayment of instalment. (4) Sufficient number of loan schemes. (5) Convenient purchase of assets through bank finance. (6) Need meeting loan schemes. (7) Standard product purchase through bank finance. F_2 (10.88%) (1) Sufficient number of deposit schemes.	F_6 = (25.34%) (1) Attractive and adequate interest rates. (2) Motivating deposit interest rates. (3) Authentic interest calculations. (4) Quick information regarding new interest rates. F_7 (54.55%) (1) Reasonable loan interest rates.	F_8 = (1.36%) (1) Branch location at hitherto. unbanked areas. (2) Reasonable market aröund branch location. (3) Satisfactory bank's staff. F_9 = (1.36%) (1) Competent and efficient employees. (2) Co-operative and friendly employees. (3) Convenient branch location. F_{10} = (76.35%) (1) Adequate present bank's staff.	F_{11} = (92.52%) (1) Fieldworkers convincing skill. (2) Promotion through fieldworkers. (3) Customer awareness meets. F_{12} (95.24%) (1) Promotion through personal involvement. (2) Employees cooperation in educating clients about new interest rates. (3) Employees cooperation in educating clients about new schemes. (4) Attractive promotional gifts.

Contd. . .

Table 6.9 *(Contd.)*

Product (A)	*Price (B)*	*Place (C)*	*Promotion (D)*
(2) Bank proves to be a good prime bank.			F_{13} (99.32%)
(3) Need meeting deposit schemes.			(1) Frequent advertisements.
F_3 (63.64%)			(2) Promotion of schemes through posters.
(1) Loan procedure easy even to layman.			(3) Heavy ads. of new interest rates.
(2) Simple loan formalities.			F_{14} (99.32%)
(3) Timely purchase of assets through bank finance.			(1) Effective T. V. & Radio ads.
F_5 (10.20%)			(2) Heavy promotion through newspapers & magazines.
(1) Quick withdrawal facility.			
(2) No delay in depositing cash.			
(3) Timely encashment of cheques.			

Table 6.10
Marketing-Mix Variables Obtaining Average Score—Non-Target Group

Product (A)	*Price (B)*	*Place (C)*	*Promotion (D)*
F_3 = (9.09%)	F_6 = (7.53%)	F_{10} = (18.24%)	F_{12} = (0.68%)
(1) Loan procedure easy even to a layman.	(1) Attractive and adequate interest rates.	(1) Adequate bank's staff.	(1) Promotion through personal involvement.
(2) Simple loan formalities.	(2) Motivating deposit interest rates.		(2) Employees co-operation in educating clients about new interest rates.
(3) Timely purchase through bank.	(3) Accurate interest calculations.		(3) Employees co-operation in educating clients about new schemes.
F_2 = (15.38%)	(4) Quick information regarding new interest rates.		(4) Attractive promotional gifts.
(1) Quick withdrawal facilities.	F_7 = (9.09%)		
(2) No delay in depositing cash rates.	(1) Reasonable loan interest rates.		
(3) Timely encashment of cheques.			

Table 6.11
Marketing-Mix Variables Obtaining Less than Average Score—Non-Target Group

Product (A)	*Price (B)*	*Place (C)*	*Promotion (D)*
F_1 = (33.33%) (1) Comfortable loan security and guarantee. (2) Easy loan recovery policy. (3) Easy repayment of instalment. (4) Sufficient number of loan schemes. (5) Convenient purchase of assets through bank finance. (6) Need meeting loan schemes. (7) Standard product purchase through bank finance. F_2 = (89.12%) Sufficient number of deposit schemes.	F_6 = (67.12%) (1) Attractive and adequate interest rates. (2) Motivating deposit interest rates. (3) Authentic interest calculations. (4) Quick information regarding new interest rates. F_7 = (36.36%) (1) Reasonable loan interest rates.	F_8 = (98.64%) (1) Branch at hitherto unbanked areas. (2) Reasonable market around branch location. (3) Satisfactory bank's staff. F_9 = (98.64%) (1) Competent and efficient employees. (2) Co-operative and friendly employees. (3) Convenient branch location. F_{10} = (5.41%) (1) Adequate present bank's staff.	F_{11} = (7.48%) (1) Promotion through fieldworkers. (2) Fieldworkers convincing skill. (3) Customer awareness meets. F_{12} = (4.08%) (1) Promotion through personal involvement. (2) Employees cooperation in educating clients about new interest rates. (3) Employees cooperation in educating clients about new (1) schemes. (4) Attractive promotional gifts.

Table 6.11 *(Contd.)*

Product (A)	*Price (B)*	*Place (C)*	*Promotion (D)*
(2) Bank proves to be a good prime bank. (3) Need meeting deposit schemes. F_3 = (27.27%) (1) Loan procedure easy even to layman. (2) Simple loan formalities. (3) Timely purchase of assets through bank finance. F_4 = (100%) (1) Accurate passbook entries. (2) Timely updating of pass-book. F_5 = (88.44%) (1) Quick withdrawal facilities. (2) No delay in depositing cash. (3) Timely encashment of cheques.			F_{13} = (0.68%) (1) Frequent advertise-ments. (2) Promotion of sche-mes through posters. (3) Heavy ads. of new interest rates. F_{14} = (0.68%) (1) Effective T. V. & Radio ads. (2) Heavy promotion through newspapers & magazines.

Table 6.12
Service Quality and Overall Performance-wise Marketing Orientation

Marketing Mix Factors ↓	*Service Quality* BA>3	*Service Quality* A=3	*Service Quality* AA<3	*Overall Performance* BA>3	*Overall Performance* A=3	*Overall Performance* AA<3
PRDMEAN 1	2.22	2.31	2.99	2.44	1.5	2.85
PRDMEAN 2	2.39	3.19	4.01	2.75	3.61	3.88
PRDMEAN 3	2.18	2.49	2.88	1.67	2.4	2.86
PRDMEAN 4	4.14	4.36	4.70	3.86	4.55	4.67
PRDMEAN 5	3.79	4.14	4.08	3.56	4.05	4.09
GRPRDMEAN	2.94	3.298	3.73	2.86	3.22	3.67
PRIMEAN 1	3.0	3.26	3.38	3.05	3.18	3.38
PRIMEAN 2	3.0	3.0	2.73	3.06	2.67	2.74
GRPRIMEAN	3.0	3.13	3.60	3.33	2.93	3.06
PLAMEAN 1	3.696	3.76	3.96	3.35	3.88	3.95
PLAMEAN 2	4.24	4.17	4.33	4.19	4.23	4.32
PLAMEAN 3	2.64	2.44	2.697	2.63	2.42	2.07
GRPLAMEAN	3.53	3.46	3.66	3.39	3.51	3.66
PRMMEAN 1	1.55	1.69	1.69	1.42	1.84	1.68
PRMMEAN 2	1.71	1.92	1.88	1.5	1.71	1.91
PRMMEAN 3	1.81	1.69	1.56	1.62	1.56	1.59
PRMMEAN 4	1.61	1.44	1.69	1.58	1.79	1.65
GRPRMMEAN	1.67	1.69	1.71	1.53	1.73	1.71
MKTORIENT	**2.79**	**2.89**	**3.04**	**2.78**	**2.85**	**3.03**
No. & % age of Respondents	**14(7%)**	**18(10%)**	**152(83%)**	**6(3%)**	**19(11%)**	**158(86%)**

Chapter—7

Measurement of Marketing Orientation in SKGB with Reference to Underdeveloped Rural Area

BACKGROUND

The present section evaluated the nature and extent of marketing orientation in a Regional Rural Bank operating in an underdeveloped area (Ambala Jattan) (Exhibit 7.1) with 38% households living below poverty line, 32% illiteracy rate, poor infrastructural facilities such as muddy roads, frequent power cuts, one government school, no private school and the branch of SKGB had accumulated loss of Rs. 1.21 lakhs as on 31.3.97 (Exhibit 7.2).

Though the deposits and advances of SKGB Ambala Jattan branch have increased year after year from 1990-91 onwards (Exhibit 7.2) but credit-deposit ratio started declining after 1992-93 when it was highest (64) with the profit being highest at Rs. 1.96 lakhs. This branch has extended primarily the agricultural loans but, due to low quintal per hectare yield (35 qtl/hec) when compared with other two area under studies of the same district, the farmers repaying capacity is comparatively lower, consequently resulting into huge bad debts and finally landing the bank branch into losses.

The data for study has been gathered from 100 randomly selected customers of SKGB with as many as 60 initial statements within the paradigm of MKTORIENT. After reduction and purification through factor analysis, 46 statements got grouped under 16 dimensions—6 product, 2 price, 2 place and 6 promotion (Table 7.0).

Exhibit 7.1

Brief Profile of the Village Ambala Jattan of Hoshiarpur District as on 31.3.97

1. Total Population	:	1486
2. Male : Female	:	827 : 659
3. Total Households	:	282
4. Tentative Economic Status		
(a) Below poverty line	:	38%
(b) Above poverty line	:	62%
5. Literacy level	:	
(a) Literate	:	68%
(b) Illiterate	:	32%
6. Infrastructural Facilities		
(a) Roads—Muddy		
(b) Electricity—frequent cuts		
(c) Govt. School - I		
(d) Private School - nil		

7. Land soil suitable for growing wheat, maize, potato and sun flower.

8. Per hectare yield-

	Irrigated	*Non-irrigated*
Wheat	—	34 qtl/hec.
Maize	—	20 qtl/hec.
Potato	—	68 qtl/hec.
Sunflower	—	18 qtl/hec.

Exhibit 7.2
Brief Profile of the Branch Ambala Jattan of SKGB

Amount in '000

Year	*Deposits*		*Advances*		*C.D.*	*Profit/*
	A/C	*Rs.*	*A/C*	*Rs.*	*Ratio*	*Loss Rs.*
1990-91	1634	3864	476	2086	54	P-55
1991-92	2002	5160	605	3123	61	P-59.9
1992-93	2306	6251	657	3991	64	P-196
1993-94	2786	8701	620	4116	47	P-80
1994-95	2872	11458	588	4743	41	L-60
1995-96	1823	13728	554	4943	36	L-163
1996-97	1917	16904	508	4816	28	L-121
1997-98	2162	21009	453	5519	26	P-83

(1) Branches of other banks at a distance of 2 kms.

(2) Number of projects financed-

	1996-97	*1997-98*
(a) Agriculture	62	58
(b) Allied to Agriculture	41	37

Table 7.0
Summary of Results from Scale Purification—
Loading and Variance Explained

Bank Marketing Mix	*Factor-Wise Dimension*	*Factor Loadings*	*% of Variance Explained*
1	2	3	4
Product	**First Factor-**		**28.4**
	Need meeting deposit schemes.	.87	
	Sufficient number of deposit schemes.	.86	
	Bank proves to be a good prime bank.	.85	
	Second Factor-		**11.4**
	Simple loan formalities.	.77	
	Comfortable loan security and guarantee.	.58	
	No switching intentions for loans.	.66	

Contd. . .

1	2	3	4
	Loan procedure easy even to a layman	.74	
	Timely purchase through bank.	.74	
	Third Factor-		**11.2**
	Accurate passbook entries.	.79	
	Timely updating of passbooks.	.87	
	Quick withdrawal facilities.	.64	
	No delay in depositing money.	.56	
	Fourth Factor-		**10.1**
	Need meeting loan schemes.	.96	
	Sufficient number of loan schemes.	.96	
	Fifth Factor-		**7.6**
	Comfortable loan recovery policy.	.91	
	Easy repayment of instalments.	.92	
	Sixth Factor-		**6.7**
	Simple account opening formalities.	.75	
	Immediate issuance of new passbooks.	.81	
	Total variance explained = 75.4%		
Price	**First Factor-**		**47.0**
	Attractive and adequate interest rates.	.89	
	Reasonable loan interest rates.	.77	
	Motivating deposit interest rates.	.86	
	Second Factor-		**24.2**
	Authentic interest calculations.	.77	
	Quick information regarding new interest rates.	.74	
	Total variance explained = 71.2%		
Place	**First Factor-**		**36.4**
	Convenient branch location.	-.78	
	Branch location at hitherto unbanked area.	.62	
	Nearest location.	.51	
	Reasonable market around branch location.	.66	
	Co-operative and friendly employees.	.57	

Contd. . .

1	2	3	4
	Employees have sufficient information.	.64	
	Second Factor-		**15.6**
	Adequate bank's staff.	-.59	
	Competent and efficient employees.	.78	
	Satisfactory present bank's staff.	.79	
	Total variance explained = 52 %		
Promotion	**First Factor-**		**19.2**
	Promotion through fieldworkers.	.92	
	Fieldworkers convincing skill.	.88	
	Attractive promotional gifts.	-.63	
	Second Factor-		**17.2**
	Employees co-operation in educating clients about new schemes.	.59	
	Employees co-operation in educating clients about new interest rates.	.94	
	Third Factor-		**12.6**
	Heavy advertisements of new interest rates.	.79	
	Promotional through personal involvement	.77	
	Customer awareness meets.	.51	
	Fourth Factor-		**11.9**
	Effective T.V. and radio advertisements	-.78	
	Promotional of schemes through attractive posters.	.77	
	Fifth Factor-		
	Employees assistance in filing withdrawal/deposit forms.	.71	
	Employees cooperation in completing loan formalities.	.77	
	Sixth Factor-		**7.3**
	Frequent advertisements	.86	
	Heavy promoting through newspapers and magazines.	-.79	
	Total variance explained = 78.1%		

Table 7.1
Overall Marketing Orientation—Customers Assessment

				Education										*Overall Mean*				
				LITERATE					*ILLITERATE*									
Income	*Land Holding*	*Gender*	*Occupation*	*A*	*B*	*C*	*D*	*M*	*A*	*B*	*C*	*D*	*M*	*A*	*B*	*C*	*D*	*M*
	Small Farmers	Male	Agricul ture	3.86	2.9	3.06	1.81	2.91	-	-	-	-	-	3.86	2.9	3.06	1.81	2.91
Target Group	Male		Allied to Agriculture	3.81	2.79	3.28	2.04	2.98	4.08	2.6	3.39	1.97	3.01	3.95	2.7	3.34	2.01	3.0
	Female		Allied to Agriculture	4.11	3.17	3.31	1.74	3.08	3.76	3.14	3.43	1.79	3.03	3.94	3.16	3.37	1.77	3.06
	Target Group Mean			3.93	2.95	3.22	1.86	2.99	3.92	2.87	3.41	1.88	3.02	3.93	2.91	3.32	1.87	3.01
	Small Farmers	Male	Agriculture	4.05	2.64	3.33	1.86	2.97	3.6	3.0	3.38	1.82	2.95	3.83	2.82	3.36	1.84	2.96
Non-Target Group	Male		Allied to Agriculture	4.02	3.15	3.41	2.09	3.17	-	-	-	-	-	4.02	3.15	3.41	2.09	3.17
	Female		Allied to Agriculture	3.98	3.15	3.35	2.05	3.13	4.03	3.25	3.36	1.86	3.13	4.01	3.20	3.36	1.96	3.13

Table 7.1 *(Contd.)*

				Education										*Overall Mean*				
				LITERATE					*ILLITERATE*									
In-come	*Land Holding*	*Gender*	*Occupa-tion*	*A*	*B*	*C*	*D*	*M*	*A*	*B*	*C*	*D*	*M*	*A*	*B*	*C*	*D*	*M*
	Mean			4.02	2.98	3.36	2.0	3.09	3.82	3.13	3.37	1.84	3.04	3.92	3.06	3.37	1.92	3.07
	Medium Farmers	Male	Agricul-ture	4.16	3.23	3.48	2.14	3.25	4.3	4.0	3.33	2.0	3.41	4.23	3.62	3.41	2.07	3.33
Non Target Group	Male		Allied to Agricul-ture	4.42	3.44	3.54	2.16	3.39	-	-	-	-	-	4.42	3.44	3.54	2.16	3.39
	Female		Allied to Agricul-ture	4.02	3.19	3.51	2.12	3.21	4.03	3.15	3.51	1.91	3.15	4.03	3.17	3.51	2.02	3.18
	Mean			4.2	3.29	3.51	2.14	3.28	4.17	3.58	3.42	1.96	3.28	4.19	3.44	3.47	2.05	3.28
	Non-Target Group Mean			4.11	3.14	3.44	2.07	3.19	3.99	3.36	3.40	1.90	3.16	4.05	3.25	3.42	1.99	3.18
	Overall Mean			4.05	3.07	3.36	2.0	3.12	3.97	3.19	3.40	1.89	3.11	4.01	3.13	3.38	1.95	3.12

Abbreviations used-
A=Product B=Price C=Place D=Promotion M=Mean of four Ps.

STATUS OF MARKETING ORIENTATION

The extent and nature of marketing orientation has been worked out separately under the following two broad heads-

1. Target Group

Among total sample customers from the village under reference, 34% belong to target group, indicating thereby SKGB's better contribution to the socio-economic development of those people for whom RRBs were primarily established.

Literate male small farmers belonging to target group have observed highest level of satisfaction (Table 7.1) with regard to 'product mix' of SKGB (3.86) followed by 'place effectiveness' (3.06), 'price reasonability' (2.90) and lowest mean value assigned to 'promotion optimality' (1.81) for the items such as 'frequent and effective communication', 'fieldworkers promotional skill', 'promotion for high interest on deposit and need based loan schemes,' 'adequate and educative advertisements for favourable changes' and 'employees personal involvement.'

Both literate and illiterate male customers having income below Rs. 11,000 p.a. under agricultural allied activities have attributed highest mean score to 'product mix' (3.81 & 4.08) followed by 'place mix' (3.28 & 3.39), 'price mix' (2.79 & 2.6) and lowest score responded to 'promotional elements' (2.04 & 1.97) such as 'timely and efficacious promotional communication', 'fieldworkers promotional competence', 'interest focused and motivating new schemes', 'effective advertisements' and 'competent personal selling effort'.

Female literate and illiterate customers engaged in agricultural allied activities have given highest marks to 'product adequacy' (4.11 & 3.76) followed by 'place effectiveness' (3.31 & 3.43), 'price reasonability' (3.17 & 3.14) and lowest score obtained by 'promotion mix' variables (1.74

& 1.79) i.e., 'prompt and result oriented promotional communication,' 'fieldworkers performance,' 'promotion for interest focused and need based new schemes,' 'sufficient and informative advertisements' and 'personal selling efforts'.

Table 7.2

Sixteen Dimensions of the Construct Falling under Two Orientation Regions of Target Customers Satisfaction and the Respective Mean Values Revealing the Extent of MKTORIENT

Below Average (-3 points)	*Above Average (+3 points)*
F_1 = 'Sufficient and need based deposite schemes' (4.07).	F_7 = "Reasonable and attractive interest rates' (2.60)
F_2 = 'Convenient purchase schemes' (3.56)	F_{11} = "Fieldworkers promotional skill' (1.58).
F_3 = 'Efficient and timely bank service' (4.59).	F_{12} = 'Promotion for interest oriented an innovative new schemes' (2.06).
F_4 = 'Adequate and need satisfying loan schemes' (3.08).	F_3 = 'Personal involvement and customer meets' (1.57).
F_5 = 'Easy loan recovery policy' (3.67).	F_{14} = 'Effective advertisements and attractive posters' (1.59).
F_6 = 'Time efficient and hasslefree procedure' (4.12).	F_{16} = 'Frequent and effective promotional communication' (1.65).
F_8 = 'Accurate interest calculations' (3.96).	
F_9 = 'Convenient and nearest branch location' (4.09).	
F_{10} = 'Adequate staff and satisfactory performance' (3.58).	
F_{15} = 'Employees co-operation in completing formalities' (3.66).	

Sixteen dimensions of MKTORIENT grouped under four Ps of marketing mix variables subdivided into two orientation regions of customer satisfaction within the framework of marketing orientation revealing the extent of MKTORIENT (Table 7.2) highlights that target customers of SKGB are highly satisfied with regard to 'sufficient and need based deposit schemes', 'convenient purchase schemes,' 'efficient and timely bank services,' 'adequate and need satisfying loan schemes,' 'easy loan recovery policy,' 'time efficient and hasslefree procedure', 'accurate interest calculations,' 'convenient and nearest branch location,' 'adequate staff and satisfactory performance,' 'employees co-operation in completing formalities'. These customers are least satisfied due to 'unreasonable and unattractive interest rates,' 'absence of fieldworkers promotional skill', 'inadequate promotion for high interest and innovative new schemes,' 'lack of personnel involvement,' 'ineffective advertisements and absence of attractive posters' and 'infrequent and ineffective promotional communication'.

The number of target customers falling in different regions of marketing orientation (Table 7.3) reveals that three dimensions viz., 'sufficient and need based deposit schemes,' 'convenient and nearest branch location' and 'efficient and timely bank services', have fallen in the highest range of MKTORIENT with as high as 67.65% , 61.76% and 85.30% of the sample respondents. Similarly the majority of respondents have given their ratings between "3-4" range of MKTORIENT with respect to 'easy loan recovery policy' (83.33%), 'employees co-operation in completing formalities' (70.59%), 'adequate staff and satisfactory performance' (91.18%), 'time efficient and hasslefree procedure' (67.65%) and 'accurate interest calculations' (67.65%). Beside these dimensions one statement viz., 'convenient purchase schemes' has also received more than average score of MKTORIENT from 68.75% respondents.

Among the dimensions obtaining below average score, about 83% of sample respondents have valued the 'adequate and need satisfying loan schemes' between "2-3" region of MKTORIENT. This table has again proved the inadequacy of marketing orientation in the said RRB branch with regard to the promotion of banking schemes. Majority of respondents have given poor values just between "1-2" range of MKTORIENT to the 'fieldworkers promotional skill" (95%), 'frequent and effective promotional communication' (94.12%), 'effective advertisements and attractive posters' (93.75%), 'personnel involvement and customer meets' ((90%), 'promotion for interest oriented and innovative new schemes' (73.53%). Likewise 'reasonable and attractive interest rates' has secured less than average score from 84.85% of respondents.

Table 7.3
Number of Target Customers under Dimension-wise MKTORIENT Regions

Orientation Regions →	*1-2*		*2-3*		*3-4*		*4-5*	
Dimensions ↓	*No.*	*(%)*	*No*	*(%)*	*No.*	*(%)*	*No.*	*(%)*
F_1 (34)	—	—	3	8.82	8	23.53	23	67.65
F_2 (32)	3	9.38	7	21.87	14	43.75	8	25
F_3 (34)	—	—	1	2.94	4	11.76	29	85.30
F_4 (6)	—	—	5	83.33	1	16.67	—	—
F_5 (6)	—	—	1	16.67	5	83.33	—	—
F_6 (34)	—	—	1	2.94	23	67.65	10	29.41
F_7 (33)	13	39.39	50	45.46	5	15.15	—	—
F_8 (34)	—	—	2	5.88	23	67.65	9	26.47
F_9 (34)	—	—	—	—	13	38.24	21	61.76
F_{10} (34)	—	—	3	8.82	31	91.18	—	—
F_{11} (20)	19	95	—	—	1	5	—	—
F_{12} (34)	25	73.53	6	17.65	3	8.82	—	—
F_{13} (20)	18	90	2	10	—	—	—	—
F_{14} (16)	15	93.75	1	6.25	—	—	—	—
F_{15} (34)	5	14.71	2	5.88	24	70.59	—	—
F_{16} (17)	16	94.12	1	5.88	—	—	—	—

Overall marketing orientation is SKGB branch as obtained from the level of satisfaction pertaining to four Ps of bank marketing mix among target customers arrived at

3.01 (Table 7.1). The highest mean score was given to 'product adequacy' (3.93) followed by 'place effectiveness' (3.32) 'price reasonability' (2.91) and 'promotion of optimality' (1.87).

2. Non-Target Group

From the village under reference, out of total sample customers, 60% belong to non-target group. Literate and illiterate male small farmers belonging to non-target group have assigned higher mean value (Table 7.1) to 'product adequacy' (4.05 & 3.6) followed by 'place effectiveness' (3.33 & 3.38), 'price reasonability' (1.86 & 1.82) and lowest mean score awarded to 'promotion mix variables' (1.86 & 1.82) viz., 'frequent and effective promotional communication', 'fieldworkers promotional aptitude', 'promotion for interest emphasising new schemes,' 'efficacious and informative advertisements' and 'interaction with customers'.

Literate and customers belonging to non-target group engaged in activities allied to agriculture have given highest score of MKTORIENT to 'product mix' (4.02) followed by 'place mix' (3.41) 'price mix' (3.15) and less than average mean value to 'promotion mix' (2.09) for the items such as 'recurrent and effective promotional communication,' 'fieldworkers promotional expertise', 'high interest on deposit and need based loan schemes,' 'competent and productive advertisements' and 'face to face communication'.

Both literate and illiterate female customers associated with agricultural allied activities have shown their highest satisfaction towards 'product variable' (3.98 & 4.03) followed by 'place variable' (3.35 & 3.36), 'price variable' (3.15 & 3.25) and lowest mean score awarded to 'promotion variable' (2.05 & 1.86) for the elements such as 'frequent and result-oriented promotional communication,' 'fieldworkers promotional ability', 'promotion for high interest deposit and low interest on loans', 'sufficient and informative advertisements' and 'personal involvement'.

Male literate medium farmers belonging to non-target group engaged in agricultural business have exhibited highest mean value to 'product adequacy' (4.16) followed by 'place effectiveness' (3.48), 'price reasonability' (3.23) and 'promotional optimality' (2.14) whereas it is illiterate counterpart has assigned highest mean score to 'product mix' (4.3) followed by 'price mix' (4.0), 'place mix (3.33) and 'promotion mix' (2.0). Thus both categories of customers have awarded lowest score to 'promotional aspect' of rural banking which incorporate 'convincing promotional communication', 'fieldworkers promotional efficiency', 'promotion for interest focused and motivating new schemes,' 'requisite and instructive advertisements' and 'personal participation in banking services.'

Literate male non-farmers who have taken loan for various activities allied to agriculture have accorded highest mean value to 'product mix' (4.42) followed by 'place mix' (3.54), 'price mix' (3.44) and lowest mean score to 'promotion mix variables' (2.16) viz., 'continual and operative promotional communication', 'fieldworkers promotional proficiency', 'promotion for interest exhibiting new schemes,' 'adequate and informative advertisements' and 'personal selling efforts'.

Both literate and illiterate female non-farmers having income above Rs. 11,000 p.a. have reflected their highest satisfaction towards 'product adequacy' (4.02 & 4.03) followed by 'place effectiveness' (3.51 & 3.51), 'price reasonability' (3.19 & 3.15) and feel highly dissatisfied towards 'promotional variable' (2.12 & 1.91) viz., 'persistent and effectiveness promotional communication,' 'fieldworkers promotional intelligence', 'promotion for new schemes', 'adequate and educative advertisements' and 'fieldworkers selling efforts'.

Marketing orientation dimensions grouped under four Ps of marketing mix divided into two orientation regions of customer satisfaction within the jurisdiction of MKTORIENT (Table 7.4) exhibits that non-target customers of SKGB have given 'above average' response to ten dimensions viz., 'sufficient and need based deposit schemes,' 'convenient purchase schemes,' 'efficient and timely bank services,' 'sufficient and need satisfying loan schemes,' 'easy loan recovery policy,' 'time efficient and hasslefree procedure', 'authentic interest calculations,' 'convenient and nearest location,' 'adequate staff and satisfactory performance' and 'employees co-operation in completing formalities'. These customers are least satisfied due to 'unreasonable and unattractive interest rates', 'absence of fieldworkers business promotion calibre', 'inadequate promotion for interest oriented new schemes', 'lack of adequate and educative advertisements', 'infrequent and ineffective promotional communication' and 'impersonal selling of banking schemes'.

Table 7.4
Sixteen Dimensions of the Construct Falling under Two Orientation Regions of Non-Target Customers Satisfaction and the Respective Mean Values Revealing the Extent of MKTORIENT

Below Average (-3 points)	*Above Average (+3 points)*
F_7 = 'Reasonable and attractive interest rates' (2.48).	F_1 = 'Sufficient and need based deposit schemes' (4.11).
F_{11} = 'Fieldworkers promotional skill' (1.57).	F_2 = 'Convenient purchase scheme' (3.76).
F_{12} = 'Promotion for interest oriented and innovative new schemes' (2.17).	F_3 = 'Efficient and timely bank services' (4.74).
F_{13} = 'Personnel involvement and customer meets' (1.69).	F_4 = 'Adequate and need satisfying loan schemes' (3.13).
F_{14} = 'Effective advertisements and attractive posters' (1.69).	F_5 = 'Easy loan recovery policy' (3.56).
F_{16} = 'Frequent and effective promotional communication' (1.65).	F_6 = 'Time efficient and hasslefree procedure' (4.19).
	F_8 = 'Accurate interest calculations' (4.06).
	F_9 = 'Convenient and nearest location' (4.22).
	F_{10} = 'Adequate staff and satisfactory performance' (3.56).
	F_{15} = 'Employees co-operation in completing formalities' (3.91).

The number of non-target customers falling in different regions of MKTORIENT (Table 7.5) reflects that three dimensions viz., 'efficient and timely bank services', 'sufficient and need based deposit schemes' and 'convenient and nearest location' have obtained highest score on MKTORIENT with 90.63%, 76.92% and 74.24% of the sample customers. Similarly the majority of respondents have given their high scores falling in the "3-4" range of MKTORIENT with respect to 'adequate staff and satisfactory performance' (90.77%), 'easy loan recovery policy' (72.22%), 'time efficient and hasslefree procedure' (64.06%) 'accurate interest calculations' (63.64%), 'employees co-operation in completing formalities' (53.12%) and 'convenient purchase schemes' (51.51%).

One dimension viz., 'adequate and need satisfying loan schemes' has fallen in the "2-3" range of marketing orientation with 75% of sample customers. Like target customers, non-target ones have also shown their dissatisfaction regarding various dimensions of 'promotion mix' i.e., 'frequent and effective promotional communication' (95%) 'fieldworkers promotional ability' (93.10%), 'effective and attractive advertisements' (90.48%), 'personal involvement and customer meets' (89.65%) and 'promotion for interest oriented and innovative new schemes' (73.02%). One dimension viz., 'reasonable and attractive interest rates' has obtained below average score from majority of the customers (90%).

Overall marketing orientation, as figured out on the basis of responses obtained from non-target customers, (Table 7.1) towards four Ps of marketing mix, arrived at 3.18. This category of customers have given highest mean value to 'product adequacy' (4.05) followed by 'place effectiveness' (3.42) 'price reasonability' (3.25) and 'promotion optimality' (1.99).

On the basis of responses generated from both 'target and non-target customers' towards various banking services of SKGB residing in the village Ambala Jattan, the overall marketing orientation worked out to be 3.12 (Table 7.1). They have assigned highest mean score to 'product mix' (4.01) followed by 'place mix' (3.38), 'price mix' (3.13) and 'promotion mix' (1.95). Thus promotional variable need to be strengthened in order to enhance the overall marketing orientation in these banks.

The association between rural bank's marketing orientation and sixteen dimensions in the scale grouped under four Ps of marketing mix established with a statistical technique of Multiple Regression is as under:

MKTORIENT = 4.04 + 2.15 (PRDMEAN 1) + 593 (PLAMEAN2) - .086 (PRMMEAN1) - .134 (PRMMEAN2) - .003 (PRMMEAN3) - .146 (PRMMEAN4) + .169 (PRMMEAN5) + .069 (PRMMEAN6) - .235 (PRDMEAN2) + .118 (PRDMEAN3) - .0776 (PRDMEAN4) - .079 (PRDMEAN5) + .072 (PRDMEAN6) - .019 (PRIMEAN1) - .208 (PRIMEAN2) - .309 (PLAMEAN 1).

The relative significance of 16 dimensions in estimating the overall marketing orientation indicates that second dimension of place mix is the most critical one. Next two ranks in order of merit have gone to first and second dimensions of product mix. Fourth dimension of product mix appears to be least important (-1.776).

VALIDITY AND RELIABILITY

Convergent validity has been worked out by analysing the degree of association between service quality, overall performance and marketing orientation of SKGB branch under study. Thus service quality and overall performance have been converged with the remaining important aspects of four Ps. Marketing orientation in terms of four Ps has received 3.12 score (Table 7.1) from the SKGB customers residing in underdeveloped area (Ambala Jattan) of Hoshiarpur district which has been proved convergently valid because this score from 94% and 92% respondents falling under 'above average' range of service quality and overall performance have respectively obtained 3.30 and 3.33 values (Table 7.12).

Table 7.5
Number of Non-Target Customers under Dimension—wise MKTORIENT Regions

Orientation Regions →	*1-2*		*2-3*		*3-4*		*4-5*	
Dimensions ↓	*No.*	*(%)*	*No*	*(%)*	*No.*	*(%)*	*No.*	*(%)*
F_1 (65)	—	—	6	9.23	9	13.85	50	76.92
F_2 (66)	4	6.06	7	10.61	34	51.51	21	31.82
F_3 (64)	—	—	1	1.56	5	7.81	58	90.63
F_4 (16)	1	6.25	12	75	3	18.75	—	—
F_5 (18)	3	16.67	—	—	13	72.22	2	11.11
F_6 (64)	—	—	1	1.56	41	64.06	22	34.38
F_7 (62)	28	45.16	28	45.16	6	9.68	—	—
F_8 (66)	—	—	3	4.54	42	63.64	21	31.82
F_9 (66)	—	—	—	—	17	25.76	49	74.24
F_{10} (65)	—	—	6	9.23	59	90.77	—	—
F_{11} (29)	27	93.10	2	6.90	—	—	—	—
F_{12} (63)	46	73.02	10	15.87	7	11.11	—	—
F_{13} (29)	26	89.65	2	6.90	1	3.45	—	—
F_{14} (21)	19	90.48	1	4.76	1	4.76	—	—
F_{15} (64)	3	4.69	11	17.19	34	53.12	15	25
F_{16} (20)	19	95	—	—	1	5	—	—

Multiple correlation (R) between independent and dependent variables worked out to be .52 which exhibits high degree of association between marketing orientation and four Ps of marketing mix. The value off co-efficient of determination (R^2) arrived at .26 which implies that 26% of the variation in marketing orientation can be justified by four variables in the linear equation.

Since the calculated value (1.85) of 'F' is smaller than the tabulated value (2.44) at 1% level of significance (df $v_1 v_2$ 15,99) so the hypothesis of equality of 16 dimensions is accepted. Thus these dimensions have equal impact on overall marketing orientation.

Table - 7.6

Marketing -Mix Variables Obtaining Less than Average Score—Target Group

Product (A)	*Price (B)*	*Place (C)*	*Promotion (D)*
F_1 = (2.94%) (1) Need meeting deposit schemes. (2) Sufficient number of deposit schemes. (3) Bank proves to be a good prime bank. F_2 = (12.5%) (1) Simple loan formalities. (2) Comfortable loan security and guarantee. (3) No switching intentions for loans. (4) Loan procedure easy even to a layman. (5) Timely purchase through banks. bank. F_3 = (2.94%) (1) Accurate passbook entries.	F_7 = (54.55%) (1) Attractive and adequate interest rates. (2) Reasonable loan interest rates. (3) Motivating deposit interest rates. F_8 = (5.88%) (1) Authentic interest calculations. (2) Quick information regarding new interest rates.	F_{10} = (2.94%) (1) Adequate bank's staff. (2) Competent and efficient employees. (3) Satisfactory present bank's staff.	F_{11} = (95%) (1) Promotion through fieldworkers. (2) Fieldworkers convincing skill. (3) Attractive promotional gifts. F_{12} = (79.41%) (1) Employees co-operation in educating clients about new schemes. (2) Employees co-operation in educating clients about new interest rates. F13 = (95%) Heavy advertisemet of new interest rates (2) Promotion through personal involvement.

Contd. . .

Table 7.6 *(Contd.)*

Product (A)	*Price (B)*	*Place (C)*	*Promotion (D)*
			(3) Customer awareness meet.
(2) Timely updating of passbook.			F_{14} = (93.75%)
(3) Quick withdrawal facilities.			(1) Effective T.V. and radio ads.
(4) No delay in depositing money.			(2) Promotion of schemes through attractive posters.
F_4 (16.67%)			F_{15} = (14.71%)
(1) Need meeting loan scheme.			(1) Employees assistance in filing withdrawal/ deposit forms.
(2) Sufficient number of loan schemes.			(2) Employees co-operation in completing loan formalities.
			F_{16} = (94.12%)
			(1) Frequent advertisements.
			(2) Heavy promotion through newspapers and magazines.

Table 7.7
Marketing-Mix Variables Obtaining Average Score—Target Group

Product (A)	*Price (B)*	*Place (C)*	*Promotion (D)*
F_1 = (5.88%) (1) Need meeting deposit schemes. (2) Sufficient number of deposit schemes. (3) Bank proves to be a good prime bank. F_2 = (18.75%) (1) Simple loan formalities. (2) Comfortable loan security and guarantee. (3) No switching intentions for loans. (4) Loan procedure easy even to a layman. (5) Timely purchase of assets through bank. F_4 = (66.66%) (1) Need meeting loan scheme.	F_7 = (30.30%) (1) Attractive and adequate interest rates. (2) Reasonable loan interest rates. (3) Motivating deposit interest rates.	F_{10} = (5.88%) (1) Adequate bank's staff. (2) Competent and efficient employees. (3) Satisfactory present bank's staff.	F_{12} = (11.77%) (1) Employees co-operation in educating clients about new schemes. (2) Employees co-operation in educating clients about new interest rates. F_{13} = (5%) (1) Heavy advertisements of new interest rates. (2) Promotion through personal involvement. (3) Customer awareness meets. F_{14} = (6.25%)

Contd. . .

Table 7.7 *(Contd.)*

Product (A)	*Price (B)*	*Place (C)*	*Promotion (D)*
(2) Sufficient number of loan schemes. F_5 = (16.67%) (1) Comfortable loan recovery policy. (2) Easy repayment of instalments. F_6 = (2.94%) (1) Simple account opening formalities. (2) Immediate issuance of passbooks.			(1) Effective T.V. and radio ads. (2) Promotion of schemes through attractive posters. F_{15} = (5.88%) (1) Employees assistance in filing withdrawal/deposit forms. (2) Employees co-operation in completing loan formalaties. F_{16} = (5.88%) (1) Frequent advertisements. (2) Heavy promotion through newspapers and magazines.

Table 7.8
Marketing-Mix Variables Obtaining More than Average Score—Target Group

Product (A)	*Price (B)*	*Place (C)*	*Promotion (D)*
F_1 = (91.18%)	F_7 = (15.15%)	F_9 = (100%)	F_{11} = (5%)
(1) Need meeting deposit schemes.	(1) Attractive and adequate interest rates.	(1) Convenient branch location.	(1) Promotion through fieldworkers.
(2) Sufficient number of deposit schemes.	(2) Reasonable loan interest rates.	(2) Branch location at hitherto unbanked area.	(2) Fieldworkers convincing skill.
(3) Bank proves to be a good prime bank.	(3) Motivating deposit interest rates.	(3) Nearest location.	(3) Attractive promotional gifts.
F_2 = (44%)	F_8 = (94.15%)	(4) Reasonable market around branch location.	F_{12} = (8.82%)
(1) Simple loan formalities.	(1) Authentic interest calculations.	(5) Co-operative and friendly employees.	(1) Employees co-operation in educating clients about new schemes.
(2) Comfortable loan security and guarantee.	(2) Quick information regarding new interest rates.	(6) Employees have sufficient information.	(2) Employees co-operation in educating clients about new interest rates.
(3) No switching intentions for loans.		F_{10} = (91.18%)	F_{15} = (70.59%)
(4) Loan procedure easy even to a layman.		(1) Adequate bank's staff.	(1) Employees assistance in filing withdrawal/deposit forms.
(5) Timely purchase through bank.		(2) Competent and efficient employees.	
F_3 = (97.06%)		(3) Satisfactory present bank's staff.	
(1) Accurate passbook entries.			
(2) Timely updating of passbook.			

Contd. . .

Table 7.8 *(Contd.)*

Product (A)	*Price (B)*	*Place (C)*	*Promotion (D)*
(3) Quick withdrawal facilities. (4) No delay in depositing money. F_4 (16.67%) (1) Need meeting loan scheme. (2) Sufficient number of loan schemes. F_5 = (83.33%) (1) Comfortable loan recovery. (2) Easy repayment instal-ments. F_6 = (97.06%) (1) Simple account opening formalities. (2) Immediate issuance of new passbooks.			(2) Employees co-operation in completing loan formalities.

Table 7.9
Marketing-Mix Variables Obtaining Less than Average Score—Non-Target Group

Product (A)	*Price (B)*	*Place (C)*	*Promotion (D)*
F_1 = (6.15%) (1) Need meeting deposit schemes. (2) Sufficient number of deposit schemes. (3) Bank proves to be a good prime bank.	F_7 = (54.84%) (1) Attractive and adequate interest rates. (2) Reasonable loan interest rates. (3) Motivating deposit interest rates.	F_{10} = (3.08%) (1) Adequate bank's staff. (2) Competent and efficient employees. (3) Satisfactory present bank's staff.	F_{11} = (96.55%) (1) Promotion through fieldworkers. (2) Fieldworkers convincing skill. (3) Attractive promotional gifts.
F_{10} = (10.61%) (1) Simple loan formalities. (2) Comfortable loan security and guarantee. (3) No switching intentions for loans. (4) Loan procedure easy even to a layman. (5) Timely purchase through bank.	F_8 = (3.03%) (1) Authentic interest calculations. (2) Quick information regarding new interest rates.		F_{12} = (74.60%) (1) Employees co-operation in educating clients about new schemes. (2) Employees co-operation in educating clients about new interest rates.
F_3 = (1.56%) (1) Accurate passbook entries. (2) Timely updating of passbook.			F_{13} = (96.55%) (1) Heavy ads of new interest rates. (2) Promotion through personal involvement.

Contd. . .

Table 7.9 *(Contd.)*

Product (A)	*Price (B)*	*Place (C)*	*Promotion (D)*
(3) Quick withdrawal facilities. (4) No delay in depositing money. F_4 (16.25%) (1) Need meeting loan scheme. (2) Sufficient number of loan schemes. F_5 = (16.67%) (1) Comfortable loan recovery policy. (2) Easy repayment insfal-ments.			F_{14} = (90.48%) (1) Effective T.V. and radio ads. (2) Promotion of sche-mes through attrac-tive posters. F_{15} = (6.25%) (1) Employees assis-tance in filing with-drawal/deposits forms. (2) Employees co-operation in completing loan formalities. F_{16} = (95%) (1) Frequent advertise-ments. (2) Heavy promotion through news-papers and magazines.

Further the values of 't' were tested both at 1% and 5% level of significance (df $v_1$14). All the dimensions have fallen in the acceptance region both at 1% (2.98) and 5% (2.15) level of significance. This highlights that all the factors of four Ps have their significant contribution in the calculation of bank marketing orientation.

STRATEGIC ACTION

The level of marketing orientation in SKGB branch, under review, figured out here (Table 7.1) implies three types of strategies for enhancing marketing culture in the working of RRBs.

This first type of strategy is a marketing plan for those dimensions which have generated 'below average' score from both target and non-target customers of SKGB.

54.69% sample customers have given 'below average' score to 'reasonable and attractive interest rates' of rural banks. In order to face competition from commercial and co-operative bank branches operating in rural areas, rural banks should offer the schemes at an attractive prices (Menezes 1979).

About 96% of the sample respondents have shown their dissonance towards 'fieldworkers promotional skills'. Sponsor banks should initiate to make requisite arrangements for training the rural field staff.

'Below average' score has been obtained by 'promotion for interest oriented and innovative new schemes' from 77% sample customers. Thus there is a need to introduce new schemes at reasonable rates and promoted through proper techniques (Vyas 1991).

95.78% of the sample respondents have given less than 3 points on MKTORIENT towards 'personal selling efforts'. The bank staff should be provided an adequate opportunity for career advancement and also financial incentives in order to improve their efficiency (Venkateswarlu 1987) thereby extending full co-operation towards their customers.

Out of total sample, 92.12% respondents feel dissatisfied with the present advertising tools of the rural banks. Had there been an effective advertising media, there would have been much awareness among rural people, resulting into increased bank clientele.

94.56% sample respondents view, `promotional communication ineffective' in rural banks. If it is to be effective, the communication strategy need to be designed in the light of customer profile their needs, values, way of life (Bhatnagar 1983).

Second type of marketing strategy has been planned for the dimensions securing 'average' values on MKTORIENT scale.

Just average value has been obtained by the fourth dimension of 'product mix' viz., 'adequate and need satisfying loan schemes' from 70.83% sample respondents. Thus sufficient and timely credit at reasonable rate of interest should be made available to a large segment of rural population (Rangarajan 1996).

Third type of strategic action incorporates those dimensions which have scored 'above average' values from the customers of SKGB.

90.98% sample customers have given 'above average' response to 'sufficient and need based deposit schemes'. Therefore, efforts should be made to introduce more need satisfying deposit schemes (Mandanna & Chengappa 1993).

Both 'efficient and timely bank services' and 'time efficient and hasslefree procedure' have generated above three points on likert scale from about 98% of total sample size. Still there is a need to provide more cost effective and efficient services (Bhattacharyay 1989) to the rural clientele so that they do not feel any hurdle in complying with the procedural formalities.

Table 7.10
Marketing Mix Variables Obtaining Average Score—Non-Target Group

Product (A)	*Price (B)*	*Place (C)*	*Promotion (D)*
F_1 = (3.08%)	F_7 = (35.48%)	F_{10} = (6.15%)	F_{11} = (3.45%)
(1) Need meeting deposit schemes. (2) Sufficient number of deposit schemes. (3) Bank proves to be a good prime bank.	(1) Attractive and adequate interest rates. (2) Reasonable loan interest rates. (3) Motivating deposit interest rates.	(1) Adequate bank's staff. (2) Competent and efficient employees. (3) Satisfactory present bank's staff.	(1) Promotion through fieldworkers. (2) Fieldworkers convincing skill. (3) Attractive promotional gifts.
F_{10} = (6.06%)	F_8 = (1.51%)		F_{12} = (14.29%)
(1) Simple loan formalities. (2) Comfortable loan security and guarantee. (3) No switching intentions for loans. (4) Loan procedure easy even to a layman. (5) Timely purchase through bank.	(1) Authentic interest calculations. (2) Quick information regarding new interest rates.		(1) Employees co-operation in educating clients about new schemes. (2) Employees co-operation in educating clients about new interest rates.
			F_{14} = (4.76%)

Contd. . .

Table 7.10 *(Contd.)*

Product (A)	*Price (B)*	*Place (C)*	*Promotion (D)*
F_4 = (75%) (1) Need meeting loan schemes. (2) Sufficient number of loan schemes. F_6 = (1.56%) (1) Simple account opening formalities. (2) Immediate issuance of new passbooks.			(1) Effective T.V. and radio ads. (2) Promotion of schemes through attractive posters. F_{15} = (15.631%) (1) Employees assistance in filing withdrawal/deposits forms. (2) Employees co-operation in completing loan formalities.

Table 7.11
Marketing-Mix Variables Obtaining More than Average Score—Non-Target Group

Product (A)	*Price (B)*	*Place (C)*	*Promotion (D)*
F_1 = (90.77%)	F_7 = (9.68%)	F_9 = (100%)	F_{12} = (11.11%)
(1) Need meeting deposit schemes.	(1) Attractive and adequate interest rates.	(1) Convenient branch location. (2) Branch location at hitherto unbanked area.	(1) Employees co-operation in educating clients about new schemes.
(2) Sufficient number of deposit schemes.	(2) Reasonable loan interest rates.	(3) Nearest location.	
(3) Bank proves to be a good prime bank.	(3) Motivating deposit interest rates.	(4) Reasonable market around branch location.	(2) Employees co-operation in educating clients about new interest rates.
F_2 = (83.33%)	F_8 = (95.46%)	(5) Co-operation and friendly employees.	
(1) Simple loan formalities.	(1) Authentic interest calculations.		
(2) Comfortable loan security and guarantee.	(2) Quick information regarding new interest rates.	(6) Employees have sufficient information.	F_{13} = (3.45%)
(3) No switching intentions for loans.		F_{10} = (90.77%)	(1) Heavy advertisements of new interest rates.
		(1) Adequate bank's staff.	
(4) Loan procedure easy even to a layman.		(2) Competent and efficient employees.	(2) Promotion through personal involvement.
(5) Timely purchase of through bank.		(3) Satisfactory present bank's staff.	(3) Customer awareness meet.
F_3 = (98.44%)			
(1) Accurate passbook entries.			F_{14} = (4.76%)

Contd. . .

Table 7.11 *(Contd.)*

Product (A)	*Price (B)*	*Place (C)*	*Promotion (D)*
(2) Timely updating of passbook. (3) Quick withdrawal facilities. (4) No delay in depositing money. F_4 = (18.75%)			(1) Effective T.V. and radio ads. (2) Promotion of schemes through attractive posters. F_{15} = (78.12%)
(1) Need meeting loan schemes. (2) Sufficient number of loan schemes. F_5 = (83.33%)			(1) Employees assistance in filing withdrawal/deposit forms. (2) Employees co-operation in completing loan formalities. F_{16} = (5%)
(1) Comfortable loan recovery policy. F_6 = (98.44%)			
(1) Simple account opening formalities. (2) Immediate issuance of new passbooks.			(1) Frequent advertisements. (2) Heavy promotion through newspapers and magazines.

Table 7.12
Service Quality and Overall Performance-wise Marketing Orientation

Marketing	*Service*	*Quality*		*Overall*	*Performance*	
Mix Factors ↓	*BA*	*A*	*AA*	*BA*	*A*	*AA*
PRDMEAN1	2.5	2.38	3.86	—	2.88	3.88
PRDMEAN2	2.25	2.37	3.81	—	2.35	3.84
PRDMEAN3	4.0	4.25	4.72	—	3.88	4.76
PRDMEAN4	—	2.0	3.17	—	2.0	3.13
PRDMEAN5	—	2.75	3.67	—	3.5	3.57
PRDMEAN6	3.5	4.2	5.17	—	4.06	4.16
GRPRDMEAN	3.06	2.99	3.9	—	3.11	3.89
PRIMEAN1	2.5	2.4	2.53	—	2.35	2.52
PRIMEAN2	3.0	3.7	4.05	—	3.19	4.11
GRPRIMEAN	2.75	3.05	3.29	—	2.77	3.32
PLAMEAN1	3.4	4.08	4.19	—	3.53	4.23
PLAMEAN2	3.0	3.07	3.61	—	3.04	3.63
GRPLAMEAN	3.2	3.58	3.9	—	3.29	3.93
PRMMEAN1	2.0	1.7	2.16	—	1.69	2.17
PRMMEAN2	1.25	1.83	1.59	—	1.44	1.64
PRMMEAN3	2.0	1.2	1.58	—	1.63	1.53
PRMMEAN4	2.0	2.37	3.50	—	1.78	3.58
PRMMEAN5	1.5	1.5	1.67	—	1.5	1.68
PRMMEAN6	1.32	1.95	2.23	—	1.85	2.47
GRPRMMEAN	1.68	1.76	2.12	—	1.65	2.18
MKTORIENT	**2.67**	**2.85**	**3.30**	—	**2.71**	**3.33**
No. & % age of Respondents	**01(1%)**	**05(5%)**	**93(94%)**	—	**08(8%)**	**89(92%)**

83% sample customers do not feel any difficulty in repaying the loans taken from rural banks, they infact appreciate R.B.I. policy of recovering loans. But for remaining customers, loan recovery policy should be made in accordance with the repaying capacity.

Out of total sample, 90.98% have shown full satisfaction towards 'rural bank staff and its performance'. The manpower should be redistributed to ensure need based availability of staff at branches (Goiporia Committee 1996) in order to attain 100% satisfaction in this regard.

74% sample respondents feel satisfied about 'employees co-operation in completing bank formalities' but remaining customers still demand customer friendly behaviour of bank personnel and easy procedural formalities.

'Accurate interest calculations' have obtained 'above average' score from approximately 95% sample size. In order to gain the confidence of remaining 5% sample customers, employees should educate customers about interest calculations in order to clear their doubts and confusions.

REFERENCES

1. Bhatnagar, Deepti (1983), "Diffusion of Banking Innovations and Communication Strategies for Rural Areas", *Prajnan,* July-Sept., Vol. XII, 205.
2. Bhattacharyay, B. N. (1989), "Marketing Approach to Promoting Banking Services," *Vikalpa,* Apr.-June, Vol. 14, 39.
3. Goiporia Committee (1996), "Customer Service in Banks", *Planning Bulletin,* June-July, 286-297.
4. Mandanna, P.K. and P.G. Chengappa (1993), "Marketing Approach in Rural Banking," *Economic Review,* June, 06.
5. Menezes, J.S. William (1979), "Marketing of Bank Services", *Prajnan,* Apr.-June, Vol. VIII, 135.
6. Rangarajan, C. (1996), "Rural India: The Role of Credit", *The Banker,* March, 15-17.
7. Sharma, R.D.; Desh Bandhu and Gurjeet Kaur (1998), "Marketing Orientation Strategy in Rural Banks: A Case Study", *Prajnan,* Apr.-June, Vol. XXVII, No. 1, 47-58.
8. Venkateswarlu, P.K. (1987), "Customer Service in Commercial Banks", *Southern Economist,* Oct., Vol. 26, 06.
9. Vyas, Vijay Shanker (1991), *"Marketing Management in Commercial Banks with Special Reference to Customer Service"*, Unpublished Thesis, Dept. of Commerce and Management, Univ. of Jodhpur, 73.

Chapter—8

Measurement of Marketing Orientation in SKGB—With Reference to Developing Rural Area

BACKGROUND

The extent and nature of marketing orientation in RRBs operating in developing rural areas has been studied from information obtained from 125 randomly selected respondents belonging to the villages viz., Pandori Mall, Dhalewal and Mirzapur of Hoshiarpur district falling within the operational jurisdiction of Shivalik Kshetriya Gramin Bank (SKGB) Pandori Mall. At the time of survey Pandori Mall had a population of 536, with 289 males, 98 households, 22% level of poverty and 78% literacy level. The population of Dhalewal was 507 (250 males and 257 females) with 86 households, 24% house below poverty line and just 24% level of illiteracy. Similarly Mirzapur had the highest population of 845, with 106 households, 20% people living below poverty line and 80% literacy rate. This rural sector is about 12 kms away from the main city as a result of which it has quite good literacy and very less poverty. The deposits and advances of SKGB, Pandori Mall increased from 1990-91 onwards (Exhibit 8.2) but credit-deposit ratio started declining from 1991-92. The branch had a nominal profit of 2690 as on 31.3.97.

The data gathered from the aforesaid 125 randomly selected customers of SKGB with 60 initial statements within the paradigm of MKTORIENT was purified through factor analysis. It resulted into 36 statements which got grouped under 16 dimensions (6 product, 2 price, 2 place and 6 promotion) (Table 8.0).

Exhibit 8.1

Brief Profile of the Villages viz. Pandori Mall, Dhalewal and Mirzapur of Hoshiarpur District as on 31.3.97

	Demographic Profile	*Pandori Mall*	*Dhalewal*	*Mirzapur*
(1)	Population	536	507	845
(2)	Male : Female	289 : 247	250 : 257	498 : 347
(3)	Households	98	86	106
(4)	Poverty	22%	24%	20%
(5)	Literacy	78%	76%	80%
(6)	Infrastructural facilities			
	(a) Roads	Pacca	Good	Pacca
	(b) Electricity	Few cuts	Average	Normal cuts
	(c) Govt. School	One	One	Three
	(d) Private School	—	—	One
(7)	Land soil suitable for growing wheat, maize, potato and sugarcane.			
(8)	Per hectare yield-			
	(a) Wheat	—	36 qtl/hec	
	(b) Maize	—	20 qtl/hec	
	(c) Potato	—	107 qtl/hec	

Exhibit 8.2
Brief Profile of the Branch Pandori Mall of SKGB

(Rs in '000)

Year	*Deposits*		*Advances*		*Profit (Rs.)*	*C.D. Ratio*
	A/C	*Rs*	*A/C*	*Rs*		
1990-91	2563	4687	973	4326	15.8	92
1991-92	2856	5524	1033	5088	10.6	92
1992-93	3127	7657	855	4511	4.1	59
1993-94	2885	10260	717	4215	9.7	41
1994-95	2862	13518	576	4173	7.3	31
1995-96	2965	18422	591	5299	31.1	29
1996-97	2727	21891	535	5009	26.9	23
1997-98	2689	25023	471	4641	56.8	19

(1) Two branches of other banks at a distance of 2 kms.

(2) Number of projects financed:

	1996-97	*1997-98*
(a) Agriculture	55	60
(b) Retail trade	17	18
(c) S.S.I.	9	10

STATUS OF MARKETING ORIENTATION

The extent and nature of marketing orientation has been worked out separately under the following two broad heads.

1. Target Group

Among total sample customers from the villages under reference, 17% belong to target group, indicating thereby SKGB's better contribution to the socio-economic development of those people for whom RRBs were primarily established. Male literate small farmers belonging to target group have assigned highest mean score to `place effectiveness' (3.5) (Table 8.1) followed by `product adequacy'

(3.19), less than average values to `price reasonability' (2.85) for the items such as `reasonable and attractive interest rates' and `accurate loan interest calculation' and lowest mean value accorded to `promotion optimality' (1.65) viz., `fieldworkers promotional skill', `frequent and educative advertisements', `promotion for high interest deposit and low interest need based loan schemes'.

Literate male non farmers having income below Rs. 11,000 p.a. engaged in activities allied to agriculture have been highest response to `place mix' (3.81) followed by `product mix' (3.20), `price mix' (3.17) and less than average score obtained by `promotion mix' elements (1.87) whereas its illiterate counterpart has given highest mean score to `product adequacy' (3.20) and less than 3-point to `place effectiveness' (2.50) followed by `price reasonability' (2.25) and `promotion optimality' (1.64). Thus both categories of customers have attributed lowest mean value to `promotional aspect' of rural banking which includes `fieldworkers performance', `sufficient and informative advertisements', `promotion for interest focusing new schemes' and `personal selling efforts'.

Literate female customers belonging to target group associated with agricultural allied activities have shown highest satisfaction towards `product mix' (4.15) followed by `place mix' (3.95), `price mix' (3.46) and lowest satisfaction with regard to `promotion mix' (1.78) whereas its illiterate group has given highest mean value to `place mix' (3.75) followed by `product mix' (3.71), `price mix' (3.23) and lowest mean score to `promotion mix' (1.69). Thus both literate and illiterate female customers have shown dissatisfaction towards `promotion mix' elements viz., `fieldworkers promotional competence', `promotion for interest emphasising new schemes', `efficacious and educative advertisements' and `interaction with customers'.

Table 8.0
Summary of Results from Scale Purification—Loading and Variance Explained

Bank Marketing Mix	*Factor-Wise Dimension*	*Factor Loadings*	*% of Variance Explained*
1	2	3	4
Product	**Factor First-**		**26.4**
	Need meeting deposit schemes.	.83	
	Sufficient number of deposit schemes.	.77	
	Bank proves to be a good prime bank.	.64	
	Simple loan formalities.	.56	
	No switching intentions for loans	.54	
	Factor Second-		**13.4**
	Need meeting loan schemes.	.87	
	Sufficient number of loan schemes.	.87	
	Loan procedure easy even to a layman.	.51	
	Factor Third-		**9.7**
	No delay in depositing money.	.88	
	Immediate issuance of new cheque/ passbooks.	.72	
	Quick withdrawal facilities	.64	
	Easy procedure for fixed deposit schemes.		
	Factor Fourth-		**8.4**
	Timely encashment of cheques.	.84	
	Simple account opening formalities.	.69	
	Factor Fifth-		**7.0**
	Comfortable loan recovery policy.	.91	
	Easy repayment of instalments.	.71	
	Total variance explained = 64.9%		
Price	**Factor First-**		**46.0**
	Attractive and adequate interest rates.	.84	
	Motivating deposit interest rates.	.80	
	Quick information regarding new interest rates.	.73	
	Factor Second-		**21.3**
	Reasonable loan interest rates.	.91	

Contd. . .

1	2	3	4
	Authentic interest calculations.	.58	
	Total variance explained =67.4%		
Place	**Factor First-**		**36.7**
	Nearest location	.91	
	Branch location at hitherto unbanked area.	.88	
	Reasonable market around branch location.	.69	
	Factor Second-		
	Co-operative and friendly employees.	.85	
	Satisfactory present bank's staff.	.74	
	Competent and efficient employees.	.71	
	Employees have sufficient information.	.58	
	Factor Third-		**12.6**
	Adequate bank's staff.	.77	
	Convenient branch location.	-.65	
	Total variance explained =66.6%		
Promotion	**Factor First-**		**29.4**
	Promotion through fieldworkers.	.94	
	Fieldworkers convincing skill.	.93	
	Promotion through personal involvement.	.71	
	Factor Second-		**14.6**
	Frequent advertisements.	.74	
	Customer awareness meets.	.67	
	Employees assistance in filing withdrawal/deposit forms.	.66	
	Heavy ads of new interest rates.	.57	
	Promotion of schemes through attractive posters.	.57	
	Factor Third-		**12.8**
	Employees co-operation in educating clients about new schemes.	.84	
	Attractive promotional gifts.	.55	
	Factor Fourth-		**9.9**
	Effective T.V. and radio ads.	.91	
	Heavy promotion through newspapers and magazines.	.90	
	Total variance explained = 66.7%		

Table 8.1
Overall Marketing Orientation—Customers Assessment

				Education										*Overall Mean*				
				LITERATE					*ILLITERATE*									
Income	*Land Holding*	*Gender*	*Occupation*	*A*	*B*	*C*	*D*	*M*	*A*	*B*	*C*	*D*	*M*	*A*	*B*	*C*	*D*	*M*
	Small Farmers	Male	Agriculture	3.19	2.83	3.5	1.65	2.79	-	-	-	-	-	3.19	2.83	3.5	1.65	2.79
Target Group	Male		Allied to Agriculture	3.8	3.17	3.81	1.87	3.03	3.2	2.25	2.50	1.64	2.4	3.24	2.71	3.16	1.76	2.72
	Female		Allied to Agriculture	4.15	3.46	3.95	1.78	3.34	3.71	3.23	3.75	1.69	3.10	3.93	3.35	3.85	1.74	3.22
	Target Group Mean			3.54	3.15	3.75	1.77	3.05	3.46	2.74	3.13	1.67	2.75	3.5	2.95	3.44	1.72	2.9
	Small Farmers	Male	Agriculture	4.56	4.0	4.22	2.15	3.73	-	-	-	-	-	4.56	4.0	4.22	2.15	3.73
Non-Target Group	Male		Allied to Agriculture	3.8	3.48	3.96	2.03	3.32	3.8	3.25	3.75	20.9	3.22	3.8	3.37	3.86	2.06	3.27
	Female		Allied to Agriculture	3.92	3.35	3.82	1.89	3.25	3.99	3.3	4.04	1.71	3.26	3.96	3.33	3.93	1.8	3.26

Table 8.1 *(Contd.)*

				Education										*Overall Mean*				
				LITERATE					*ILLITERATE*									
Income	*Land Holding*	*Gender*	*Occupation*	*A*	*B*	*C*	*D*	*M*	*A*	*B*	*C*	*D*	*M*	*A*	*B*	*C*	*D*	*M*
	Mean			4.09	3.62	4.0	2.02	3.43	3.9	3.13	3.9	1.9	3.24	3.99	3.38	3.95	1.96	3.39
	Medium Farmers	Male	Agriculture	4.07	3.72	3.93	2.43	3.54	-	-	-	-	-	4.07	3.72	3.93	2.43	3.54
Non-Target Group	Male		Allied to Agriculture	3.96	3.54	3.95	2.25	3.43	-	-	-	-	-	3.96	3.54	3.95	2.25	3.43
	Female		Allied to Agriculture	3.83	3.54	3.87	2.07	3.33	4.0	3.67	4.0	1.85	3.38	3.92	3.61	3.94	1.96	3.36
	Mean			3.95	3.6	3.92	2.25	3.43	4.0	3.67	4.0	1.85	3.38	3.98	3.64	3.96	2.05	3.41
	Non-Target Group Mean			4.02	3.61	3.96	2.14	3.43	3.95	3.4	3.95	1.88	3.31	3.99	3.51	3.96	2.01	3.37
	Overall Mean			3.86	3.46	3.89	2.01	3.30	3.79	3.18	3.68	1.81	3.12	3.83	3.32	3.76	1.91	3.21

Abbreviations used-
A=Product B=Price C=Place D=Promotion M=Mean of four Ps.

Table 8.2
Fourteen Dimensions of the Construct Falling under Two Orientation Regions of Target Customers Satisfaction and the Respective Mean Values Revealing the Extent of MKTORIENT

Below Average (-3 points)	*Above Average (+3 points)*
F_2 = "Need based and convenient purchase schemes" (2.5).	F_1 = "Need satisfying deposit schemes and simple loan formalities" (3.36).
F_5 = "Easy loan recovery policy" (2.83).	F_4 = "Efficient and adequate bank service" (4.19).
F_{11} = "Fieldworkers promotional skill" (1.60).	F_3 = "Time efficient and hassle-free procedure" (4.18).
F_{12} = "Frequent and effective promotional communication" (1.99).	F_6 = "Reasonable and attractive interest rates" (3.11).
F_{13} = "Promotion for interest oriented and innovative new schemes" (1.52).	F_7 = "Accurate loan interest rates and calculations" (3.38).
F_{14} = "Adequate and educative advertisement" (1.53).	F_8 = "Nearest branch location" (3.17).
	F_9 = "Co-operative, informative and efficient employees" (3.75).
	F_{10} = "Adequate staff and reasonable market" (3.34).

Fourteen marketing orientation dimensions grouped under four Ps marketing mix, segregated into two orientation regions of customer satisfaction within the paradigm of MKTORIENT (Table 8.2) reflects that target customers of SKGB are highly satisfied with respect to eight dimensions viz., `need satisfying deposit schemes and simple loan formalities', `efficient and adequate bank services', `time efficient and hasslefree procedure', `reasonable and attractive interest rates', `accurate loan interest rate calculations', `nearest branch location', `co-operative, informative and efficient employees', `adequate staff and reasonable market'.

However these customers have exhibited their dissatisfaction due to `complicated loan schemes', `inconvenient loan recovery policy', `absence of fieldworkers promotional skill', `lack of educative advertisements', `infrequent and ineffective promotional communication', `lack of promotion for interest oriented and innovative new schemes' and `personal selling efforts in the bank'.

The number of target customers, under study falling in four marketing orientation regions (Table 8.3) reveals that majority of the respondents have given their ranking in "3-4" range of MKTORIENT to `adequate staff and reasonable market' (70%), `need satisfying deposit schemes and simple loan formalities' (66%), `efficient and adequate bank services' (62%) and `co-operative, informative and efficient employees' (60%). Beside other dimensions securing `above average' score and `time efficient and hasslefree procedure' (96%) and `nearest branch location' (81%).

Table 8.3
Number of Target Customers under Dimensions-wise MKTORIENT Regions

Orientation Regions →	*1-2*		*2-3*		*3-4*		*4-5*	
Dimensions ↓	*No.*	*(%)*	*No.*	*(%)*	*No.*	*(%)*	*No.*	*(%)*
F_1 (21)	01	5	05	24	14	66	01	5
F_2 (20)	10	50	02	10	05	25	03	15
F_3 (21)	—	—	01	4	10	48	10	48
F_4 (21)	—	—	02	9	13	62	06	29
F_5 (3)	01	33	01	33	01	33	—	—
F_6 (20)	03	15	08	40	09	45	—	—
F_7 (20)	03	15	07	35	08	40	02	10
F_8 (21)	03	14	01	5	09	43	08	38
F_9 (20)	—	—	02	10	12	60	06	30
F_{10} (21)	—	—	06	29	15	71	—	—
F_{11} (21)	20	95	—	—	01	5	—	—
F_{12} (21)	11	52	10	48	—	—	—	—
F_{13} (21)	20	95	01	5	—	—	—	—
F_{14} (18)	17	94	01	6	—	—	—	—

Maximum of the respondents have given their responses between "1-2" range of MKTORIENT with respect to `fieldworkers promotional ability' (95%) `promotion for interest focusing new schemes' (95%), `adequate and informative advertisements' (94%), `frequent and result oriented promotional communication' (52%) and `need based and convenient purchase schemes' (50%). Apart from these, other dimensions obtaining `below average' score are `easy loan recovery policy' (67%) and `reasonable and attractive interest rates' (55%).

Out of fourteen dimensions, one dimension viz., `attractive loan interest rates' and `accurate calculation' has generated `above average' and `below average' score from equal number of respondents (50%).

Overall marketing orientation in given SKGB branch, pertaining to four Ps of marketing mix arrived at 2.90 (Table 8.1). The highest mean value, has been given to `product adequacy and suitability' (3.5) followed by `place effectiveness' (3.44) and less than average value to `price reasonability' (2.95) and `promotion optimality' (1.72).

2. Non-Target Group

From the village under study, out of total sample customers of 125, 83% belong to non-target group indicating thereby that till the date of survey RRBs had not been able to reach target customers for the purpose of which they were basically established.

Male literate small farmers having income above Rs. 11,000 p.a. have assigned higher mean values (Table 8.1) to `product mix' (4.56) followed by `place mix' (4.22), `price mix' (4.0) and lower mean score awarded to `promotional mix' (2.15) viz., `fieldworkers promotional expertise', `promotion for high interest deposit and need based loan schemes', `competent and productive advertisements' and `frequent and effective promotional communication'.

Literate male non-farmers belonging to non-target group under agricultural allied activities have shown highest satisfaction with regard to `place effectiveness' (3.98) followed by `product adequacy' (3.8), `price reasonability' (3.48) and less than average value obtained by `promotion optimality' (2.03) whereas its illiterate group has assigned highest score to `product mix' (3.8) followed by `place mix' (3.75), `price mix' (3.25) and lowest score given to `promotion mix' (2.09). Thus both categories of customers have accorded lowest mean values to promotional variable for the items such as `fieldworkers promotional proficiency', `promotion for interest exhibiting new schemes', `adequate and informative advertisements' and `face to face communication'.

Literate female customers belonging to non-target group who have taken loans for various activities allied to agriculture have exhibited their highest satisfaction towards `product adequacy' (3.92) followed by `place effectiveness; (3.82), `price reasonability' (3.35) and `promotion optimality' (1.89) whereas its illiterate group has assigned highest score to `place mix' (4.04) followed by `product mix' (3.99), `price mix' (3.3) and `promotion mix' (1.71). Thus both categories of customers have given less than 3-point to promotional aspect of rural banking which involve fieldworkers promotional ability, promotion for interest oriented new schemes, adequate and resulted oriented advertisements and sufficient and productive promotional communication.

Literate male customers having income above Rs. 11,000 p.a. engaged in both agricultural and its allied activities have reflected their highest satisfaction with respect to `product adequacy' (4.07 & 3.96) followed by `place effectiveness' (3.93 & 3.95), `price reasonability' (3.72 & 3.54) but feel highly dissatisfied with regard to `promotional elements' (2.43 & 2.25) viz., `fieldworkers promotional skill', `competent and effective advertisements', `interest focused and motivating new schemes' and `personal selling efforts'.

Table 8.4
Fourteen Dimensions of the Construct Falling under Two Orientation Regions of Non-Target Customers Satisfaction and the Respective Mean Value Revealing the Extent of MKTORIENT

Below Average (-3 points)	*Above Average (+3 points)*
F_{11} = "Fieldworkers promotional skill" (2.12).	F_1 = "Need satisfying deposit schemes and simple loan formalities" (3.88).
F_{12} = "Frequent and effective promotional communication" (2.30).	F_2 = "Need based and convenient purchase schemes" (3.32).
F_{13} = "Promotion for interest oriented and innovative new schemes" (1.97).	F_3 = "Time efficient and hassle-free procedure" (4.43).
F_{14} = "Adequate and educative advertisements" (1.79).	F_4 = "Efficient and adequate bank services" (4.36).
	F_5 = "Easy loan recovery policy" (3.22).
	F_6 = "Reasonable and attractive interest rates" (3.47).
	F_7 = "Accurate loan interest rates and calculation" (3.70).
	F_8 = "Nearest branch location" (4.03).
	F_9 = "Co-operative, informative and efficient employees" (4.03).
	F_{10} = "Adequate staff and reasonable market" (3.49).

Both literate and illiterate female customers belonging to non-target group under agricultural allied activities have highlighted their maximum satisfaction towards `place mix' (3.87 & 4.0) followed by `product mix' (3.83 & 4.0), `price mix' (3.54 & 3.67) and less than average score on MKTORIENT scale to the `promotion mix' (2.07 & 1.85) which includes `fieldworkers promotional competence', `promotion for interest oriented and innovative new schemes', `frequent and effective advertisements' and `field selling efforts'.

Fourteen dimensions of MKTORIENT grouped under four Ps of marketing mix separated into two orientation regions of customer satisfaction within the framework of MKTORIENT (Table 8.4) reveals that non-target customers of SKGB have given `above average' response with respect to ten dimensions viz., `need satisfying deposit schemes and simple loan formalities', `need based and convenient purchase schemes', `time efficient and hasselfree procedure', `efficient and adequate bank services, `reasonable and attractive interest rates', `accurate loan interest rates and calculations', `nearest branch location', `co-operative, informative and efficient employees' and `adequate staff and reasonable market'. These customers have given `below average' score to the remaining four dimensions due to `lack of fieldworkers promotional skill', `infrequent and ineffective promotional communication', `absence of promotion for interest oriented and innovative new schemes' and `inadequate and uneducated advertisements'.

The number of non-target customers falling indifferent regions of MKTORIENT (Table 8.5) highlights that four dimensions viz., `time efficient and hasslefree procedure', `nearest branch location', `co-operative, informative and efficient employees' and `efficient and adequate bank services' have secured highest range of MKTORIENT ("4-5") with 76%, 64%, 61%, and 59% of the sample customers. Further the majority of respondents have given their high ratings in the "3-4" range of MKTORIENT with respect to 'adequate staff and reasonable market' (64%), `accurate loan interest rates and calculations' (62%), `reasonable and attractive interest rates' (58%), `need satisfying deposit schemes and simple loan formalities' (55%), ` need based and convenient purchase schemes' (50%) and `easy loan recovery policy' (50%). Thus only 50% respondents have fallen in the said range for `need based and convenient purchase schemes' and `easy loan recovery policy'.

Similarly `frequent and effective promotional communication' has received score between "2-3" range of orientation region from respectively 64% of sample respondents. Likewise, maximum of non-target customers have responded between "1-2" range of MKTORIENT to the 'fieldworkers promotional skill' (66%), `promotion for interest oriented and innovative new schemes' (68%) and `adequate and educative advertisements' (83%).

Overall marketing orientation in the SKGB branch, under reference, as judged by non-target customers on the basis of their responses towards four Ps of rural bank marketing (Table 8.1) arrived at 3.37. They have assigned highest mean score to `product mix' (3.99) followed by `place mix' (3.96), `price mix' (3.51) and lowest value accorded to `promotion mix' (2.01).

On the basis of both target and non-target customers assessment towards four Ps of bank marketing mix, overall marketing orientation in the aforesaid SKGB branch worked out to be 3.21. They have attributed highest mean value to `product adequacy' (3.83) followed by `place effectiveness' (3.76), `price reasonability' (3.32) and lowest mean score awarded to `promotion optimality' (1.91). Thus, promotional variable of marketing mix has generated below 2-point on MKTORIENT, which indicates that in order to improve marketing orientation in the rural banking industry `promotional element' has to be geared up more effectively.

The relationship between rural bank marketing orientation and fourteen dimensions in the scale grouped under four Ps of marketing mix established with the help of a statistical tool of multiple regression is as under:

MKTORIENT : .419 + .240 (PRDMEAN1) + .103 (PLAMEAN3) + .039 (PRMMEAN1) - .197 (PRMMEAN2) + .259 (PRMMEAN3) - .014 (PRMMEAN4) - .045 (PRDMEAN2) + .318 (PRDMEAN3) - .007 (PRDMEAN4) + .079 (PRDMEAN5) - .086 (PRIMEAN1) + 0.79 (PRIMEAN2) + .068 (PLAMEAN1) + .174 (PLAMEAN2).

Aforesaid discussion indicates that third dimension of product mix is the most important one and next rank in order of merit has gone to third dimension of promotion mix. Second dimension of promotion mix appears to be least significant (-.197).

VALIDITY AND RELIABILITY OF DATA

`Service quality' and `overall performance' have been converged with the remaining aspects of marketing orientation (Table 8.12). Marketing Orientation, which worked out to be 3.21 (Table 8.1), has been proved convergently valid because majority of SKGB customers have fallen under `above average' region of `service quality' (81%) and `overall performance' (95%) by assigning 3.38 and 3.34 values respectively.

Multiple correlation (R) between overall marketing orientation and four Ps of marketing mix arrived at .70 which implies very high degree of association between these variables. The value of co-efficient of determination (R^2) figured out to be .49 which indicates that 49% of the variation in marketing orientation can be explained by four variables in the linear equation.

Since the calculated value (7.60) of `F' is greater than the tabulated value (3.17) at 1% level of significance (df_{v1v2} 13, 124) so the hypothesis of equality of 14 dimensions is rejected. Thus these dimensions don't have equal impact on overall MKTORIENT.

The values of `t' were tested both at 1% and 5% level of significance ($df_{v1}$12). Except for the first and third dimension of `product mix' and third dimension of `promotion mix', 11 dimensions have fallen in the acceptance region at 5% level of significance (2.18) where as except third dimensions of `product mix' and `promotion mix' all the 12 dimensions have fallen in the acceptance region at 1% level of significance (3.06). Beside three dimensions, rest have their significant contribution in the calculation of bank MKTORIENT both the 1% & 5% level of significance.

STRATEGIC ACTION

The extent of marketing orientation, measured in the said SKGB branch (Table 8.1) necessitated the following strategies for increasing the level of marketing orientation in the functioning of RRBs.

At the first stage efforts be made not only to maintain the present status of marketing culture with respect to those aspects where SKGB customers enjoy 'above average' response of orientation but also to take it to the highest point on MKTORIENT scale.

Table 8.5
Number of Non-Target Customers under Dimensions-wise MKTORIENT Regions

Orientation Regions →	*1-2*		*2-3*		*3-4*		*4-5*	
Dimensions ↓	*No.*	*(%)*	*No.*	*(%)*	*No.*	*(%)*	*No.*	*(%)*
F_1 (104)	01	1	06	6	57	55	40	38
F_2 (97)	17	18	20	21	49	50	11	11
F_3 (104)	—	—	01	1	24	23	79	76
F_4 (104)	05	5	04	4	34	32	61	59
F_5 (28)	03	11	10	36	14	50	01	3
F_6 (102)	04	4	28	27	59	58	11	11
F_7 (103)	02	2	22	21	64	62	15	15
F_8 (104)	11	11	02	2	24	23	67	64
F_9 (104)	—	—	07	7	33	32	64	61
F_{10} (104)	—	—	30	29	67	64	07	7
F_{11} (104)	69	66	14	14	21	20	—	—
F_{12} (21)	32	31	67	64	05	5	—	—
F_{13} (21)	71	68	19	18	14	14	—	—
F_{14} (18)	80	83	08	8	18	19	—	—

Table 8.6
Marketing-Mix Variables Obtaining Less than Average Score—Target Group

Production (A)	*Price (B)*	*Place (C)*	*Promotion (D)*
F_1 = (24%) (1) Need meeting deposit schemes. fieldworkers. interest deposit schemes. (3) Bank proves to be a good prime bank. (4) Simple loan formalities. (5) No switching intentions for loans. F_2 = (50%) (1) Need meeting loan schemes. (2) Sufficient number of loan schemes. (3) Loan procedure easy even to a layman. F_5 = (67%) (1) Comfortable loan recovery policy.	F_6 = (30%) (1) Attractive and adequate interest rates. (2) unbanked area. rates. (3) Quick information regarding new interest rates. F_7 = (20%) (1) Reasonable loan interest rates. (2) Authentic interest calculations.	F_8 = (19%) (1) Nearest location. (2) Branch location at hitherto Sufficient number of (2) Fieldworkers con- (3) Reasonable market around branch location. F_9 = (10%) (1) Co-operative and friendly employees. (2) Satisfactory present bank's staff. (3) Competent and efficient employees. (4) Employees have sufficient information. F_{10} = (10%) (1) Adequate bank's staff. (2) Convenient branch location.	F_{11} = (95%) (1) Promotion through (2) Motivating deposit vincing skill. (3) Promotion through personal involvement. F_{12} = (100%) (1) Frequent advertisements. (2) Customer awareness meet. (3) Employees assistance in filing deposit/withdrawal forms. (4) Heavy ads of new interest rates.

Contd. . .

Table 8.6 *(Contd.)*

Product (A)	*Price (B)*	*Place (C)*	*Promotion (D)*
(2) Easy repayment of of instalments.			(5) Promotion of schemes through attractive posters. F_{13} = (100%) (1) Employees co-operation in educating clients about new schemes. (2) Employees co-operation in educating clients about new interest rates. (3) Attractive promotional gifts. F_{14} = (100%) (1) Effective T.V. and Radio ads. (2) Heavy promotion through newspapers and magazines.

Table 8.7
Marketing-Mix Variables Obtaining Average Score—Target Group

Product (A)	*Price (B)*	*Place (C)*	*Promotion (D)*
F_1 = (5%)	F_6 = (25%)	F_{10} =(19%)	
(1) Need meeting deposit schemes.	(1) Attractive and adequate interest rates	(1) Adequate bank's staff.	
(2) Sufficient number of deposit schemes	(2) Motivating deposit interest rates.	(2) Convenient branch location.	
(3) Bank proves to be a good prime bank.	(3) Quick information regarding new interest rates.		
(4) Simple loan formalities.	F_7 = (30%)		
(5) No switching intentions for loans	(1) Reasonable loan interest rates.		
F_2 = (10%)	(2) Authentic interest calculations.		
(1) Need meeting loan schemes.			
(2) Sufficient number of loan schemes.			
(3) Loan procedure easy even to a layman.			
F_3 = (5%)			
(1) No delay in depositing cash.			
(2) Immediate issuance of new cheque/passbooks.			
(3) Quick withdrawal facilities.			
(4) Easy procedure for fixed deposit schemes.			
F_4 = (9%)			
(1) Timely encashment of cheques.			
(2) Simple account opening formalities.			

Table 8.8
Marketing-Mix Variables Obtaining More than Average Score—Target Group

Product (A)	*Price (B)*	*Place (C)*	*Promotion (D)*
F_1 = (71%) (1) Need meeting deposit scheme. (2) Sufficient number of deposit schemes. (3) Bank proves to be a good prime bank. (4) Simple loan formalities. (5) No switching intentions for loans. F_2 = (40%) (1) Need meeting loan schemes. (2) Sufficient number of loan schemes. (3) Loan procedure easy even to a layman. F_3 = (96%) (1) No delay in depositing cash.	F_6 = (45%) (1) Attractive and adequate interest rates. (2) Motivating deposit interest rates. (3) Quick information regarding new interest rates. F_7 = (50%) (1) Reasonable loan interest rates. (2) Authentic interest calculations.	F_8 = (81%) (1) Nearest location. (2) Branch location at hitherto unbanked area. (3) Reasonable market around branch location. F_9 = (90%) (1) Co-operative and friendly employees. (2) Satisfactory present bank's staff. (3) Competent and efficient employees. (4) Employees have sufficient information. F_{10} = (71%) (1) Adequate bank's staff. (2) Convenient branch location.	F_{11} = (5%) (1) Promotion through fieldworkers. (2) Fieldworkers convincing skill. (3) Promotion through personal involvement.

Contd. . .

Table 8.8 *(Contd.)*

Product (A)	*Price (B)*	*Place (C)*	*Promotion (D)*
(2) Immediate issuance of new cheque/passbooks.			
(3) Quick withdrawal facilities.			
(4) Easy procedure for fixed deposit schemes.			
F_4 = (91%)			
(1) Timely encashment of cheques.			
(2) Simple account opening formalities.			
F_5 = (33%)			
(1) Comfortable loan recovery policy.			
(2) Easy repayment of instalment.			

Table - 8.9

Marketing-Mix Variables Obtaining Less than Average Score—Non-Target Group

Product (A)	*Price (B)*	*Place (C)*	*Promotion (D)*
F_1 = (5%)	F_6 = (16%)	F_8 = (12%)	F_{11} = (77%)
(1) Need meeting deposit scheme.	(1) Attractive and adequate interest rates.	(1) Nearest location.	(1) Promotion through fieldworkers.
(2) Sufficient number of deposit schemes.	(2) Motivating deposit interest rates.	(2) Branch location at hitherto unbanked area.	(2) Fieldworkers convincing skill.
(3) Bank proves to be a good prime bank.	(3) Quick information regarding new interest rates.	(3) Reasonable market around branch location.	(3) Promotion through personal involvement.
(4) Simple loan formalities.	F_7 = (4%)	F_9 = (5%)	
(5) No switching intentions for loans.	(1) Reasonable loan interest rates.	(1) Co-operative and friendly employees.	
F_2 = (20%)	(2) Authentic interest calculations.	(2) Satisfactory present bank's staff.	
(1) Need Meeting loan schemes.		(3) Competent and efficient employees.	
(2) Sufficient number of loan schemes.		(4) Employees have sufficient information.	
(3) Loan procedure easy even to a layman.		F_{10} = (1%)	
F_3 = (1%)		(1) Adequate bank's staff.	
(1) No delay in depositing cash.		(2) Convenient branch location.	

Contd. . .

Table 8.9 *(Contd.)*

Product (A)	*Price (B)*	*Place (C)*	*Promotion (D)*
(2) Immediate issuance of new cheque/passbooks.			
(3) Quick withdrawal facilities.			
(4) Easy procedure for fixed deposit schemes.			
F_4 = (5%)			
(1) Timely encashment of cheques.			
(2) Simple account opening formalities.			
F_5 = (47%)			
(1) Comfortable loan recovery policy.			
(2) Easy repayment of instal-ment.			

Table 8.10
Marketing-Mix Variables Obtaining Average Score—Non-Target Group

Product (A)	*Price (B)*	*Place (C)*	*Promotion (D)*
F_1 = (2%) (1) Need meeting deposit schemes. (2) Sufficient number of deposit schemes. (3) Bank proves to be a good prime bank. (4) Simple loan formalities. (5) No switching intentions for loans. F_2 = (19%) (1) Need meeting loan schemes. (2) Sufficient number of loan schemes. (3) Loan procedure easy even to a layman. F_4 = (4%) (1) Timely encashment of cheques.	F_6 = (16%) (1) Attractive and adequate interest rates. (2) Motivating deposit interest rates. (3) Quick information regarding new interest rates. F_7 = (19%) (1) Reasonable loan interest rates. (2) Authentic interest calculations.	F_8 = (1%) (1) Nearest location. (2) Branch location at hitherto unbanked area. (3) Reasonable market around branch location. F_9 = (2%) (1) Co-operative and friendly employees. (2) Satisfactory present bank's staff. (3) Competent and efficient employees. (4) Employees have sufficient information. F_{10} = (28%) (1) Adequate bank's staff. (2) Convenient branch location.	F_{11} = (3%) (1) Promotion through fieldworkers. (2) Fieldworkers convincing skill. (3) Promotion through personal involvement. F_{12} = (9%) (1) Frequent advertisements. (2) Customer awareness meets. (3) Employees assistance in filing deposit/withdrawal forms. (4) Heavy ads of new interest rates.

Contd. . .

Table 8.10 *(Contd.)*

Product (A)	*Price (B)*	*Place (C)*	*Promotion (D)*
(2) Simple accounts opening formalities.			(5) Promotion of schemes through attractive posters. F_{13} = (9%) (1) Employees co-operation in educating clients about new schemes. (2) Employees co-operation in educating clients about new interest rates. (3) Attractive promotional gifts. F_{14} = (4%) (1) Effective T.V. and Radio ads. (2) Heavy promotion through newspapers and magazines.

Table 8.11
Marketing-Mix Variables Obtaining More than Average Score—Non-Target Group

Product (A)	*Price (B)*	*Place (C)*	*Promotion (D)*
F_1 = (93%) (1) Need meeting deposit scheme. (2) Sufficient number of deposit schemes. (3) Bank proves to be a good prime bank. (4) Simple loan formalities. (5) No switching intentions for loans. F_2 = (61%) (1) Need Meeting loan schemes. (2) Sufficient number of loan schemes. (3) Loan procedure easy even to a layman. F_3 = (99%) (1) No delay in depositing cash.	F_6 = (68%) (1) Attractive and adequate interest rates. (2) Motivating deposit interest rates. (3) Quick information regarding new interest rates. F_7 = (77%) (1) Reasonable loan interest rates. (2) Authentic interest calculations.	F_8 = (12%) (1) Nearest location. (2) Branch location at hitherto unbanked area. (3) Reasonable market around branch location. F_9 = (5%) (1) Co-operative and friendly employees. (2) Satisfactory present bank's staff. (3) Competent and efficient employees. (4) Employees have sufficient information. F_{10} = (1%) (1) Adequate bank's staff. (2) Convenient branch location.	F_{11} = (20%) (1) Promotion through fieldworkers. (2) Fieldworkers convincing skill. (3) Promotion through personal involvement. F_{12} = (5%) (1) Frequent advertisement. (2) Customer awareness meets. (3) Employees assistance in filing withdrawal/deposit schemes. (4) Heavy ads of new interest rates.

Contd. . .

Table 8.11 *(Contd.)*

Product (A)	*Price (B)*	*Place (C)*	*Promotion (D)*
(2) Immediate issuance of new cheque/passbooks. (3) Quick withdrawal facilities. (4) Easy procedure for fixed deposit schemes. F_4 = (91%) (1) Timely encashment of cheques. (2) Simple account opening formalities. F_5 = (53%) (1) Comfortable loan recovery policy. (2) Easy repayment of instalment.			(5) Promotion of schemes through attractive posters. F_{13} = (14%) (1) Employees co-operation in educating clients about new interest rates. (2) Employees co-operation in educating clients about new schemes. (3) Attractive promotional gifts. F_{14} = (19%) (1) Effective T.V. and Radio ads. (2) Heavy promotion through newspapers and magazines.

Table 8.12
Service Quality and Overall Performance-wise Marketing Orientation

Marketing Mix Factors	*Service Quality* BA	A	AA	*Overall Performance* BA	A	AA
PRDMEAN 1	2.49	3.37	3.98	—	2.71	3.87
PRDMEAN 2	2.0	3.24	3.37	—	1.93	3.35
PRDMEAN 3	3.83	4.29	4.49	—	3.83	4.46
PRDMEAN 4	3.71	4.44	4.40	—	3.75	4.39
PRDMEAN 5	1.5	3.17	3.37	—	2.0	3.38
GRPRDMEAN	2.71	3.70	3.92	—	2.84	3.89
PRIMEAN 1	2.52	3.21	3.54	—	2.67	3.48
PRIMEAN 2	3.08	3.53	3.74	—	3.4	3.69
GRPRIMEAN	2.8	3.37	3.64	—	3.04	3.59
PLAMEAN 1	3.48	3.46	4.13	—	3.28	4.04
PLAMEAN 2	3.31	3.73	4.13	—	3.28	4.04
PLAMEAN 3	3.5	3.11	4.11	—	3.22	4.05
GRPRMMEAN	3.43	3.5	3.92	—	3.36	3.86
PRMMEAN 1	2.05	1.81	2.09	—	1.83	2.06
PRMMEAN 2	1.57	2.1	2.34	—	1.57	2.30
PLAMEAN 3	1.57	1.77	1196	—	1.17	1.95
PRMMEAN 4	1.64	1.77	1.77	—	2.0	1.75
GRPRMMEAN	1.71	1.86	2.04	—	1.64	2.02
MKTORIENT	**2.66**	**3.11**	**3.38**	—	**2.72**	**3.34**
No. & % age of Respondents	**01 (6%)**	**16 (13%)**	**102 (81%)**	—	**06 (5%)**	**119 (95%)**

82% sample customers have shown their satisfaction towards 'need satisfying deposit schemes and simple loan formalities.

New need based schemes should be introduced or old schemes need to be revised.

Only 51% sample respondents feel that major loans through from rural banks are more convenient whereas remaining sample respondents indicate lack of timely advice and assistance on the financial matters (Kshirsagar 1976).

`Time efficient and hasslefree procedure' and `efficient and adequate bank services' have obtained `above average' score from about 98% and 91% of the total sample. Through more efficient services and less cumbersome procedure, new customers can be encouraged to deal with an RRB (Hebbar 1998). 57% and 64% sample customers have highlighted their satisfaction towards `reasonable and attractive interest rates' and `accurate loan interest rates' but for the remaining lot there is a need to make interest rates more acceptable keeping in view the customers' expectations towards `price element' of marketing mix.

Out of the total sample, 84% customers are fully satisfied with regard to the branch location of rural banks. In order to get 100% customer satisfaction branches should be shifted to more convenient places.

Approximately 92% sample respondents have reflected their satisfaction towards `co-operative, informative and efficient employees'. The working style of RRB employees should be based on the local environment (Kalkundrikar 1990) so as to make banking operations more successful.

`Adequate staff and reasonable market' has generated `above average' score from 71% sample customers. Adequate staff should be available as per the needs of the banking operations (Goiporia Committee 1996).

Second type of strategic action necessitates adequate attention of the bank towards all those dimensions of four Ps which scored `below average' level of orientation. 57% sample customers have exhibited their dissatisfaction towards `easy loan recovery policy'. The flexibility given to the co-operatives to determine interest rates (Rangarajan 1966) should also be provided to RRBs so that high interest rates may not come in the way of repaying the loans.

About 86% sample respondents have given `below average' response to `fieldworkers promotional skill'. "On-the-job-training" should be provided to fieldworkers (Venkateswarlu 1987) so that they feel confident while approaching the people in areas of their jurisdiction.

Out of the total sample 93% and 89% customers feel dissatisfied respectively about promotional communication in rural banks and `promotion for interest oriented and innovative new schemes'. Thus there is a need for effective promotion of bank schemes and respective interest rates (Kshirsagar 1976).

`Adequate and educating advertisements' have obtained `below average' responses from 86% sample respondents. Customer education programmes should be introduced where in banks' employees should launch effective advertisements for customers awareness (Goiporia Committee 1996).

REFERENCES

1. Goiporia Committee (1996) "Customer Service in Banks" *Planning Bulletin*, June/July, 258-259.
2. Hebbar C. Kusumakara (1988), "Bank Marketing Strategy in Commercial Banks", *Southern Economist* Oct., Vol. 27, 18.
3. Kalkundrikar, A.B. (1990), "RRBs and Economic Development", *Prajnan*, July-Sept., Vol. XIX, 319.
4. Kalkundrikar, A.B. (1990), "Improving Customer Service of Banks", *Prajnan*, Apr.-June, Vol. VI, 146-155.
5. Menezes, J. S. William (1979), "Marketing of Bank Services", *Prajnan*, Apr.-June Vol. VIII, 135.
6. Rangarajan, C. (1996), "Rural India: The Role of Credit", *The Banker*, March, 17.
7. Venkateswarlu, P.K. (1987), "Customer Service in Commercial Banks", *Southern Economist*, Oct., Vol. 26, 06.

Chapter—9

Measurement of Marketing Orientation in SKGB with Reference to Developed Rural Area

BACKGROUND

The status of marketing orientation in RRBs functioning in developed sector has been worked out from the data collected from 175 randomly selected respondents belonging to the villages viz., Baghpur and Sataur of Hoshiarpur district falling within the operational jurisdiction of SKGB (Baghpur). Baghpur had total population of 3128, with 309 households, 82% literacy rate, just 16% households living below poverty line, very good infrastructural facilities such as a pacca roads, regular power supply, 3 government and one private school and a dispensary and Sataur had 5233 population, 375 households, 86% literacy level, 15% poverty rate, good infrastructural facilities such as quit good roads, few power cuts, one government and a private school (Exhibit 9.1). A branch of SKGB (Baghpur) operates in the area, at a profit of about Rs. 5 lacs as on 31-3-97 (Exhibit 9.2), alongwith a co-operative bank branch. The deposits and advances of SKGB Baghpur have shown an increasing trends but credit deposit ratio declined from 1990-91 onwards (Exhibit 9.2). This village is approximately 7 kms away from the main city as a result of which it has high literacy, low poverty and high per hectare yield (61 qtl/hec) and all these factors help on institution like SKGB to enjoy comparatively better and knowledgeable target market.

The data for this chapter was collected through the pretested schedule of 60 statements falling within the paradigm of MKTORIENT. After the process of reduction through factor analysis, 39 statements got grouped under 15 dimensions (5 product, 2 price, 3 place and 5 promotion) of MKTORIENT (Table 9.0).

STATUS OF MARKETING ORIENTATION

Extent of marketing orientation has been analysed on the basis of the judgement by 98 males and 77 females of SKGB living in the village Baghpur of Hoshiarpur district and the same has been worked out separately under the following two main heads.

1. Target Group

Out of total sample customers from the village under reference, 34% belong to target group. It reflects that adequate number of target customers are availing rural banking services.

Literate male small farmers having income below Rs. 11,000 p.a have accorded highest mean value to `product adequacy and suitability' (3.94) (Table 9.1) followed by `price reasonability' (3.6) `place effectiveness' (3.56) and lowest mean score assigned to `promotion optimality' (1.93) for the items such as `frequent and effective promotional communication', `fieldworkers promotional efficiency', `promotion for interest oriented and motivating new schemes', `requisite and instructive advertisements' and `personal selling efforts'.

Literate male customers belonging to target group under agricultural allied activities have attributed highest value to `place mix' (3.93) followed by `product mix' (3.92), `price mix' (3.12) and lowest score responded to `promotional elements' (1.90) such as `persistent and effective promotional communication', `fieldworkers promotional intelligence', `promotion for new scheme', `sufficient and informative advertisements' and `employees' efforts in selling banking services'.

Literate female customers engaged in agricultural allied activities, have given highest response to `place mix effectiveness' (3.94), followed by `product mix effectiveness' (3.91) `price mix effectiveness' (2.96) and least score obtained by `promotion mix variables' (1.96) i.e., `frequent and effective promotional communication', `fieldworkers promotional skill', `promotion for high interest deposit and low interest loan schemes', `adequate and educative advertisements for favourable changes' and `field selling efforts'.

Illiterate female non farmers belonging to target group have ranked `product adequacy' (4.21) at the top, second rank accorded to `place effectiveness' (3.78), followed by `price reasonability' (3.50) and last rank went to `promotion mix' (1.58) for the items such as `timely and efficacious promotional competence', `interest focused and motivating new schemes', `competent and effective advertisements' and `personal selling efforts'.

Fifteen dimensions of MKTORIENT grouped under four Ps of marketing mix variables segregated into two orientation regions of customer satisfaction within the jurisdiction of marketing orientation revealing the extent of MKTORIENT (Table 9.2) exhibits that target customers of SKGB are highly satisfied with regard to `time efficient and hasslefree procedure', `simple loan recovery policy', `efficient and adequate bank services', `correct and timely passbook entries', `easy purchase schemes', `co-operative, informative and efficient employees', `adequate staff and satisfactory performance', `staff co-operation in completing bank formalities'. These customers are least satisfied due to `unreasonable and unattractive interest rates', `inconvenient branch location', `inadequate and fieldworkers promotional skill', `inadequate and ineffective advertisements', `insufficient promotion for interest oriented and innovative new schemes', `infrequent and ineffective promotional communication'.

The number of target customers falling in different marketing orientation regions (Table 9.3) reveals that one dimension viz., `correct an timely passbook entries' has fallen in the highest range of MKTORIENT with as high as 83% of the sample respondents. Similarly majority of respondents have given `above average' assessment with respect to `time efficient and hasslefree procedure' (96%), `easy loan recovery policy' (65%), `efficient and adequate bank services' (95%), `timely information on new interest rates' (88%), `co-operative, informative and efficient employees' (86%), `adequate staff and satisfactory performance' (98%) and `employees co-operation in completing bank formalities' (75%).

Among the dimensions obtaining below average score, two factors viz., `reasonable and attractive interest rates' (92%) and `convenient purchase schemes' (58%) have fallen in this orientation region. Further majority of respondents have given poor values just between "1-2" scale of MKTORIENT to the `adequate and educative advertisements' (100%), `fieldworkers promotional skill' (97%), `frequent and effective promotional communication' (97%), `promotion for interest oriented and innovative new schemes' (87%) and `nearest branch location in unbanked area' (97%).

Overall marketing orientation in SKGB branch as worked out from the extent of satisfaction pertaining to four Ps of bank marketing mix among target customers figured out to be 3.24 (Table 9.1). The highest mean score given to `product adequacy and its suitability' (4.07) followed by `place effectiveness' (3.80), `price reasonability' (3.37) and `promotion optimality' (1.75). Thus among all the four Ps promotion mix is the critical one, which demands more planned efforts and resources for strengthening overall marketing orientation in rural banks.

2. Non-Target Group

From the village under study, out of total sample of 175 customers, 66% belong to non-target group. Male literate small farmers having income above Rs. 11,000 p.a. have given highest score to `place effectiveness' (4.17) (Table 9.1) followed by `product adequacy' (3.83), just average mean value to `promotional optimality' (3.0) and less than average mean score to `price reasonability' (2.6) for the items such as `reasonable and attractive interest rates' and `timely information on new interest rates'.

Illiterate male small farmers belonging to non-target group have awarded higher mean value to `product mix' (4.38) followed by `price mix' (4.25), `place mix' (3.44) and lower mean score assigned to the `promotion mix variables' (2.0) viz., `prompt and result oriented promotional communication', `fieldworkers performance', `promotion for interest focused and need based new schemes', `sufficient and informative advertisements' and `field selling efforts'.

Both male and female literate customers belonging to non-target group engaged in activities allied to agriculture have shown their highest satisfaction with regard to `place effectiveness' (4.0 & 4.04) followed by `product adequacy' (3.91 & 3.91), `price reasonability' (3.04 & 2.71) and `promotion optimality' scored lowest mean score (2.05 & 1.81) for the items such as `recurrent and effective promotional communication', `fieldworkers promotional expertise', `high interest on deposit and need satisfying loan schemes', `competent and productive advertisements' and `face to face communication'.

Male literate and illiterate medium farmers engaged in agricultural business have exhibited highest satisfaction with respect to 'product mix' (4.08 & 4.54) folloed by 'place mix' (4.06 & 4.06), 'price mix' (2.97 & 3.4) and less than average value obtained by the elements of 'promotion mix' (1.98 & 2.0) viz., 'speedy and compelling promotional communication', 'fieldworkers promotional ability', 'promotion for new schemes', 'adequate and result oriented advertisements' and 'personal involvement'.

Literate male non-farmers who have taken loan for various activities allied to agriculture have shown highest satisfaction with regard to `product mix effectiveness' (4.09) followed by `place mix effectiveness' (4.01), `price mix effectiveness' (3.10) and feel highly dissatisfied towards, `promotion mix variables' (2.08) viz., `frequent and effective promotional communication', `fieldworkers promotional aptitude', `promotion for interest emphasising new schemes', `efficacious and informative advertisements' and `interaction with customers'.

Literate female non-farmers having income above Rs. 11,000 p.a engaged in allied agricultural activities have reflected their highest satisfaction towards `place effectiveness' (3.78) followed by `product adequacy' (3.66), less than average mean score to `price reasonability' (2.93) and lower mean value to `promotion optimality' (2.05) whereas its illiterate counterpart has assigned highest mean value to `price mix' (4.5) followed by `place mix' (4.27), `product mix' (4.25) and less than 3 point on MKTORIENT scale to `promotion mix' (2.13). Thus both categories of customers have assigned lowest mean score to promotional aspect of rural banking which include `convincing and operative promotional communication', `fieldworkers promotional proficiency', `promotion for interest oriented new schemes', `adequate and informative advertisements' and `field selling efforts'.

Fifteen dimensions of MKTORIENT clubbed under four Ps of marketing mix segregated into two orientation regions of customer satisfaction within the paradigm of MKTORIENT (Table 9.4) highlights that non-target customers of SKGB have been given "above average" response to the nine dimensions viz., `time efficient and hasslefree procedure', `easy loan recovery policy', `efficient and adequate bank services', `accurate and timely passbook entries', `convenient purchase schemes', `timely information on new interest rates', `co-operative, informative and efficient employees', `adequate staff and satisfactory performance', `staff assistance in completing bank formalities'. However these customers feel least satisfied due to `unreasonable and unattractive interest rates', `branch location in unbanked area', `fieldworkers ineffective promotional skill', `inadequate and uneducative advertisements', `ineffective promotional communication', `inadequate promotion for interest oriented and innovative new schemes.'

The number of non-target customers falling in different regions of MKTORIENT (Table 9.5) exhibits that three dimensions viz., `time efficient and hasslefree procedure', `efficient and adequate bank services' and `accurate and timely passbook entries' have secured highest score on MKTORIENT with 55%, 68% and 84% of the sample customers. Similarly majority of respondents have given their high scores falling in the "3-4" range of MKTORIENT with respect to `adequate staff and satisfactory performance' (80%), `timely information on new interest rates' (63%), `easy loan recovery policy' (59%), `promotion for interest oriented and innovative new schemes' (53%) and co-operative, informative and efficient employees' (52%). Beside these dimensions, one dimensions viz., `convenient purchase schemes' has scored "above average" response from majority of the customers (60%).

One dimension viz., `reasonable and attractive interest rates has fallen in the "2-3" range of MKTORIENT with 55% of sample customers. Like target customers, non-target ones have also expressed their dissatisfaction regarding various dimensions of `promotion mix' i.e., `fieldworkers promotional skill' (95%), `adequate and educative advertisement' (95%), `frequent and effective promotional communication' (90%) and `promotion for interest oriented and innovative new schemes" (72%).

Overall marketing orientation as worked out on the basis of responses extracted from non-target customers towards four Ps of marketing mix arrived at 3.39. This category of customers have given highest mean value to `place mix' (4.13) followed by `product mix' (3.90), `price mix' (3.43) and `promotion mix' (2.10).

On the basis of responses obtained from both `target and non-target customers', towards various banking services of SKGB, residing in the village Baghpur, the overall marketing orientation worked out to be 3.34. They have assigned highest mean score to `product adequacy' (4.11) followed by `place effectiveness' (3.86), `price reasonability' (3.41) and `promotion optimality' (1.98). Thus promotion mix variables need to be strengthened in order to enhance the overall marketing orientation in these banks.

The relationship between rural bank's marketing orientation and fifteen dimensions in the scale combined under four Ps of marketing mix formulated with a statistical technique of Multiple Regression is as under:—

MKTORIENT = 1.69 + 1.08 (PRDMEAN1) +.069 (PLAMEAN3) +.053 (PRMMEAN1) +.008 (PRMMEAN3) -.138 (PRMMEAN4) -.028 (PRMMEAN5) +.099 (PRDMEAN3) -.020 (PRDMEAN4) +.045 (PRDMEAN5) -.028 (PRIMEAN1) +.300 (PRIMEAN2) +.037 (PLAMEAN1) +.076 (PLAMEAN2).

The relative importance of 15 dimensions estimating the overall marketing orientation highlights that second dimension of price mix is the most critical one. Next two ranks in order of merit have gone to first and third dimensions of product mix. Fourth dimension of promotion mix appears to be least important (-138).

VALIDITY AND RELIABILITY

`Service quality' and `overall performance' have been converged with other important aspects of marketing orientation (Table 9.12). Marketing Orientation, which worked out to be 3.34 (Table 9.1), has been proved convergently valid because majority of SKGB customers have fallen under `above average' region of `service quality' (80%) and `overall performance' (93%) by attributing 3.31 and 3.27 values respectively. (3.01), all other dimensions have fallen in the acceptance region. This exhibits that out of fifteen dimensions, 13 have their important contribution in the computation of marketing orientation in rural banks.

STRATEGIC ACTION

The extent of marketing orientation estimated in SKGB branch under study indicates two types of marketing strategy to increase the present status of marketing orientation in the RRBs' operations of RRBs under similar conditions.

Firstly marketing strategy incorporates all those dimensions of four Ps which have generated `below average' score from majority of the SKGB customers.

55.5% of sample customers have exhibited dissatisfaction towards interest rates charged and provided by rural banks. Different interest rates should be quoted depending upon the standard of living of rural people. Those living below or at just above poverty line should be provided more or charged less interest rates.

Out of total sample, 87.5% customers felt branch location quite inconvenient, as it is about 2 kms away from the village and moreover a branch of cooperative bank is also functioning at the place. Thus there is a need to relocate the rural bank branches at an accessible place (Vijay Kumar 1991) and to transfer the business of rural branches of all commercial/co-operative banks in the operation to the branches of RRBs (Kalkundrikar 1990).

All the customers contacted have expressed their dissatisfaction towards fieldworkers promotional skill. Adequate reward and recognition system should be used effectively (Gioporia Committee 1996) in order to promote fieldworkers selling efforts and communicational ability.

About 98% sample respondents viewed that rural banks do not advertise their new schemes and interest rates. If advertising is a costly affair to one RRB branch, a joint advertising programme can be initiated by two or more RRBs (Hebbar 1989).

84% sample customers have been `below average' values to `promotion for interest oriented and innovative new schemes'. Innovation of suitable credit and deposit related financial products (Mandanna & Chengappa 1993) and changes in interest rates should be made known to customers (Goiporia Committee 1996) at the earliest possible.

Almost all the respondents contacted were least satisfied with the promotional communication of RRBs staff. Thus there is a need to strengthen RRBs with more dedicated (Hebbar 1989) and trained staff (Bhattacharyay 1989).

Similarly marketing plan should aim at enhancing marketing culture in RRBs by taking the dimensions of four Ps upto 4-point on MKTORIENT scale, which have otherwise secured `above average' values.

`Time efficient and hasslefree operation' and `efficient and adequate bank services' have obtained `above average' score from 96.5% and 97% of sample respondents. In order to take their satisfaction level upto highest point on the construct, there is a need to make banking operations more convenient and to provide with more need satisfying services by way of rewarding best branches from customer satisfaction point of view (Goiporia Committee 1996).

63% sample customers felt contented with loan recovery policy of rural banks but remaining lot still desires cross subsidy facility which is available to commercial banks (Rangarajan 1996) so as to relieve themselves from the burden of repaying huge debts.

Only 51% customers contacted have shown their satisfaction towards `convenient purchase of product through rural bank finance' but 49% sample customers feel very cumbersome to procure product through rural banks. Thus at least for illiterate small, marginal farmers and persons of low income group, employees should extend full co-operation which will help customers obtain products without much difficulty.

About 91% sample respondents opined that timely information is provided on new interest rates but still there is a need to effectively communicate new services and interest rates to customers (Kshirsagar 1976).

`Co-operative, informative and efficient employees; and `staff assistance in completing bank formalities' have secured `above average' score from 83% and 77% sample respondents, which implies that employees have to be exposed to increasing interaction with clientele so that they develop needed marketing orientation (Vaghul 1976).

`Adequate staff and satisfactory performance' has fallen in above average MKTORIENT with 96% sample customers. In order to improve their performance training programmes should be launched in line with customers service orientation.

REFERENCES

1. Bhattacharyay, B. N. (1989), "Marketing Approach to Promoting Banking Services", *Vikalpa*, Apr.-June, Vol. 14, 39.
2. Goiporia Committee (1966), "Customer Services in Banks", *Planning Bulletin*, June-July, 293.
3. Hebbar, C. Kusumakara (1988), "Bank Marketing Strategy in Commercial Banks", *Southern Economist*, Oct., Vol. 14, 39.
4. Hebbar, A.R.K (1989), "Problems of RRBs", *Yojana*, April, Vol. 33, 24.
5. Kalkundrikar, A. B. (1990), Regional Rural Banks and Economic Development", Reviewed by N. B. Shete, *Prajnan*, July-Sept., Vol, XIX, No. 3, 319.
6. Kshirsagar (1976), "Improving Customer Service of Banks", *Prajnan*, Apr.-June, Vol. VI, 146.
7. Mandanna, P.K. and P.G. Chengappa (1993), "Marketing Approach in Rural Banking", *Economic Review*, June, 06.
8. Rangarajan, C (1996), "Rural India: The Role of Credit", *The Banker*, March, 15-17.
9. Vaghul, N (1976), "Employees Development for Efficient Customers Services", *Prajnan*, Apr.-June, Vol. VI, 175.
10. Vijay Kumar, M.K. & H.J. Gurunath (1991), "RRBs: An Analysis", *Southern Economist*, Mar., Vol. 29, 17.

Exhibit 9.1

Brief Profile of the Villages viz., Baghpur and Sataur of Hoshiarpur District as on 31.3.97

Baghpur	*Sataur*
(1) Total Population - 3128	(1) Total Population - 5233
(2) Male : Female - 1645 : 1483	(2) Male : Female - 2721 : 2512
(3) Total Households - 309	(3) Total Households - 375
(4) Tentative Economic Status-	(4) Tentative economic status-
(a) Below poverty line - 16%	(a) Below poverty line - 15%
(b) Above poverty line - 84%	(b) Above poverty line - 85%
(5) Literacy Rate -	(5) Literacy Rate -
(a) Literate = 82%	(a) Literate - 86%
(b) Illiterate = 18%	(b) Illiterate - 14%
(6) Infrastructural facilities-	(6) Infrastructural facilities-
(a) Roads—pacca	(a) Roads - quite good condition
(b) Electricity—quite good	(b) Electricity - few cuts
(c) Govt. School -3	(c) Govt. school - one
(d) Private School -1	(d) Private school - one

(7) Land solid suitable for growing wheat, maize, potato and rice.

(8) Per hectare yield-

(a) Wheat	—	40 qtl/hec
(b) Maize	—	25 qtl/hec
(c) Potato	—	160 qtl/hec
(d) Rice	—	50 qtl/hec.

Exhibit 9.2
Brief Profile of the Branch Baghpur of SKGB

(Rs. in '000)

Year	*Deposits*		*Advances*		*C.D.*	*Profit*
	A/c	*Rs.*	*A/c*	*Rs.*	*Ratio*	*Rs.*
1990-91	2790	4925	913	3808	77	110
1991-92	3195	6924	957	4467	65	128
1992-93	3471	9013	860	4827	54	53
1993-94	3366	12545	777	4886	40	256
1994-95	3585	17271	861	5042	29	180
1995-96	3569	23507	640	6633	28	341
1996-97	3596	28212	608	6900	24	500
1997-98	3551	35545	552	6972	20	1020

(1) One branch of co-operation bank in the same area.

(2) Number of projects financed:

	1996-97	*1997-98*
(a) Agriculture	153	164
(b) Allied to Agriculture	87	95

Table 9.0
Summary of Results from Scale Purification—Loading and Variance Explained

Bank Marketing Mix	*Factor-Wise Dimension*	*Factor Loadings*	*% of Variance Explained*
1	2	3	4
Product	**Factor First -**		23.0
	Quick withdrawal facilities.	.88	
	No delay in depositing money.	.86	
	Need meeting deposit schemes.	.51	
	Factor Second -		16.1
	Comfortable loan recovery policy.	.94	
	Easy repayment of instalments.	.94	

Contd. . .

1	2	3	4
	Factor Third -		**11.8**
	Immediate issuance of new cheque/ passbooks.	.81	
	Simple account opening formalities.	.76	
	Factor Fourth -		**10.1**
	Timely updating of passbook.	.87	
	Accurate passbook entries.	.80	
	Factor Fifth -		**8.5**
	Timely purchase through bank.	.74	
	Standard product purchase through bank finance.	.67	
	Loan procedure easy even to a layman.	.53	
	Total variance explained = 69.6%		
Price	**Factor First -**		**44.8**
	Attractive and adequate interest rates.	.87	
	Motivating deposit interest rates.	.87	
	Reasonable loan interest rates.	.76	
	Factor Second -		**22.7**
	Quick information regarding new interest rates.	.86	
	Authentic interest calculations.	.69	
	Total variance explained = 67.6%		
Place	**Factor First -**		**24.9**
	Competent and efficient employees.	.74	
	Co-operative and friendly employees.	.71	
	Employees have sufficient information.	.68	
	Reasonable market around branch location.	.68	
	Factor Second -		**20.7**
	Branch location at hitherto unbanked area.	.90	
	Nearest location	.89	

Contd. . .

1	2	3	4
	Factor Third -		**13.4**
	Satisfactory present bank's staff.	.63	
	Convenient branch location.	.61	
	Adequate bank's staff.	.55	
	Total variance explained = 59%		
Promotion	**Factor First -**		**13.4**
	Fieldworkers convincing skill.	.94	
	Promotion through fieldworkers.	.94	
	Attractive promotional gifts.	-.74	
	Factor Second -		**18.2**
	Heavy promotion through newspaper and magazines.	.94	
	Effective T.V. and Radio ads.	.94	
	Factor Third -		**12.3**
	Employees co-operation in educating clients about new schemes.	.95	
	Employees co-operation in education clients about new interest rates.	.95	
	Factor Fourth -		**11.1**
	Heavy ads of new interest rates.	.69	
	Customer awareness meets.	.65	
	Promotion of schemes through attractive posters.	.59	
	Frequent advertisements.	.57	
	Factor Fifth -		**10.0**
	Employees co-operation in completing loan formalities.	.81	
	Employees assistance in filing withdrawal/deposit forms.	.79	
	Total variance explained = 74%		

Table 9.1
Overall Marketing Orientation—Customers Assessment

				Education										*Overall Mean*				
				LITERATE					*ILLITERATE*									
Income	*Land Holding*	*Gender*	*Occupation*	*A*	*B*	*C*	*D*	*M*	*A*	*B*	*C*	*D*	*M*	*A*	*B*	*C*	*D*	*M*
	Small Farmers	Male	Agricul ture	3.94	3.6	3.56	1.93	3.26	—	—	—	—	—	3.94	3.6	3.56	1.93	3.26
Target Group	Male		Allied to Agriculture	3.92	3.12	3.93	1.90	3.22	—	—	—	—	—	3.92	3.12	3.93	1.90	3.22
	Female		Allied to Agriculture	3.91	2.96	3.94	1.93	3.19	4.21	3.5	3.78	1.58	3.27	4.06	3.23	3.86	1.76	3.23
	Target Group Mean			3.92	3.23	3.81	1.92	3.22	4.21	3.5	3.78	1.58	3.27	4.07	3.37	3.80	1.75	3.24
	Small Farmers	Male	Agriculture	3.83	2.60	4.17	3.0	3.40	4.38	4.25	3.44	2.0	3.52	4.11	3.43	3.81	2.50	3.46
Non-Target Group	Male		Allied to Agriculture	3.91	3.04	4.0	2.05	3.25	—	—	—	—	—	3.91	3.04	4.0	2.05	3.25
	Female		Allied to Agriculture	3.91	2.71	4.04	1.81	3.12	—	—	—	—	—	3.92	2.71	4.04	1.81	3.12

Contd. . .

Table 9.1 *(Contd.)*

				Education										*Overall Mean*				
				LITERATE					*ILLITERATE*									
Income	*Land Holding*	*Gender*	*Occupation*	*A*	*B*	*C*	*D*	*M*	*A*	*B*	*C*	*D*	*M*	*A*	*B*	*C*	*D*	*M*
	Mean			3.88	2.78	4.07	2.29	3.26	4.38	4.25	3.44	2.0	3.52	4.13	3.51	3.76	2.15	3.39
	Medium Farmers	Male	Agriculture	4.08	2.97	4.06	1.98	3.27	4.54	3.4	4.06	2.0	3.50	4.31	3.19	4.06	1.99	3.39
Non-Target Group	Male		Allied to Agriculture	4.09	3.10	4.01	2.08	3.32	—	—	—	—	—	4.09	3.10	4.01	2.08	3.32
	Female		Allied to Agriculture	3.66	2.93	3.78	2.05	3.11	4.27	4.5	4.25	2.13	3.79	3.97	3.72	4.02	2.09	3.45
	Mean			3.94	3.0	3.95	2.04	3.23	4.41	3.95	4.16	2.07	3.65	4.12	3.34	4.03	2.05	3.39
	Non-Target Group Mean			3.92	2.89	4.01	2.17	3.25	4.40	4.10	3.80	2.04	3.59	4.13	3.43	3.90	2.10	3.39
	Overall Mean			3.92	3.0	3.94	2.08	3.24	4.33	3.90	3.79	1.88	3.48	4.11	3.41	3.86	1.98	3.34

Abbreviations used-
A=Product B=Price C=Place D=Promotion M=Mean of four Ps.

Table 9.2
Sixteen Dimensions of the Construct Falling under Two Orientation Regions of Target Customers Satisfaction and the Respective Mean Values Revealing the Extent of MKTORIENT

Below Average (-3 points)	*Above Average* (+3 points)
F_6 = "Reasonable and attractive interest rates" (2.45).	F_1 = "Time efficient and hassle-free procedure" (4.08).
F_9 = "Nearest branch location in unbanked area" (1.93).	F_2 = "Easy loan recovery policy" (3.18).
F_{11} = "Fieldworkers promotional skill" (1.51).	F_3 = "Efficient and adequate bank services" (4.13).
F_{12} = "Adequate and educative advertisements" (1.28).	F_4 = "Accurate and timely passbook entries" (4.69).
F_{13} = "Promotion for interest oriented and innovative new schemes" (1.86).	F_5 = "Convenient purchase schemes" (3.25).
F_{14} = "Frequent and effective promotional communication" (1.62).	F_7 = "Timely information on new interest rates" (3.83).
	F_8 = "Cooperative, informative and efficient employees" (3.81).
	F_{10} = "Adequate staff and satisfactory performance" (3.17).
	F_{15} = "Staff assistance in completing bank formalities" (3.8).

Table 9.3
Number of Target Customers under Dimension-wise MKTORIENT Regions

Orientation Regions →	*1-2*		*2-3*		*3-4*		*4-5*	
Dimensions ↓	*No.*	*(%)*	*No.*	*(%)*	*No.*	*(%)*	*No.*	*(%)*
F_1 (60)	—	—	02	4	29	48	29	48
F_2 (17)	03	16	05	29	11	65	—	—
F_3 (60)	—	—	03	5	35	58	22	37
F_4 (60)	—	—	01	02	09	15	50	83
F_5 (53)	09	17	22	41	18	34	04	8
F_6 (49)	22	45	23	47	04	08	—	—
F_7 (60)	—	—	07	12	48	80	05	8
F_8 (60)	01	2	07	12	27	45	25	41
F_9 (56)	44	79	09	16	—	—	03	05
F_{10} (60)	—	—	01	2	54	90	05	8
F_{11} (60)	58	97	02	3	—	—	—	—
F_{12} (36)	36	100	—	—	—	—	—	—
F_{13} (59)	51	87	06	10	02	3	—	—
F_{14} (60)	58	97	02	3	—	—	—	—
F_{15} (60)	02	3	13	22	36	60	09	15

Table 9.4

Sixteen Dimensions of the Construct Falling under Two Orientation Regions of Non-Target Customers Satisfaction and the Respective Mean Values Revealing the Extent of MKTORIENT

Below Average (-3 points)	*Above Average (+3 points)*
F_6 = "Reasonable and attractive interest rates" (2.58).	F_1 = "Time efficient and hassle-free procedure" (4.15).
F_9 = "Nearest branch location in unbanked area" (2.13).	F_2 = "Easy loan recovery policy" (3.36).
F_{11} = "Fieldworkers promotional skill" (1.58).	F_3 = "Efficient and adequate bank services" (4.52).
F_{12} = "Adequate and educative advertisements" (1.51).	F_4 = "Accurate and timely passbook entries" (4.73).
F_{13} = "Promotion for interest oriented and innovative new schemes" (1.86).	F_5 = "Convenient purchase schemes" (3.47).
F_{14} = "Frequent and effective promotional communication" (1.62).	F_7 = "Timely information on new interest rates" (4.07).
	F_8 = "Cooperative, informative and efficient employees" (3.86).
	F_{10} = "Adequate staff and satisfactory performance" (3.76)
	F_{15} = "Staff assistance in completing bank formalities" (3.94).

Table 9.5
Number of Non-Target Customers under Dimension-wise MKTORIENT Regions

Orientation Regions →	*1-2*		*2-3*		*3-4*		*4-5*	
Dimensions ↓	*No.*	*(%)*	*No.*	*(%)*	*No.*	*(%)*	*No.*	*(%)*
F_1 (115)	—	—	06	0	45	39	63	55
F_2 (39)	08	21	07	18	23	59	01	02
F_3 (114)	—	—	01	1	35	31	78	68
F_4 (113)	—	—	—	—	18	16	95	84
F_5 (109)	16	14	28	26	50	46	15	14
F_6 (93)	30	32	51	55	12	13	—	—
F_7 (114)	—	—	06	5	72	63	36	32
F_8 (114)	—	—	12	10	59	52	43	38
F_9 (94)	62	66	28	30	02	2	02	2
F_{10} (114)	—	—	07	6	91	80	16	14
F_{11} (113)	107	95	06	5	—	—	—	—
F_{12} (98)	93	95	04	4	01	1	—	—
F_{13} (113)	81	72	21	18	11	10	—	—
F_{14} (113)	102	90	10	9	10	1	—	—
F_{15} (113)	07	7	16	14	60	53	30	26

Table 9.6
Marketing-Mix Variables Obtaining Less than Average Score—Target Group

Product (A)	*Price (B)*	*Place (C)*	*Promotion (D)*
F_1 = (4)	F_6 = (57%)	F_8 = (9%)	F_{11} = (100%)
(1) Quick withdrawal facility.	(1) Attractive and adequate interest rates.	(1) Competent and efficient employees.	(1) Fieldworkers convincing
(2) No delay in depositing skill. cash.	(2) Motivating deposit interest rates.	(2) Co-operative and friendly employees.	(2) Promotion through fieldworkers.
(3) Need meeting deposit schemes.	(3) Reasonable loan interest rates.	(3) Employees have sufficient information.	(3) Attractive promotional gifts.
F_2 = (29%)	F_7 = (2%)	(4) Reasonable market around branch location.	F_{12} = (100%)
(1) Comfortable loan recovery policy.	(1) Quick information regarding new interest rates.	F_9 = (93%)	(1) Heavy promotion through newspapers and magazines.
(2) Easy repayment of instalments.	(2) Authentic interest calculations.	(1) Branch location at hitherto unbanked area.	(2) Effective T.V. and Radio ads.
F_4 = (2%)		(2) Nearest location.	F_{13} = (88%)
(1) Timely updating of passbooks.		F_{10} = (2%)	(1) Employees co-operation in educating clients about new interest rates.
(2) Accurate passbook entries.		(1) Satisfactory present bank's staff.	
F_5 = (24%)		(2) Convenient branch location.	
(1) Timely purchase through bank.		(3) Adequate bank's staff.	

Contd. . .

Table 9.6 *(Contd.)*

Product (A)	*Price (B)*	*Place (C)*	*Promotion (D)*
(2) Standard purchase through bank finance. (3) Loan procedure easy to a layman.			(2) Employees co-operation in educating clients about new schemes. F_{14} = (100%) (1) Heavy ads of new interest rates. (2) Customer awareness meets. (3) Promotion of schemes through attractive posters. (4) Frequent advertisements. F_{15} = (8%) (1) Employees co-operation in completing loan formalities. (2) Employees assistance in filing withdrawal/deposit forms.

Table 9.7

Marketing-Mix Variables Obtaining Average Score—Target Group

Product (A)	*Price (B)*	*Place (C)*	*Promotion (D)*
F_2 = (16)	F_6 = (35%)	F_8 = (5%)	F_{13} = (9%)
(1) Comfortable loan recovery policy.	(1) Attractive and adequate interest rates.	(1) Competent and efficient employees.	(1) Employees co-operation in educating clients about interest new rates.
(2) Easy repayment of instalments.	(2) Motivating deposit interest rates.	(2) Co-operative and friendly employees.	(2) Employees co-operation in educating clients about new schemes.
F_3 = (5%)	(3) Reasonable loan interest rates.	(3) Employees have sufficient information.	F_{15} = (17%)
(1) Immediate issuance of new cheque/passbooks.	F_7 = (10%)	(4) Reasonable market around branch location.	(1) Employees co-operation in completing loan formalities.
(2) Simple account opening formalities.	(1) Quick information regarding new interest rates.	F_9 = (2%)	(2) Employees assistance in filing withdrawal/deposit forms.
F_5 = (34%)	(2) Authentic interest calculations.	(1) Branch location at hitherto unbanked area.	
(1) Timely purchase through bank.		(2) Nearest location.	
(2) Standard purchase through bank finance.			
(3) Loan procedure easy to a layman.			

Table - 9.8

Marketing-Mix Variables Obtaining More than Average Score—Target Group

Product (A)	*Price (B)*	*Place (C)*	*Promotion (D)*
F_1 = (96%)	F_6 = (8%)	F_8 = (86%)	F_{13} = (3%)
(1) Quick withdrawal facility.	(1) Attractive and adequate interest rates.	(1) Competent and efficient employees.	(1) Employees co-operation in clients about new interest rates.
(2) No delay in depositing educating cash.	(2) Motivating deposit interest rates.	(2) Co-operative and friendly employees.	(2) Employees co-operation in educating clients about new schemes.
(3) Need meeting deposit scheme.	(3) Reasonable loan interest rates.	(3) Employees have sufficient information.	F_{15} = (75%)
F_2 = (65%)	F_7 = (88%)	(4) Reasonable market around branch location.	(1) Employees co-operation in completing loan formalities.
(1) Comfortable loan recovery policy.	(1) Quick information regarding new interest rates.	F_9 = (5%)	(2) Employees assistance in filing withdrawal/deposit forms.
(2) Easy repayment of instalments.	(2) Authentic interest calculations.	(1) Branch location at hitherto unbanked area.	
F_2 = (95%)		(2) Nearest location.	
(1) Immediate issuance of new cheques/passbooks.		F_{10} = (98%)	
(2) Simple account opening formalities.		(1) Satisfactory present bank's staff.	
F_4 = (98%)		(2) Convenient branch location.	
(1) Timely updating of passbooks.		(3) Adequate bank's staff.	

Contd. . . .

Table 9.8 *(Contd.)*

Product (A)	*Price (B)*	*Place (C)*	*Promotion (D)*
(2) Accurate passbook entries.			
F_5 = (42%)			
(1) Timely purchase through bank.			
(2) Standard purchase through bank finance.			
(3) Loan procedure easy to a layman.			

Table 9.9
Marketing-Mix Variables Obtaining Less than Average Score—Target Group

Product (A)	*Price (B)*	*Place (C)*	*Promotion (D)*
F_1 = (2%) (1) Quick withdrawal facility. (2) No delay in depositing cash. (3) Need meeting deposit scheme.	F_6 = (54%) (1) Attractive and adequate interest rates. (2) Motivating deposit interest rates. (3) Reasonable loan interest rates	F_8 = (3%) (1) Competent and efficient employees. (2) Co-operative and friendly employees. (3) Employees have sufficient information. (4) Reasonable market around branch location.	F_{11} = (100%) (1) Fieldworkers convincing skill. (2) Promotion through fieldworkers. (3) Attractive promotional gifts.
F_2 (26%) (1) Comfortable loan recovery policy. (2) Easy repayment of instalments.	F_7 (3%) (1) Quick information regarding new interest rates. (2) Authentic interest calculations.	F_9 (82%) (1) Branch location at hitherto unbanked area. (2) Nearest location.	F_{12} (95%) (1) Heavy promotion through newspapers and magazines. (2) Effective T.V. and Radio ads.
F_5 (20%) (1) Timely purchase through bank. (2) Standard purchase through bank finance. (3) Loan procedure easy even about new to a layman.			F_{13} (80%) (1) Employees co-operation in educating clients interest rates.

Contd. . . .

Table 9.9 *(Contd.)*

Product (A)	*Price (B)*	*Place (C)*	*Promotion (D)*
			(2) Employees co-operation in educating clients about new schemes. F_{14} (99%) (1) Heavy ads of new interest rates. (2) Customer awareness meets. (3) Promotion of schemes through attractive posters. (4) Frequent advertisements. F_{15} (9%) (1) Employees co-operation in completing loan formalities. (2) Employees assistance in filing withdrawal/deposit forms.

Table 9.10
Marketing-Mix Variables Obtaining Average Score—Non-Target Group

Product (A)	*Price (B)*	*Place (C)*	*Promotion (D)*
F_1 = (3%) (1) Quick withdrawal facility. (2) No delay in depositing cash. (3) Need meeting deposit scheme. F_2 (13%) (1) Comfortable loan recovery policy. (2) Easy repayment of instalments. F_{13} (1%) (1) Immediate issuance of new cheque/passbooks. (2) Simple account opening formalities. F_5 = (20%) (1) Timely purchase through bank. (2) Standard purchase through bank finance. (3) Loan procedure easy even to a layman.	F_6 = (33%) (1) Attractive and adequate interest rates. (2) Motivating deposit interest rates. (3) Reasonable loan interest rates F_7 (3%) (1) Quick information regarding new interest rates. (2) Authentic interest calculations.	F_8 = (7%) (1) Competent and efficient employees. (2) Co-operative and friendly employees. (3) Employees have sufficient information. (4) Reasonable market around branch location. F_9 (14%) (1) Branch location at hitherto unbanked area. (2) Nearest location. F_{10} = (6%) (1) Satisfactory present bank's staff. (2) Convenient branch location. (3) Adequate bank's staff.	F_{12} = (4%) (1) Heavy promotion through newspapers and magazines. (2) Effective T.V. and Radio ads. F_{13} = (10%) (3) Employees co-operation in educating clients about new interest rates. (2) Employees co-operation in educating clients about new schemes. F_{15} (12%) (1) Employees co-operation in completing loan formalities. (2) Employees assistance in filing withdrawal/deposit forms.

Table 9.11
Marketing-Mix Variables Obtaining More than Average Score—Non-Target Group

Product (A)	*Price (B)*	*Place (C)*	*Promotion (D)*
F_1 = (95%) (1) Quick withdrawal facility. (2) No delay in depositing cash. (3) Need meeting deposit scheme. F_2 = (61%) (1) Comfortable loan recovery policy. (2) Easy repayment of instalments. F_{13} = (99%) (1) Immediate issuance of new cheque/passbooks. (2) Simple account opening formalities. F_4 = (100%) (1) Timely updating of pass-books. (2) Accurate passbook entries. F_5 = (60%)	F_6 = (13%) (1) Attractive and adequate interest rates. (2) Motivating deposit interest rates. (3) Reasonable loan interest rates F_7 = (94%) (1) Quick information regarding new interest rates. (2) Authentic interest calculations.	F_8 = (80%) (1) Competent and efficient employees. (2) Co-operative and friendly employees. (3) Employees have sufficient information. (4) Reasonable market around branch location. F_9 = (4%) (1) Branch location at hitherto unbanked area. (2) Nearest location. F_{10} = (94%) (1) Satisfactory present bank's staff. (2) Convenient branch location. (3) Adequate bank's staff.	F_{12} = (1%) (1) Heavy promotion through newspapers and magazines. (2) Effective T.V. and Radio ads. F_{13} = (10%) (3) Employees co-operation in educating clients about new interest rates. (2) Employees co-operation in educating clients about new schemes. F_{14} = (1%) (1) Heavy ads of new interest rates. (2) Customer awareness meets. (3) Promotion of schemes through attractive posters.

Contd. . .

Table 9.9 *(Contd.)*

Product (A)	*Price (B)*	*Place (C)*	*Promotion (D)*
(1) Timely purchase through bank. 2) Standard purchase through bank finance. (3) Loan procedure easy even to a layman.			(4) Frequent advertisements. F_{15} = (79%) (1) Employees co-operation in completing loan formalities. (2) Employees assistance in filing withdrawal/deposit forms.

Table 9.12
Service Quality and Overall Performance-wise Marketing Orientation

Marketing Mix Factors ↓	*Service Quality* *BA*	*A*	*AA*	*Overall Performance* *BA*	*A*	*AA*
PRDMEAN 1	3.25	3.53	4.22	—	3.69	4.16
PRDMEAN 2	3.53	3.95	4.27	—	3.61	4.19
PRDMEAN 3	3.46	4.25	4.38	—	4.08	4.40
PRDMEAN 4	3.64	4.46	4.75	—	4.5	4.73
PRDMEAN 5	3.76	4.23	4.66	—	4.08	4.71
GRPRDMEAN	3.53	4.08	4.46	—	3.99	4.44
PRIMEAN 1	2.33	2.0	2.59	—	2.32	2.55
PRIMEAN 2	3.04	3.46	4.04	—	3.42	4.03
GRPRIMEAN	2.69	2.73	3.32	—	2.87	3.29
PLAMEAN 1	3.21	3.28	3.92	—	3.32	3.89
PLAMEAN 2	2.02	2.0	2.05	—	1.96	2.06
PLAMEAN 3	3.17	3.56	3.76	—	3.61	3.75
GRPLAMEAN	2.80	2.95	3.24	—	2.96	3.23
PRMMEAN 1	1.52	1.51	1.56	—	1.5	1.56
PRMMEAN 2	1.58	1.63	1.78	—	1.31	1.46
PRMMEAN 3	1.38	1.63	2.01	—	1.71	1.98
PRMMEAN 4	1.61	1.40	1.72	—	1.65	1.70
PRMMEAN 5	3.04	3.08	4.01	—	3.5	3.94
GRPRMMEAN	1.83	1.85	2.22	—	1.88	2.13
MKTORIENT	**2.71**	**2.90**	**3.31**	—	**2.93**	**3.27**
No. & Persentage of Respondents	**09 (5%)**	**25 (15%)**	**137 (80%)**	—	**12 (7%)**	**162 (93%)**

Chapter—10

Measurement of Marketing Orientation in Rural Banks Through Management Opinion

BACKGROUND

Marketing Orientation is an exercise which begins with the management efforts to understand the target customers' current and future needs and to satisfy these unfulfilled needs better and sooner than the competitors (Shiffman and Kanuk 1995; Stanto, Etzel and Walker 1991; Leader and Kyritisis 1989; Cundiff, Still and Govoni 1980; Fox and Wheatley 1978). It lays continuous emphasis on interfunctional co-ordination (Narver and Slater 1990) or co-ordinated marketing (Kohli, Jaworski and Kumar 1992) as such the greater the departmental connectedness, the greater the marketing orientation in an organisation (Kohli and Jaworski 1990). Management can ensure long run profits, survival and success of an institution if it practices marketing orientation (Kotler 1996) on continual basis. In this chapter an effort has been made to measure the present status of marketing culture in RRBs through a survey of management opinion pertaining to six Ps of bank marketing mix.

Marketing orientation in RRBs has been worked out on the basis of responses obtained from the JRB and SKGB branch managers working in Jammu (J&K) and Hoshiarpur (Punjab) districts on five-point (5<—>1) Scale. A separate questionnaire for management (Annexure-II) was prepared and personally distributed to all the branch managers operating in aforesaid two districts and finally got 24 questionnaires from JRB and 17 from SKGB managers completely filled in. The response of RRBs managers have been segregated into 6 Ps viz; `product adequacy and suitability', `price reasonability', `place managing effectiveness', `promotion optimality', `customers-bank relations', and `procedural effectiveness', to measure marketing orientation separately for each `P' and finally both the RRBs put together, on the premises that both extend same services, similar schemes and to identical group of clientele. The views of two RRBs chairmen towards inherent marketing orientation in R.B.I. policy regulating rural banking (Annexure-III) have also been collected personally. The generalisation of overall marketing orientation in RRBs has been done for application and formulation of marketing orientation strategies in similar other rural bank settings.

MARKETING ORIENTATION IN TERMS OF `PRODUCT ADEQUACY'

83% of JRB mangers exhibited their satisfaction ("3-4" range) (Table 10.1) towards `product adequacy and its suitability'. 13% of them rated `below average' and remaining (4%) feel highly satisfied ("4-5")]with this aspect of rural banking. Similarly 76% SKGB managers have placed their responses between "3-4" range to the various items of `product mix' (Table 10.1) followed by 18% responses between "2-3" range and 6% respondents falling between "4-5" orientation region. Thus the managers of two RRBs opined that their present bank schemes are suitable, sufficient to meet the customers financial requirements and customers are satisfied with regard to the deposit and loan schemes.

The product adequacy has received 5, 4, 3, 2 and 1 points of orientation scores respectively from 17 & 15%, 43 & 44%, 20 & 20%, 16 & 14% and 4 & 70% of JRB and SKGB managers (Table 10.2). On the whole the respondents have shown their satisfaction towards rural banks product mix.

One statement viz; 'government policy of waiving off the loan' has received 2.0 and 2.33 scores respectively from SKGB and JRB managers and `banks simple loan recovery policy' has obtained `below average' (2.76) value from SKGB managers. Some of the statements viz., sufficient number of advance schemes, favourable policy of financing products instead of releasing cash, simple loan recovery policy, government policy of forgiving the loans, complicated loan procurement formalities have generated `below average' degree of MKTORIENT from few managers of both the RRBs. Thus in order to strengthen overall marketing orientation in rural banks, these aspects of product variable require considerable attention of both R.B.I. and sponsor banks. The remaining statements viz; adequacy and suitability of deposit schemes, customers primary bank, suitability of advance schemes have procured `above average' score from JRB and SKGB managers.

Both the RRB's managers have assigned `above average' score to product mix. JRB managers have given 3.53 and SKGB 3.45 (Table 10.9) and thus overall mean score with regard to product schemes of rural banks worked out to be 3.49.

The score of `product adequacy and its suitability obtained from the chairman of both JRB and SKGB on five-point likert scale comprising all important aspects of the product mix has arrived at 3.28. In this process of measurement they have assigned `below average' value to two statements viz; need based schemes introduced by R.B.I. and R.B.I. as a sole controller to introduce the schemes for RRBs. One statement of product mix viz., implementation of RRB's suggestion by R.B.I. has obtained `average' score on MKTORIENT scale. Rest of the statements of product adequacy viz., RRBs' efforts of customer-oriented schemes, introduction of different packages for different set of customers by R.B.I. regular market research by RRBs to assist R.B.I in the introduction of new schemes, bank's knowledge about the profitability of schemes, bank's attempt to identify the schemes to be added or screened out from its schemes lines, introduction of short-term packages, schemes planned by sponsor banks in the light of socio-economic requirements of rural masses and infusion of necessary changes in the schemes in introduced by sponsor banks etc. have obtained `above average' score of MKTORIENT.

JRB and SKGB managers perception about marketing orientation has been compared with the scores obtained from their respective customers. The respective values assigned by management and customers of JRB and SKGB to `product mix' of rural banks reveal that JRB management is more satisfied as compared to its customers whereas SKGB customers are more optimistic than its management with regard to this element of marketing mix. JRB management has assigned 3.53 score to this variable (Table 10.9) whereas customers contacted from underdeveloped, developing and developed areas have given respectively 3.38, 3.34 and 3.45 (Table 4.1, 5.1 and 6.1) values whereas SKGB management has attributed 3.45 value to product adequacy (Table 10.9) and the customers surveyed from aforesaid three areas have accorded 3.83, 4.01 and 4.11 scores respectively (Tables 7.1, 8.1 and 9.1).

Measurement of differences in the scores of respondents of same sample has been done through split-half reliability (Tull and Hawkins 1993). With the help of random table, the managers of JRB and SKGB have been divided randomly and equally. In case of JRB where number of managers contacted came out to be an even number, equal number (12 each) has been segregated under two groups—A (2, 6, 7, 8, 9, 12, 14, 15, 19, 22, 23, and 24) and B (1, 3, 4, 5, 10, 11, 13, 16, 17, 18, 20, and 21). In case of SKGB, number of respondents surveyed figured out to be an odd number, therefore, the score by a respondent selected randomly has been ignored. In case of SKGB also two groups (8 each) were formed—A (2, 5, 6, 7, 8, 9, 10 and 16) and B (1, 3, 4, 11, 12, 13, 14 and 15). The responses generated from JRB managers with regard to product adequacy are more reliable than that of SKGB as both groups A and B have secured 3.53 and 3.53 from JRB and 3.82 and 3.52 from SKGB respondents. The consistency of data collected from JRB managers appeared to be more than that of SKGB managers.

Convergent validity has been worked out by examining the nature of association between both "mix component and overall orientation-wise" and responses to one important aspect of six marketing mix variables i.e. `Repeat Customers' has been converged with `product adequacy and suitability' vis-a-vis MKTORIENT. The ratings obtained on five-point scale about this aspect were converted into 3 points viz; BA, A, AA (Sharma 1996; Rastora 1995; Chahal 1994; Narver and Slater 1990) to make interpretation more meaningful.

Marketing orientation with respect to product mix of 3.49 (Table 10.9) has been proved convergently valid (Table 10.3) because this score from majority of JRB (67%) and SKGB (94%) falling under `above average' region of `repeat customers' score has respectively arrived at 4.11 and 3.67. Thus it can be concluded on the basis of management judgement, that their customers who are highly satisfied with regard to `product adequacy and its suitability' are likely to deal with the bank repeatedly in future.

The opinions of JRB managers differ significantly with regard to `product mix' and the range as a measure of dispersion in this case was worked out as 19 (Table 10.9). Similarly range value for SKGB came out at 12, which is the highest among all six Ps. The degree of variability in the views of management analysed through standard deviation indicates that product variable has received wider variations from respondents. Standard deviation is greater for JRB (3.66) as compared to SKGB (3.52). Further the co-efficient of variation (C.V.) is higher in case of JRB (11.44) in contrast to SKGB (11.35) which means that views of SKGB managers regarding adequacy and suitability of rural banking schemes are less variable, more consistent and homogenous. The measurement of sampling variability due to chance or fluctuations of random sampling has been done through standard error (S.E). It is also highest (1.13) for product variable. The reliability of standard error has been checked through t-test and it figured out at 0.07 for the items of product mix. Both at 1% (2.58) and 5% (1.96) level of significance, the generalisation is accepted i.e., there exists no significant difference between the responses of JRB and SKGB managers with respect to `product adequacy and its suitability.

MARKETING ORIENTATION IN TERMS OF `PRICE REASONABILITY'

Majority of the managers of both JRB and SKGB have accorded `above average' values to the price reasonability component of marketing orientation (Table 10.1). On an average the respondents have highlighted their positive attitude towards `price mix' items such as need-based interest rate structure and provision of attractive and reasonable interest rates on deposits and advances.

The `price rationality' has obtained 5, 4, 3 and 2 points on MKTORIENT scale respectively from 25 and 25%, 49 and 53%, 18 and 19%, 8 and 3% of JRB and SKGB managers (Table 10.2) which certifies high degree of satisfaction with respect to this aspect of rural banking. Few managers of both RRBs have awarded `below average' point to two statements of price mix variables viz., customer satisfaction towards interest rate charged/provided by the bank and customer focused present interest rate structure. The remaining statements viz; reasonable interest on advances, attractive and motivating interest rates on deposits, authentic interest calculations, deregulation of interest rates, role of interest rates in increasing the number of clientele have obtained `above average' score from the respondents of two RRBs.

Marketing orientation in two RRBs on the basis of manager judgement towards `price mix' is quite high (3.94). JRB managers have attributed value (3.87) within "3-4" range whereas SKGB managers (4.01) within "4-5" orientation regions (Table 10.9). This reflects that SKGB managers feel highly satisfied as compared to JRB so far as `price rationality' of marketing-mix is concerned.

JRB and SKGB chairmen opined that current interest rate structure of rural banks is quite satisfactory and as such they have attributed 4.06 score to all the important aspects of `price-mix'. Only one statement viz. R.B.I.'s direction of interest rate has scored `below average' (2.0) whereas remaining aspects viz. presentation of interest rate structure as per socio-economic status of customers belonging to different groups, bank's consideration of competitors while setting interest rates on the basis of rural environment after a comprehensive market research, fulfilment of the profitability objective by bank's interest rates and bank's independent pricing schemes have secured `above average' score.

JRB and SKGB managers have shown their higher satisfaction towards price-mix as compared to their respective customers. JRB managers have attributed 3.87 score to `price reasonability' (Table 10.9) whereas customers contacted from underdeveloped, developing and developed sectors of Jammu district have assigned 2.96, 3.16 and 3.17 values to this variable (Tables 4.1, 5.1 and 6.1). Similarly SKGB managers have given 4.01 score to price element of rural banking (Table 10.9) whereas this mix has obtained 3.13, 3.32 and 3.41 values (Tables 7.1, 8.1 and 9.1) from the customers belonging to above mentioned areas of Hoshiarpur district.

The split-half reliability of data collected from JRB and SKGB managers pertaining to `price reasonability' reveals that the responses of JRB respondents are more uniform than that of SKGB. Groups A and B of both JRB and SKGB have obtained 3.85 and 3.90, 3.94 and 4.02 values.

`Attractive deposit rates' has been converged with the remaining aspects of `price reasonability'. Price mix has obtained 3.94 score (Table 10.4) from the managers to two RRBs, which has been tested convergently valid (Table 10.4) because this score from majority of JRB (79%) and SKGB (88%) respondents falling under `above average' range of `attractive interest rate on deposits' score has respectively arrived at 3.96 and 4.03.

Second and third highest range was registered in case of JRB (11) and SKGB (10) managers respectively (Table 10.9). This reveals that there exists significant difference within the responses of both RRBs' managers. Standard deviation was second highest (after product adequacy) for two selected RRBs. It figured out at 2.66 and 2.69 for JRB and SKGB. Co-efficient of variation also reflects that `price mix' has procured less uniform and more variable responses from JRB (11.57) and SKGB (11.21) respondents. Standard error for `price reasonability' worked out to be second highest (0.85) among six Ps. Finally `t' values exhibit no significant difference in responses, pertaining to this mix of bank marketing, generated from SKGB and JRB managers. Both at 1% (2.58) and 5% (1.96) level of significance, the hypothesis stands accepted. In nutshell, it may be concluded that difference, in responses with regard to price mix variable is significant within the managers of JRB and SKGB whereas it is insignificant between the respondents of aforesaid RRBs.

MARKETING ORIENTATION IN TERMS OF `PLACE EFFECTIVENESS'

About 75% JRB and SKGB managers have given their responses within "3-4" range whereas 25% of them have exhibited higher satisfaction ("4-5") with regard to convenient branch location (Table 10.1).

`Place effectiveness' has obtained 5, 4, 3 & 2 points of orientation respectively from 15 & 15.5%, 57 & 63%, 20 & 15.5% and 8 & 6% of JRB and SKGB managers. On the whole, managers are satisfied with the branch locational aspect of rural banks. Some respondents have evaluated two statements of place mix viz., restrictions imposed by Service Area Approach and branch locational problem for far off villages `below average'. Majority of the managers have placed their responses `above 3' point on orientation scale for the statements such as convenient location of branches, fulfilment of customers distribution requirements by bank's branches and achievement of bank's profitability by the branch location.

Place-orientation has generated 3.58 score from both the RRBs' managers. JRB respondents have assigned 3.81 whereas SKGB attributed 3.88 to this mix of bank marketing. Thus SKGB managers are more satisfied with their branch locations as compared to that of JRB.

Chairmen of both RRBs have assigned 3.78 score to the place-mix effectiveness'. They have exhibited their dissatisfaction with regard to two statements of this variable viz., R.B.I. and sponsor banks' dictation of branch location. Remaining aspects have generated `above average' mean values towards the items viz; R.B.I.'s consideration of profitability; customers, competitors and environmental before setting up of new branches; location of bank branches as per the requirements of different categories of customers; initiation of regular market research for new location; adequate market coverage and services by the bank branches and role of top management and subordinate staff in the opening of new branches.

In an attempt to find out whether customers or managers feel highly satisfied with `place mix' aspect of rural banking, their respective scores have been compared. In this measurement, SKGB managers have displayed higher satisfaction (3.88) (Table 10.9) in contrast to its rural bank customers residing in underdeveloped (3.76), developing (3.38) and developed (3.86) areas (Tables 7.1, 8.1 and 9.1). In contrast to above finding, JRB customers belonging to aforesaid three sectors have exhibited their high level of satisfaction (3.92, 3.95 and 3.87) with regard to place variable (Tables 4.1, 5.1 & 6.1) when compared with management score (3.81) (Table 10.9).

The data received from JRB and SKGB respondents with respect to `place effectiveness' divided into two groups A and B highlights that JRB managers have accorded 3.57 & 3.67 values which varied less than that assigned by A and B groups of SKGB (3.83 and 3.95). Thus split-half reliability of data procured from JRD is better as compared to SKGB.

`Inconvenient location' vis-a-vis `place effectiveness' has been converged to prove the validity of data pertaining to this bank marketing mix (Table 10.5). MKTORIENT in terms of place mix has received 3.85 score (Table-10.9) and majority of JRB (67%) and SKGB (53%) respondents have fallen under `below average' orientation region of `inconvenient location' (without reversion) by assigning 3.89 and 3.95 score towards `place effectiveness'.

Lowest range value from JRB (6) and SKGB (3) managers was recorded in case of place managing effectiveness. It reflects that degree of variation (Table 10.9) in responses of both RRBs managers for `place mix' is quite low. Standard deviation with respect to place mix variables worked out to be less in comparison to all the Ps. There is more uniformity and consistency in the responses of SKGB managers in comparison to JRB managers for aforesaid variable as standard deviation is greater in case of JRB (1.77) than for SKGB (1.39). Co-efficient of variation figured out at 9.32 JRB & SKGB have assigned `below average' point to two statements of promotion-variable viz. employment of promotional tools in the light of customers' educational level and holding of regular meetings to determine customers' banking needs. The remaining aspects of this variable have obtained above average' score from majority of JRB and SKGB respondents viz. effectiveness of advertisements, promotion of schemes and interest rates through posters and personal involvement and fieldworkers promotional skill and performance.

Both the JRB and SKGB managers have accorded `above average' score to `promotion optimality'. JRB has assigned 3.85 whereas SKGB 3.82 (Table 10.9) and thus overall mean score with respect to utilisation of all promotional tools figured out at 3.84.

The score of `promotion mix' from both the chairmen of JRB and SKGB on 5-point likert scale consisting of all important aspects of promotion variable has arrived at 3.63. In this process they have attributed `below average' value

(2.0) to a statement viz; effective use of sales promotion tools such as loan meals. Rest of the statements of `promotion mix' have procured `above average' score viz; employment of promotional tools as per customer's educational level; effectiveness of promotional and 7.32 for JRB and SKGB, which is third highest in case of JRB and least of all Ps for SKGB. It shows variation in the responses of JRB managers towards this aspect of RRBs. Standard error was least (0.49) for place mix. Similar to product and price variable discussed earlier, t-values (0.14) pertaining to branch location leads to a conclusion that managers of both RRBs differ within and not between their responses with regard to all important items of place mix, both at 1% (2.58) and 5% (1.96) level of significance.

MARKETING ORIENTATION IN TERMS OF `PROMOTION OPTIMALITY'

Majority of JRB (75%) and SKGB (71%) managers have highlighted their views within "3-4" orientation region regarding `promotion optimality' of rural banks (Table 10.1). They have assigned above 3-point on the scale with respect to promotional tools used by the banks thereby indicating positive attitude towards various aspects of promotion mix viz; adequate promotion of schemes through advertisements, posters, personal selling and village level customer meets. The `promotion optimality' has generated 5, 4, 3, 2 points on marketing orientation scale respectively from 14 & 16%, 62 & 56%, 21 & 23% and 3 & 5% of JRB and SKGB managers (Table 10.2). To sum up, the respondents have shown their satisfaction towards rural banks promotion mix. Few managers of both tools in approaching different sets of customers; planning of promotional campaign in the light of customers, competitors and rural environment; undertaking of regular market research; adequacy of sales promotional budget; bank's performance, evaluation and compensation of its sales force; introduction of regular promotion policies and promotion programmes through field staff.

While comparing the scores obtained from the JRB and SKGB managers towards promotion-mix of bank marketing with that of their respective customers, the management appears to be quite optimistic with this aspect of rural banking whereas customers have reflected their dissatisfaction towards it. Both the JRB and SKGB managers have given `above average' values (3.85 & 3.82) to promotion variable, whereas the customers have assigned `below average' value (Tables 7.1, 8.1 and 9.1) on MKTORIENT scale. Thus management opined that promotional tools have been used optimally but the customers have displayed their dissonance towards the management views.

There is uniformity as verified through split-half reliability in the responses collected from JRB managers with regard to `promotion optimality' when compared with responses of SKGB managers. Groups A and B of JRB have received almost equal values (3.83 and 3.85) in contrast to more variation in the scores obtained by A (3.73) and B (3.87) groups of SKGB.

`Effective advertisements' has been converged with the remaining important aspect of `promotion optimality'. MKTORIENT in terms of `promotion mix' figured out at 3.84 (Table 10.9) which has been proved convergently valid (Table 10.6) as majority of JRB (54%) and SKGB (53%) managers have fallen under `above average' range of effective advertisements of according 4.17 and 3.95 scores to promotion optimality.

Range value for promotion-mix variable worked out same (7) for both the RRBs Standard deviation is also second to the least for JRB (1.85) and SKGB (2.16) (Table 10.9) which reflects that variation in the response of managers with regard to promotion optimality is quite low when compared with product, price, people and process mix of rural banking. Similarly co-efficient of variation for promotion-mix is least and third last in case of JRB (8.04) and SKGB (9.39). Standard error of 0.65 depicts that except for place mix, rest all the Ps have greater variations in the collected data from management than promotion-mix variables. Both at 1% (2.58) and 5% (1.96) level of significance, the hypothesis viz, there is no significant difference between the responses of JRB and SKGB managers towards various aspects of promotion mix, is accepted as the calculated value (0.05) is lower than tabulated values.

MARKETING ORIENTATION IN TERMS OF 'CUSTOMER-BANK RELATIONS'

Majority of JRB (54%) and SKGB (53%) respondents have attributed highest score within "4-5" range towards 'customer bank relation' (Table 10.1) whereas remaining managers have given responses within "3-4" marketing orientation region. They are of the opinion that employees are fully aware of customers banking needs, welcome customers in interaction and have been successful in providing the services satisfactorily.

'Employees efficiency' has received 5, 4, 3, 2 and 1 points on MKTORIENT scale from 27 & 28%, 62 & 55%, 8 & 12%, 2 & 4% and 1 & 1% of JRB and SKGB managers respectively (Table 10.2). Thus management of both RRBs' holds positive views regarding rural banks' employees satisfactory performance in delivering need based services to their clients.

One statement viz, scarcity of time at the disposal of bank employees to cater their customers' needs has obtained scores within "3-4" range both from JRB (3.5) and SKGB (3.53) managers. Remaining statements on 'bank employees' viz, better fulfilment of customers requirements through trained employees, satisfactory banks' present staff; employees awareness about customers financial and non-financial needs; employees co-operative behaviour and employees regular interaction with customers have secured the values within "4-5" region of MKTORIENT. Thus the respondents of JRB and SKGB are highly satisfied with the working of their bank employees and as such they have assigned 4.10 and 4.09 scores to this aspect of rural banking, which is highest among all the Ps. The overall marketing orientation in terms of `customer personal relation' figure out at 4.10.

Chairmen of JRB and SKGB feel highly satisfied with the services of their employees as a result of which they have attributed highest score (4.36) to people variable of marketing mix. They have accorded scores within "3-4" range with respect to three statements of `people effectiveness' viz. frequent evaluation of bank employees, successful coverage of market requirements by bank personnel and effective implementation of the customers' needs through rural bank staff. Rest of the statements relating to this aspect of rural banking have received values within "4-5" region of orientation viz, employees training designed to meet the needs of customers; banks focus on customers, competitions and rural atmospheres while planning its employees training; well organised employees recruitment process and presence of marketing intelligence in bank employees.

The responses of SKGB managers towards `customer bank relations' are more homogenous than the scores obtained from JRB managers. This split half reliability of responses has been checked through the values received by groups A and B of JRB (3.89 & 4.31) and SKGB (4.13 & 4.04).

One aspect of `employees effectiveness' viz, `scarcity of time at the disposal of bank employees' has been converged with its their important items (Table 10.7). MKTORIENT with regard to `customer-bank relation' of 4.10 (Table 10.9) has been proved, convergently valid because this score from majority of JRB (58%) and SKGB (65%) respondents falling under `below average' region of `over burdened bank employees' has respectively arrived at 4.12 and 4.34. In relation to nature and extent of routine work it was observed that inspite of less time with the RRBs staff, they are quite optimistic with regard to duties and responsibilities towards their customers.

There exists significant difference within the responses of JRB and SKGB managers towards `employees effectiveness' as worked out by range, which arrived at 9 & 11 for the aforesaid RRBs (Table 10.9). This statement has also been supported by standard deviation and co-efficient of variation which figured out to be 2.22 and 8.88 for JRB and 2.59 and 10.36 for SKGB. Standard error for customers bank relation of 0.77 indicates significant difference in the means of two samples. Finally the above results have been evidenced with t-value (0.01) which leads to the conclusion that there is no significant difference in the views of managers working in JRB and SKGB. This has been tested both at 1% and 5% level of significance.

MARKETING ORIENTATION IN TERMS OF `PROCEDURAL EFFECTIVENESS'

JRB and SKGB managers contacted have focused their satisfaction (2.14 & 17) with regard to `process and procedural effectiveness' as they have given `above average' response to all important aspects of this mix (Table 10.1). They feel that customers do not find it much difficult to comply with the formalities incorporated in the rural banking.

`Process mix' has generated 5, 4, 3, 2 & 1 points of orientation score from 18 & 22%, 55% & 60%, 13 & 9%, 12 & 4% and 2 & 5% of JRB and SKGB respondents respectively (Table 10.2)

Three statements of process effectiveness have received below 3 points on the scale from few managers of both RRB viz., simple rural banking processes, customer satisfying number of processes in rural banks and complicated account opening formalities. Remaining aspects of this variable have obtained 'above average' score from JRB and SKGB managers viz, quick withdrawal and depositing of cash and immediate insurance passbooks and chequebooks.

Marketing orientation in terms of `procedural effectiveness' came out at 3.84. SKGB managers are more satisfied with this element of bank marketing in comparison to JRB managers as SKGB respondents have given higher score (3.39) than that of JRB (3.74).

The score of `process and procedural effectiveness' given by the chairmen of both RRBs, incorporating all important aspects of process-mix, was 3.25. They have assigned `below average' score to the statements of process variable viz, R.B.I.'s introduction of banking services of satisfy customers financial requirements and R.B.I.'s efforts for simplifying and rationalising the procedural system in rural banks. Similarly two aspects of `process-mix' have received `average' score from the Chairmen of JRB and SKGB viz; introduction of banking processes in the light of rural conditions and consideration of rural educational level for designing loan procedure. Finally the remaining statements of process effectiveness have been placed in the `above average' region by the aforesaid respondents viz; planning of banking processes after recognising customers and rural atmosphere and follow up of R.B.I. guidelines while introducing new banking processes.

The `procedural effectiveness' has displayed more consistency in the date collected from JRB managers as compared to values assigned by SKGB managers. Group A and B of JRB have obtained approximately same values (3.75 and 3.74) whereas split-half reliability was less in the scores received from SKGB managers as reflected from the values of groups A (4.04) and B (3.89).

`Complicated account opening formalities' has been converged with the remaining aspects of `procedural effectiveness'. MKTORIENT in terms of process-mix of 3.84 has been tested and proved convergently valid (Table 10.8) because majority of JRB (54%) and SKGB (94%) managers have fallen under `below average' region of `complicated formalities' (without reversion) by assigning 4.11 and 3.94 values `procedural effectiveness'.

JRB and SKGB managers have exhibited almost equal variations in their responses towards `process effectiveness' as range estimated in this case was 9 and 10 (Table 10.9). Two measures of dispersion viz; S.D. and C.V. reveal that there exists difference within the views of JRB (2.39 and 9.19) and SKGB (2.33 & 8.32) managers with regard to `process mix'. Standard error due to fluctuations of random sampling arrived at 0.75. It further strengthened the finding that the responses generated with respect to process variable from RRBs managers differ significantly. Finally-test has been used to ascertain validity of the above findings. Process-mix has obtained 0.25 t-value which indicates no significant difference between the responses of JRB and SKGB managers both at 1% (2.58) and 5% (1.96) level of significance and hence the hypothesis set stands accepted.

Convergent validity has also been worked out by analysing the degree of association between service quality and overall marketing orientation. Thus service quality has been converged with the remaining important aspects of six Ps. MKTORIENT in terms of Ps has received 3.82 and 3.86 scores (Table 10.10) from the managers of JRB and SKGB which has been proved convergently valid because these scores from majority of JRB (71%) and SKGB (59%) respondents falling under `above average' range of `service quality' score have respectively arrived at 3.84 and 3.96 (Table 10.9).

Two-way classification of Analysis of Variance has been used in order to measures the differences both within and between the assessment of JRB and SKGB managers towards six Ps of marketing-mix indicating thereby no significant difference between and within the scores, thus the hypothesis standss accepted both at 1% and 5% level of significance (16.26 and 6.61) d.f. (1,5) and (10.97 and 5.05) df (5,5) (Table 10.11). Since the calculated values for between (.007) and within (3) the samples are lower than tabulated values both at 1% and 5% level of significance further testify the results.

Strategy for Marketing Orientation at Management Level

The nature and extent of marketing orientation in JRB and SKGB as worked out through management judgement requires the following strategies for creating and enhancing marketing culture in RRBs.

Firstly, the efforts need to be made to maintain not only the present level of marketing orientation regarding those aspects which have obtained `above average' score but also to take the bank to the highest level of customers satisfaction to ensure profitability. Such an achievement is possible by ensuring suitability and adequacy of deposit and advance schemes; simple loan formalities; reasonable and attractive interest rates on advances and deposits; correct interest calculations; convenient branch location; promotion of bank's schemes and interest rates through advertisements posters and personal involvement; co-operative, friendly and efficient bank employees; improved customers services and simple rural banking procedures viz., withdrawal and depositing of cash.

The second type of strategy demands improvement in the present status of marketing culture about all those aspects where JRB and SKGB managers scored `average' level of orientation. All the bank marketing variables falling in `average' orientation region require some modification in the present operations of rural banks. Only one aspect viz., "complicated account opening formalities" has obtained `average' score which need to be adequately simplified and rationalised.

The last type of strategy requires immediate attention of the administrators towards all those variables of marketing-mix which scored `below average' level of orientation. One aspect each of product and place mix viz., government policy of waiving off the loan and implications of Service Area Approach need to be reviewed and modified to achieve better customer satisfaction and long run viability.

REFERENCES

1. Chahal, Hardeep (1994), *"Consumer Satisfaction in Public .Health System—A Case Study of Jammu District"*, Unpublished Thesis, Department of Commerce, University of Jammu.

2. Cundiff, Edward. W. Richard. R. Still and Narman. A.P. Govoni (1980), *Fundamentals of Modern Marketing*, Prentice Hall of India, New Delhi, 3rd ed., 19.

3. Fox, Edward J. and Edward. W. Wheatly (1978), *Modern Marketing and Practices*, Scott, Foreman and Co. Glenview, Illinosis, 10.

4. Kohli, Ajay K. and Bernard J. Jaworski (1990), "Marketing Orientation: The Construct, Research Propositions and Managerial Implications", *Journal of Marketing*, Vol. 54 (April), 10.

5. Kohli, Ajay K., Bernard J. Jaworski and Ajith Kumar (1992), *"A Measure of Markst Orientation"*, December, 2-4.

6. Kolter, Philip (1966), *Marketing Management: Analysis, Planning, Implementation and Control*, Prentice Hall of India, New Delhi, 8th Ed., 241.

7. Leader, W.G and N. Kyritisis (1989), *Fundamentals of Marketing*, Hutchinson Education, London, 3-4.

8. Narver, John.C and Stanley. F Slater (1990), "The Effect of a Market Orientation on Business Profitability", *Journal of Marketing*, Oct., 21 & 25.

9. Rasotra, Poonam (1995), "Customer Satisfaction in Insurance Service—A Case Study of L.I.C in Jammu Division", Unpublished Thesis, Department of Commerce, University of Jammu.

10. Sharma, R.D (1996), "MKTEFFECT: A Multiple Item Scale for Measuring Marketing Effectiveness in American Consumer Banking Through Customer Judgement," *Vikalpa*, Jan-Mar., Vol. 1, No. 1, 61-62.

11. Shiffman, Leon. G and Leslie. Lazar Kunuk (1995), *Consumer Behaviour*, Prentice Hall of India, New Delhi, 5th ed., 93.

12. Stanton, William J. Michael J. Etzel and Bruce J. Walker (1991), *Fundamentals of Marketing*, McGraw Hill, Inc, 9th ed., 08.

13. Tull, Donald, S and Del. I. Hawkins (1993), *Market Research—Measurement and Method*, Macmillan Publishing Company, New York, 6th ed., 316.

Table 10.1

MKTORIENT Region-Wise and Marketing-Mix Variable-Wise Distribution of Respondents

Orientation								
Regions →	*1-2*		*2-3*		*3-4*		*4-5*	
Variables ↓	*JRB %*	*SKGB %*	*JRB %*	*SKGB %*	*JRB %*	*SKGB %*	*JRB %*	*SKGB %*
Product	—	—	3 (13)	3 (18)	20 (83)	13 (76)	1 (4)	1 (6)
Price	—	—	1 (4)	1 (6)	15 (63)	7 (41)	8 (33)	9 (53)
Place	—	—	— —	— —	18 (75)	13 (76)	6 (25)	4 (24)
Promotion	—	—	— —	— —	18 (75)	12 (71)	6 (25)	5 (29)
People	—	—	— —	1 (6)	11 (46)	7 (41)	13 (54)	9 (53)
Process	—	—	— —	— —	20 (83)	10 (59)	4 (17)	7 (41)

Table 10.2

MKTORIENT Point-wise and Marketing-mix Variable-wise Distribution of Respondents

Orientation 1 → *Points*	2		3		4		5			
Variables ↓	*JRB %*	*SKGB %*	*JRB %*	*SKGB %*	*JRB %*	*SKGB %*	*JRB %*	*SKGB %*	*JRB %*	*SKGB %*
Product	8 (4)	11 (7)	35 (16)	21 (14)	44 (20)	31 (20)	93 (43)	67 (44)	36 (17)	23 (15)
Price	— —	— —	12 (8)	3 (3)	26 (18)	19 (19)	69 (49)	54 (53)	35 (25)	26 (25)
Place	— —	— —	9 (8)	5 (6)	24 (20)	13 (15.5)	68 (57)	53 (63)	18 (15)	13 (15.5)
Promotion	— —	— —	5 (3)	5 (5)	30 (21)	24 (23)	88 (62)	57 (56)	20 (14)	16 (16)
People	2 (1)	1 (1)	3 (2)	3 (4)	12 (8)	10 (12)	89 (62)	47 (55)	38 (27)	24 (28)
Process	3 (3)	6 (5)	21 (12)	5 (4)	22 (13)	11 (9)	92 (55)	71 (60)	30 (18)	26 (22)

Table 10.3
Repeat Business-wise Product Adequacy

No. of Statements	*JRB*			*SKGB*		
	BA	*A*	*AA*	*BA*	*A*	*AA*
01	4.0	4.25	4.33	—	4.0	4.6
02	3.8	3.88	4.33	—	4.0	4.3
03	4.0	3.75	5.0	—	3.0	3.9
04	4.4	3.81	4.33	—	5.0	4.1
05	3.0	3.44	3.67	—	4.0	4.0
06	3.8	2.94	4.67	—	3.0	3.7
07	3.6	3.25	4.0	—	4.0	2.8
08	2.0	2.25	3.33	—	2.0	2.1
09	2.2	3.5	3.33	—	3.0	3.3
No. & Percentage of Respondents	**03 (12)**	**05 (21)**	**16 (67)**	—	**01 (6)**	**15 (9)**
MKTORIENT	**3.42**	**3.45**	**4.11**	—	**3.56**	**3.67**

Table 10.4
Attractive Deposit Rates-wise Price Reasonability

No. of Statements	*JRB*			*SKGB*		
	BA	*A*	*AA*	*BA*	*A*	*AA*
01	—	3.8	4.32	—	3.5	4.27
02	—	3.8	4.26	—	4.0	4.33
03	—	2.4	3.68	—	4.0	3.6
04	—	4.2	4.26	—	4.5	4.47
05	—	3.0	3.26	—	3.5	3.53
06	—	3.4	3.95	—	4.0	4.0
No. & % of Respondents	—	**05 (21)**	**19 (79)**	—	**02 (12)**	**15 (88)**
MKTORIENT	—	**3.43**	**3.96**	—	**3.83**	**4.03**

Table 10.5
Inconvenient Location-wise Place Effectiveness

No. of Statements	*JRB*			*SKGB*		
	BA	*A*	*AA*	*BA*	*A*	*AA*
01	4.07	4.4	4.0	4.75	3.87	4.0
02	2.93	3.6	2.5	2.75	3.56	2.75
03	4.33	3.8	2.75	4.25	3.78	4.0
04	4.4	4.0	4.0	4.0	4.22	4.0
05	3.73	3.6	3.75	4.0	3.67	4.0
No. & Percentage of Respondents	**16 (67)**	**4 (16.5)**	**4 (16.5)**	**9 (53)**	**4 (23.5)**	**04 (23.5)**
MKTORIENT	**3.89**	**3.88**	**3.4**	**3.95**	**3.82**	**3.75**

Table - 10.6
Effective Advertisement-wise Promotion Optimality

No. of Statements	*JRB*			*SKGB*		
	BA	*A*	*AA*	*BA*	*A*	*AA*
01	3.38	3.5	4.0	3.0	3.5	3.67
02	3.38	3.4	3.0	3.5	3.67	3.56
03	4.38	3.9	3.0	3.5	3.0	4.22
04	3.92	3.2	4.0	4.0	4.67	4.33
05	4.0	3.9	4.0	4.0	3.33	4.11
06	3.69	4.1	3.0	3.5	4.17	3.78
No. & Percentage of Respondents	**13 (54)**	**10 (42)**	**01 (4)**	**02 (12)**	**04 (35)**	**09 (53)**
MKTORIENT	**3.79**	**3.67**	**3.5**	**3.58**	**3.72**	**3.95**

Table 10.7
Employees Scarce Time-wise Customer-Personal Relations

No. of Statements	*JRB*			*SKGB*		
	BA	*A*	*AA*	*BA*	*A*	*AA*
01	4.4	4.4	4.07	4.18	4.33	3.67
02	4.0	4.0	4.14	4.18	4.33	4.0
03	3.8	3.8	4.43	4.36	3.33	4.0
04	4.2	4.0	4.36	4.55	4.0	4.0
05	4.2	4.2	4.5	4.45	4.0	3.67
No. & of Respondents	**14 (58)**	**5 (21)**	**5 (21)**	**11 (65)**	**3 (17.5)**	**3 (17.5)**
MKTORIENT	**4.12**	**4.08**	**4.3**	**4.34**	**3.99**	**3.87**

Table 10.8
Complicated Formalities-wise Procedural Effectiveness

No. of Statements	*JRB*			*SKGB*		
	BA	*A*	*AA*	*BA*	*A*	*AA*
01	4.08	3.83	4.0	—	4.0	3.88
02	4.25	4.67	3.6	—	3.0	4.13
03	3.08	3.5	3.4	—	4.0	3.19
04.	3.75	2.5	2.2	—	4.0	3.44
05.	4.58	3.83	3.8	—	3.0	4.44
06.	4.58	3.83	4.2	—	4.0	4.38
07	4.42	4.33	3.8	—	5.0	4.13
No. & Percentage of Respondents	13 (54)	06 (25)	05 (21)	—	01 (6)	16 (94)
MKTORIENT	4.11	3.78	3.57	—	3.86	3.94

Table 10.9
Comparative Positive of MKTORIENT in JRB and SKGB

	Mean		*Standard Deviation*		*Co-efficient of Variation*		*Range*		*Standard*	*t-*
Variables	*JRB %*	*SKGB %*	*JRB %*	*SKGB %*	*JRB %*	*SKGB %*	*JRB %*	*SKGB %*	*Error*	*Values*
Product	3.53	3.45	3.66	3.52	11.44	11.35	19	12	1.13	0.07
Price	3.87	4.01	2.66	2.69	11.57	11.21	11	10	0.85	0.16
Place	3.81	3.88	1.77	1.39	9.32	7.32	6	3	0.49	0.14
Promotion	3.85	3.82	1.85	2.16	8.04	9.39	7	7	0.65	0.05
People	4.10	1.09	2.22	2.59	8.88	10.36	9	11	0.77	0.01
Process	3.74	3.93	2.39	2.33	9.19	8.32	9	10	0.75	0.25

Level of Significance -

at 1% = 2.58

at 5% = 1.98

Table 10.10
Service Quality-wise Marketing Orientation

Orientation	*B.A*		*A*		*A.A*	
Regions→	*JRD*	*SKGB*	*JRB*	*SKGB*	*JRB*	*SKGB*
Product	—	—	3.46	3.45	3.48	3.48
Price	—	—	3.62	4.10	3.94	4.13
Place	—	—	3.63	3.77	3.8	3.88
Promotion	—	—	3.71	4.0	3.87	4.17
People	—	—	4.0	4.07	4.14	4.10
Process	—	—	3.65	3.88	3.78	4.0
No. & % of Respondents	—	—	**07 (29)**	**07 (41)**	**17 (71)**	**10 (59)**
MKTORIENT	—	—	**3.68**	**3.88**	**3.84**	**3.96**

Table 10.11
An Analysis of Significant Difference between and Within the Assessment of JRB and SKGB Managers

Significant Difference	*Degree of freedom*	*Sum of Squares*	*Mean of Squares*	*F-Values*
(a) Between the samples	1	.402	.402	.007
(b) Within the samples	5	.005	.001	3
(c) Residual or error	5	.015	.003	—
Total	11	0.422	0.406	3.007

Level of Significance—

(1) F (1,5) : 1% = 16.26; 5% = 6.61.

(2) F (5,5) : 1% = 10.97; 5% = 5.05

Chapter—11

Marketing Orientation Strategy of RRBs

BACKGROUND

Marketing orientation in Indian Rural Banking signifies the adequacy and suitability of deposit/advance schemes, at reasonable interest, available at convenient location and promoted through effective tools and techniques (Bhatt 1991; Madhukar 1991; Bhattacharyay 1989 and Mark 1988). The nature of marketing orientation examined in the first study two chapters of the study viz, `Inbuilt Marketing Orientation in Indian Rural Banking' and `Review of Literature' implies that R.B.I. and G.O.I. have taken many initiatives right from 1904 when Cooperative Credit System was introduced to cater the credit needs of rural populace. Consequently, apex institutions, committees, commissions and many banks had focused little on the marketing orientation which in real marketing sense was ineffective and non-systematic (Mandanna & Chengappa 1993 and Bhatt 1991). The rural banking schemes of R.B.I. and/or G.O.I. addressed to the needs of the different sections of rural communities have not directly focused on marketing orientation in rural banks. It is in this context that the current study undertaken primarily to work out marketing orientation strategy by identifying the strengths and weaknesses in the ongoing marketing practices of Indian rural banking through both customer judgement and management opinion. Management is quite optimistic with regard to marketing culture in rural banking and has placed six Ps of marketing mix in the `above average' orientation region (Table 10.10). The level of marketing status in the three selected areas separately and collectively from Jammu (J&K) and Hoshiarpur (Punjab) districts viz., Jakh and Ambala Jattan (Underdeveloped), Sarore and Pandori Mall (Developing) and Simbal Camp and Baghpur (Developed) reveals a positive correlation between the marketing culture and performance of RRBs, under different rural areas. Thus the greater the marketing orientation, the better the performance (Kohli & Jaworski 1990) of RRBs in Jammu and Hoshiarpur districts, marketing orientation in both JRB and SKGB is highest (Tables 4.1 & 7.1) in case of developed areas (3.07 & 3.34) where RRBs' branches were operating in profits (0.96 & 5.0 lakhs) (Exhibits 4.2 & 7.2) followed by 3.03 and 3.21 in developing areas where branches were at no profit no loss point (2.0 & 2.5 thousands) Exhibits 5.2 & 8.2) and 2.996 and 3.12 in underdeveloped areas where branches of JRB and SKGB were running in losses (2.35 & 1.21 lakhs) (Exhibis 6.2 & 9.2).

FINDINGS

The findings of the study have been discussed in detail alongwith the identified problems and the strategy to improve and maintain high level of marketing orientation in rural banks particularly in RRBs for underdeveloped, developing and developed rural areas.

1. Underdeveloped Area

It has already been stated that the area having highest poverty, lowest literacy, lowest per hectare yield and poor infrastructural facilities has been characterised as an underdeveloped area. There exists positive association between the extent of MKTORIENT in RRBs and the degree of development in the underdeveloped areas. Marketing strategy in SKGB branch operating in an underdeveloped sector is higher (3.12) (Table 7.10) as compared to that in JRB branch (2.996) (Table 4.1) as such Ambala Jattan (Hoshiarpur district) is comparatively more developed than Jakh (Jammu district) (Exhibits 4.1 & 7.1) in terms of level of literacy (68 & 58%), poverty (38 & 64%) and per hectare yield (35 & 32 qtl/hec). The marketing mix variable-wise findings are as under -

1 (a). Product

Various important aspects of product mix viz., need satisfying and adequacy of deposit and loan schemes, simple loan formalities, comfortable loan recovery policy, quick withdrawal/depositing of cash, timely encashment of cheques, immediate issuance of new chequebooks, passbooks, simple account opening formalities etc., have been dealt under two heads viz., (a) Target and (b) Non-Target groups. This variable has secured 3.38 and 4.01 values respectively from JRB and SKGB customers.

As stated earlier in the chapter `Research Design and Methodology', target group consists of the customers whose annual income is below Rs. 11,000. 50% of JRB target customers assigned 2.75 score (Tables 4.2 & 4.8) to `convenient purchase of assets through bank finance' and `easy repayment of instalments'; 54% gave 3.26 value for `simple loan formalities' and `loan procedure easy even to a layman'; 69% of them attributed 3.81 score towards `sufficient number of deposit schemes' and `bank proves to be a good prime bank' (Krishnan 1990). All of JRB respondents feel highly satisfied (4.81) with `accurate passbook entries' and `timely updating of passbooks'. Similarly 67% SKGB customers assigned `average' score to `need-satisfying and sufficiency of loan schemes'; 91% of them placed `adequacy and suitability of deposit schemes' in the `above average' region (4.07); 97% respondents highlighted `highest satisfaction' (4.12) towards `time efficient and hasslefree procedure' viz; `accurate passbook entries, `timely updating of passbooks', `simple account opening formalities' and `quick withdrawal/depositing of cash'; and 83% SKGB customers attributed 3.67 value for `comfortable loan recovery policy' and `easy repayment of instalments'. Both JRB and SKGB customers of this group accorded 3.44 and 3.93 values to `product adequacy and its suitability' which reveals higher satisfaction among SKGB customers towards this mix effectiveness when compared with that of JRB.

The non-target group comprises of the customers with income greater Rs. 11,000 p.a. All the JRB customers contacted have fallen in the `below average' orientation region (2.31) (Tables 4.4, 4.9 & 4.11) with regard to `convenient purchase of assets through bank finance' and `easy repayment of instalments'. 54% JRB respondents assigned 3.11 score to `simple loan to formalities' and `easy loan procedure even to a layman'; 79% attributed 3.81 for `sufficiency of deposit schemes' and `bank proves to be a primary bank' and 97% of them accorded 4.58 for `accurate passbook entries.' Similarly 75% SKGB customers gave 2.48 score (Tables 7.4, 7.10 & 7.11) for `adequacy and suitability of loan (Patel & Shete 1980) schemes', `time efficient and hasslefree procedure' obtained 4.19 score from 98% customers; 83% respondents assigned 3.76 and 3.56 values towards `convenient purchase of assets through bank finance' and `easy loan recovery policy' and 91% of them placed `sufficient and need based deposit schemes' in the `above average' region (4.11). `Product adequacy' has generated 3.35 and 4.05 scores from JRB and SKGB customers belonging to non-target group which implies higher satisfaction among SKGB customers towards this mix variable.

1 (b). Price

This mix of bank marketing refers to reasonable loan interest rates, motivating deposit interest rates, authentic interest calculations and quick information regarding new interest rates. The overall MKTORIENT in terms of `price reasonability' arrived at respectively 2.96 & 3.32 in JRB and SKGB (Tables 4.1 & 7.1).

54% JRB target respondents assigned `average' score (Table 4.2 & 4.8) to `reasonable and attractive interest rates' viz., `rational loan interest rates' and `motivating deposit interest rates', (Rangarajan 1996) and 62% of them attributed `above average' value (3.69) towards `quick information regarding new interest rates'. Similarly 55% of SKGB customers accorded 2.60 value (Tables 7.2, 7.6 & 7.8) to `reasonable loan interest rates' and `attractive deposit interest rates' and 94% of them gave 3.96 score for `accurate interest calculations'. This group of JRB and SKGB respondents have exhibited `average' (3.0) and `below average' (2.91) level of satisfaction (Tables 4.1 & 7.1) towards `price rationality'. It reflects that JRB customers are more satisfied with `price mix' of bank marketing as compared to SKGB.

48% JRB non-target customers ranked `reasonable and attractive interest rates on advances and deposits' `below average' (2.80) (Tables 4.4 & 4.9) whereas 62% of them feel satisfied with the `quick information regarding new interest rates' (3.68) (Table 4.10). 55% SKGB respondents assigned 2.48 score for `rational loan and motivating deposit interest rates' (Savaraiah & Thirupalu 1985) (Tables 4.4, 4.9 & 4.10) and 94% have exhibited `highest satisfaction' (4.06) towards `authentic interest calculations'. `Price mix' has generated 2.95 & 3.25 from JRB and SKGB respondents which indicates higher satisfaction among SKGB customers with respect to price-mix effectiveness of rural banking.

1 (c). Place

`Place effectiveness' has been measured through various items viz, `convenient and nearest branch location', `location at hitherto unbanked areas', `reasonable market around branch location', `co-operative and friendly employees', `competent and efficient employees', adequate bank's staff' and `satisfactory present bank's staff. It has obtained 3.92 and 3.38 scores (Tables 4.1 & 7.1) from JRB and SKGB respondents.

JRB and SKGB target customers displayed highest satisfaction (Tables 4.2 & 7.2) with regard to `convenient and nearest branch location' (Kshirsagar 1976) (4.49 & 4.09), `adequate staff and satisfactory performance' (3.54 & 3.58), `co-operative and informative employees' (3.88 & 3.66) and `competent and efficient employees' (3.54 &-) (Khandelwal 1987). All the customers contacted from both RRBs reflected full satisfaction (100%) (Tables 4.8 & 7.8) for `convenient and nearest branch location' and `branch location at hitherto unbanked areas'. 92 and 84% of JRB customers assigned `above average' score towards `co-operative and friendly employees' and `competent and efficient employees'; 91 and 92% of SKGB and JRB respondents placed `adequate bank staff' and `satisfactory present bank's staff' in `more than average' (3.51 & 3.56) orientation region. JRB customers seem to be more satisfied with the `place effectiveness' as compared to SKGB as they have assigned 3.95 value in contrast to 3.32 generated from SKGB respondents (Tables 4.1 & 7.1).

All the non-target customers contacted from both JRB and SKGB have shown their high satisfaction (100%) towards `convenient and nearest branch location' and `location at hitherto unbanked areas' by attributing 4.49 and 4.22 values (Tables 4.4, 4.11, 7.4 & 7.11). Majority of JRB (96%) and all SKGB (100%) customers placed their responses between "4-5" orientation region for `co-operative and informative employees' and 74 and 91% of them exhibited maximum satisfaction (3.51 & 3.56) towards `adequate and satisfactory present bank's staff'. 'Competent and efficient employees' has generated 3.52 score from 81% JRB respondents. `Place mix' has secured 3.89 and 3.42 values from JRB and SKGB customers which signifies greater satisfaction among JRB customers towards this variable of rural banking.

1 (d). Promotion

Important aspects of `promotion mix' have been discussed under this head viz; promotion of schemes and interest rates through effective advertisements, attractive posters, role of fieldworkers, personal involvement and customers awareness meets. This mix has received `below average' values from JRB (1.73) and SKGB (1.93) respondents (Tables 4.1 & 7.1).

`Promotion effectiveness of fieldworkers and their convincing skill' has obtained `less than average' score (1.65 & 1.58) from majority of JRB (92%) and SKGB (95%) target respondents (Tables 4.2, 4.6, 7.2 & 7.6) 77 and 79% JRB and SKGB customers assigned 2.19 and 2.06 values for `employees co-operation in educating clients about new schemes and interest rates'. `The extent of personal involvement' has procured 1.88 and 1.57 scores from JRB and SKGB respondents; `effective advertisements in television, radio, newspapers and magazines has secured 1.54 and 1.65 values respectively from 100 and 94% customers. `Heavy advertisements of new interest rates', `customer awareness meets' and `promotion through posters' have obtained 1.85 and 1.59 scores from 92 and 94% of JRB and SKGB respondents. MKTORIENT with regard to `promotion mix' as per target customers of JRB and SKGB worked out to be 1.65 and 1.87 which highlights greater dissatisfaction among JRB customers towards various items of promotion-mix variable.

`Frequent and effective promotional communication' has generated 1.62 and 1.65 values from non-target JRB and SKGB customers (Tables 4.4, 4.9, 7.4 & 7.9) and 92 and 97% respondents accorded 1.51 and 1.57 scores to `fieldworkers promotional skill', `promotion for interest oriented and innovative new schemes' has generated 2.22 and 2.17 values from respectively 69 and 75% of JRB and SKGB respondents; `adequate and educative advertisements for favourable changes' has procured 1.86 and 1.69 (Varde 1976) scores from 93 and 90% customers and `personal involvement' scored 1.13 and 1.69 values from 97% both of JRB and SKGB respondents. This group has assigned 1.77 and 1.99 scores (Tables 4.1 & 7.1) which reflects greater satisfaction among SKGB respondents with respect to `promotion mix' competent of marketing orientation.

Hence the hypothesis viz; `above average level of marketing orientation exists in SKGB whereas it is `average' in JRB, stated in the chapter `Research Design and

Methodology' stands accepted as marketing orientation in SKGB branch, operating in the underdeveloped area of Hoshiarpur district, is greater (3.12) as compared to that in JRB branch (2.996) (Tables 4.1 & 7.1). Except for `place mix' rest of three variables viz; product, price and promotion have obtained higher scores from SKGB customers residing in underdeveloped area, in contrast of JRB.

2. Developing Area

An area having average level of literacy, poverty, per hectare yield and infrastructural facilities has been identified as a developing area. MKTORIENT in SKGB branch functioning in developing area is higher (3.21) (Table 8.1) as compared to that in JRB branch (3.03) (Table 5.1). As such Pandori Mall (Hoshiarpur) is comparatively more developed than Sarore (Jammu) (Exhibits 5.1 & 8.1) with regard to the degree of literacy (78 & 71), poverty (22 & 33%) and per hectare yield (51 & 38 qtl/hec). The results derived from the study on this area are as under-

2 (a). Product

The values obtained from JRB and SKGB customers with respect to `product adequacy' arrived at 3.34 and 3.83 (Tables 5.1 & 8.1).

50 and 67% JRB and SKGB target customers assigned 2.25 and 2.83 values (Tables 5.2, 5.6, 8.2 & 8.6) to `comfortable loan recovery policy' and `easy repayment of instalments'. 76 and 71% respondents attributed 3.44 and 3.35 scores towards `need satisfying and adequacy of deposit scheme' (Sharma & Tomar 1987); `simple account opening formalities' and `timely encashment of cheques' have obtained 3.89 and 4.19 scores from 84% JRB and 91% SKGB customers respectively (Tables 5.8 & 8.8); `quick withdrawal/depositing facilities has secured 3.58 and 4.18 values from majority of JRB (60%) and SKGB (96%) respondents. `Adequacy and suitability of loan schemes' has generated 2.93 and 2.95 values from JRB (44%) and SKGB (50%) customers (Tables 5.7 %

8.7). Product mix has procured 3.30 and 3.5 values from JRB and SKGB target customers (Tables 5.1 & 8.1) which implies greater satisfaction among SKGB respondents for this element of rural banking.

`Need satisfying deposit schemes' has obtained 3.48 and 3.88 scores from majority of JRB (74%) and SKGB (93%) belonging to non-target group (Tables 5.4, 5.11, 8.4 & 8.11); 96% and 91% customers assigned 4.25 and 4.36 values for `efficient and adequate bank services '(Hundekar 1991) and 83 and 99% JRB and SKGB respondents attributed 3.92 and 4.43 values towards `time efficient and hasslefree procedure'. `Easy loan recovery policy' has received 2.82 and 3.22 (Kshirsagar 1976) from the JRB (50%) and SKGB (53%) customers (Tables 5.9 & 8.10) and `need based and convenient purchase scheme' has generated `below average' (2.96) and `above average' (3.32) scores (Thingalaya 1989) respectively from 44% of JRB and 61% SKGB customers. Non-target customers both of JRB and SKGB have attributed 3.42 and 3.99 values towards `product variable' (Tables 5.1 & 8.1) which indicates that SKGB customers are more satisfied with this mix as compared to JRB.

2 (b). Price

`Price reasonability' has obtained `above average' scores from JRB (3.16) and SKGB (3.22) customers (Table 5.1 & 8.1). `Reasonable loan interest and accurate calculations' has secured 2.96 value from 56% JRB target customers (Tables 5.2 & 5.8). 45% SKGB respondents having income below Rs. 11,000 p.a., assigned 3.11 score towards `motivating deposit interest rates' (Shankar 1993) and `quick information regarding new interest rates' and 50% of them attributed 3.38 value for `reasonable loan interest rates' and `authentic interest calculations' (Tables 8.2 & 8.8). Although values arrived at `below average' but SKGB customers have exhibited their greater satisfaction (2.95) in contrast to JRB respondents (2.88) (Tables 5.1 & 8.1) with respect to `price reasonability'. 67% JRB customers belonging to non-target group highlighted `above average' satisfaction (3.39) towards `rational and attractive interest rates on loans and deposits' and `authentic interest calculations' (Tables 5.4 & 5.11). Similarly 68% SKGB respondents accorded 3.47 value for `attractive deposit interest rates' and 77% of them scored 3.70 value towards `reasonable loan interest rates and calculations'. This mix has generated 3.33 and 3.51 scores from JRB and SKGB respondents which indicates higher satisfaction among SKGB customers pertaining to the `price variable' of rural banks.

2 (c). Place

`Place managing effectiveness' has procured 3.95 and 3.76 values from JRB and SKGB respondents (Tables 5.1 & 8.1).

`Easy access to branch location' has obtained 4.28 and 3.71 scores from respectively 100% JRB and 81% SKGB target customers (Kshirsagar 1976) (Tables 5.2, 5.8, 8.2 & 8.8). `Adequate staff and satisfactory performance' has secured 3.28 and 3.43 values from majority of JRB (52%) and SKGB (71%) respondents 90% SKGB customers assigned 3.75 score towards `co-operative nature of employees' and `competence and efficiency of employees'. `Place effectiveness' as per the judgement of this group has generated 3.89 and 3.44 values from JRB and SKGB customers. Thus JRB respondents are more satisfied in contrast of SKGB in terms of `place mix.'

Majority of SKGB (87%) and all JRB customers having income above Rs. 11,000 p.a. displayed their satisfaction (4.03 & 4.43) towards `nearest and convenient branch location' (Chadha 1994) and `branch location at hitherto unbanked areas' (Tables 5.4, 5.11, 8.4 & 8.11). 57 & 71% JRB and SKGB respondents assigned 3.35 and 3.49 values for `adequate and satisfactory present bank's staff. `Co-operation, competence and efficiency of employees' has obtained 4.03 score from 93% SKGB customers. Both the RRB's customers have exhibited equal level of satisfaction by attributing 3.96 values (Tables 5.1 & 8.1) towards `place effectiveness' component of marketing culture in rural banks.

2 (d). Promotion

`Promotion optimality' has obtained 1.66 and 1.91 scores from JRB and SKGB customers respectively (Tables 5.1 & 8.1).

`Promotion effectiveness of fieldworkers and their motivating skill' has generated `below average' values (1.6 & 1.6) from majority of JRB (92%) and all SKGB belonging to target group (Tables 5.2, 5.6, 8.2 & 8.6); `adequate and educative advertisements' procured 1.6 and 1.53 scores (Hebbar 1989) from all the customers contacted of both RRBs. All SKGB customers assigned `less than average' value (1.52) for `employees co-operation in educating clients about new schemes and interest rates' and `frequent and effective promotional communication' through employees personal touch, posters and customer awareness meets has secured 1.72 and 1.99 scores from majority of JRB (92%) and all SKGB customers. Promotion-mix effectiveness has scored 1.5 and 1.72 values from JRB and SKGB respondents (Tables 5.1 & 8.1).

Majority of JRB (97%) and SKGB (77%) non-target customers assigned 1.5 and 2.12 values (Tables 5.4, 5.9, 8.4 & 8.9) for `fieldworkers performance and their professional skill, (Rangarajan 1996) and `promotion for interest oriented and innovative new schemes' has obtained 2.5 and 1.97 scores from respectively 64% JRB and 77% SKGB respondents. 99% JRB and 77% SKGB customers attributed 1.61 and 1.79 values towards `frequent and informative advertisements' through television, radio, newspapers and magazines (Bhattacharyay 1989) and result oriented promotional communication has generated 2.0 and 2.30 scores respectively from 85% JRB and 86% SKGB respondents. SKGB customers displayed their little higher satisfaction (2.01) with regard to `promotion optimality' as compared to JRB (1.82) (Tables 5.1 & 8.1).

Thus the hypothesis viz; `above average' level of marketing orientation prevails in SKGB whereas `average' level in JRB stands accepted in case of developing areas also as marketing orientation in SKGB and JRB branches functioning in such areas worked out to be 3.21 and 3.03 (Tables 5.1 & 8.1). SKGB customers have exhibited their higher satisfaction with regard to `product adequacy', `price reasonability' and `promotion optimality' as compared to that of JRB.

3. Developed Area

An area is said to be developed when it has high level of literacy, low poverty, high per hectare yield and good infrastructural facilities. MKTORIENT in SKGB branch working in developed area is comparatively higher (3.34) in contrast to that in JRB branch (3.07) (Tables 9.1 & 6.1) because Baghpur (Hoshiarpur district) is more developed that Simbal Camp (Jammu district) with respect to literacy (82 & 74%), poverty (16 & 31%) and per hectare yield (69 & 41 qtl/hec) (Exhibits 6.1 & 9.1). The findings of the study regarding this area are as under-

3 (a). Product

The important aspects of `product mix' have obtained 3.45 & 4.11 scores from JRB and SKGB respondents (Tables 6.1 & 9.1).

`Quick withdrawal/depositing facilities' has generated 4.15 and 4.08 values from majority of JRB (89%) and SKGB (96%) target customers (Tables 6.2, 6.8, 9.2, & 9.8), `timely updating of passbooks' and `accurate passbook entries' have also procured `above average' scores (4.62 & 4.69) from 100 and 98% respondents and 2.82 and 3.25 values have been assigned by 48% and 42% JRB & SKGB customers towards `loan procedure easy even to a layman' and `timely purchase of assets through bank finance'. 89% JRB respondents attributed 3.83 value for `adequacy and suitability of deposit schemes' (Sankaranarayanan 1990) and 43% of them accorded 2.77 score towards `comfortable loan recovery policy', `easy repayment of instalments' and `need-based and suitability of loan schemes'. This group of JRB and SKGB customers assigned 3.36 and 4.07 values for `product adequacy and its suitability' (Tables 6.1 & 9.1) which reflects greater satisfaction among SKGB respondents with regard to product-mix variable of marketing-mix.

The JRB and SKGB respondents having income above Rs. 11,000 p.a. assigned 4.63 and 4.73 values (Tables 6.4, 6.11, 9.4 & 9.11) for 'timely updating of passbooks' and `accurate passbook entries.' `Quick withdrawal/depositing of cash' has obtained 4.04 and 4.15 scores from 88% and 95% JRB and SKGB customers. `Timely purchase of assets through bank finance' and `loan procedure easy even to a layman' generated `above average' (3.47) and `below average' (2.76) values respectively from 60% SKGB and 64% JRB customers (Table 6.9) 67% and 61% of JRB and SKGB respondents respectively placed `time efficient and hasslefree loan procedure' in `less than average' (2.78) (Vaghul 1976) and `more than average' (3.36) orientation region. `Need based and adequacy of deposit schemes' has procured 3.80 score from 89% JRB customers. Non-target customers of JRB and SKGB have accorded 3.50 & 4.13 values (Tables 6.1 & 9.1) for the `product adequacy and its suitability' which implies greater satisfaction among SKGB customers towards this variable of rural bank marketing.

2 (b). Price

`Price rationality' has obtained 3.17 & 3.41 scores (Tables 6.1 & 9.1) from the JRB and SKGB respondents. `Attractive interest rates on deposits', `correct interest calculations' and `quick information regarding new interest rates' have generated 3.33 value from majority of JRB (68%) target customers (Tables 6.2 & 6.8) whereas 65% of them placed `reasonable loan interest rates' in the `below average' (1.35) (Table 6.6) region of MKTORIENT. 57% SKGB customers belonging to target group assigned 2.58 score (Tables 9.2 & 9.6) towards `reasonable and attractive interest rates' and 94% (Table 9.8) attributed 4.07 value for `accurate interest calculations'. SKGB respondents have exhibited their higher satisfaction towards price-mix variable by assigning 3.37 score in contrast to 3.12 value obtained from JRB customers (Tables 6.1 & 9.1)

Majority of non-target JRB (55%) respondents accorded `below average' (2.75) value for `reasonable loan interest rates' (Tables 6.4 & 6.9) whereas `motivating deposit rates' and `accurate interest calculations' have obtained 3.34 score respectively from 67% customers (Table 6.11).

Majority of SKGB respondents (54%) assigned 2.58 score (Tables 9.4 & 9.9) to `reasonable and attractive interest rates' (Rangarajan 1996) whereas `authentic interest calculations' has secured 4.07 value from 94% customers (Table 9.11). Like the target ones, SKGB non-target respondents have reflected their higher satisfaction (3.43) with regard to `price mix' when compared with that of JRB (3.20) (Tables 6.1 & 9.1)

3 (c). Place

Place effectiveness has secured 3.87 and 3.86 values from JRB and SKGB customers (Tables 6.1 & 9.1).

Majority of SKGB (86%) and all JRB respondents under target category assigned 4.36 and 3.81 values (Tables 6.2, 6.8, 9.2 & 9.8) for `co-operation, efficiency and competence of bank employees', `convenient and nearest branch location' and `branch location at hitherto unbanked area' (Thingalaya 1989) have obtained 3.98 score from all the JRB customers contacted whereas `adequate bank's staff' generated `below average' (2.62) value (Singh 1987) from 38% respondents (Table 6.6). 93% SKGB respondents (Table 9.6) attributed 1.93 scores towards `nearest location' and `location in unbanked area' due to the fact that a co-operative bank branch is also operating in the same market. `Sufficiency and satisfactory performance of bank's staff' has procured 3.71 score from majority of SKGB (98%) customers. JRB respondents seem to be more satisfied (3.85) in contrast to SKGB (3.80) with respect to `place-mix'.

The employees' qualities like co-operative, informative and efficiency have generated 4.29 and 3.86 scores from majority of JRB (99%) and SKGB (80%) respondents belonging to non-target group (Tables 6.4, 6.11, 9.4 & 9.11). `Convenient branch location' and `reasonable market around branch location' have obtained 3.90 value from 99% JRB customers

(Krishnan 1990) and `adequacy of bank's staff' has procured 2.66 score from 76% respondents (Table 6.9). Majority of SKGB customers (82%) attributed `below average' value (2.13) (Table 9.9) to `nearest branch location in unbanked areas' and `adequate staff and satisfactory performance' secured 3.76 mean value from 94% respondents. SKGB customers belonging to this group have displayed their higher satisfaction (3.90) for `place effectiveness' in contrast to JRB (3.87) (Tables 6.1 & 9.1).

3 (d). Promotion

`Promotion mix' has obtained 1.78 and 1.98 scores from JRB and SKGB respondents (Tables 6.1 & 9.1).

`Fieldworkers promotional skill' has generated `below average' (1.56 & 1.51) values (Kothai 1995) from majority and all of JRB (97%) and SKGB (100%) customers having income below Rs. 11,000 p.a., (Tables 6.2, 6.6, 9.2 & 9.6); all the respondents of both RRBs have assigned 1.61 and 1.28 scores for `adequate and effective advertisement'. `Employees co-operation in educating clients about new schemes and interest rates' has obtained 1.69 and 1.86 respectively from 97% JRB and 88% SKGB respondents and `frequent and effective promotional communication' secured 1.63 and 1.62 values from all the customers contacted. 98% SKGB customers (Table 6.8) assigned 3.8 for `employees co-operation in completing bank formalities.' `Promotion optimality' has received 1.86 and 1.75 scores from JRB and SKGB customers.

Majority of JRB (93%) and all SKGB respondents under non-target category placed `fieldworkers convincing skill' in the `below average' (1.71 & 1.58) orientation region (Tables 6.4, 6.9, 9.4 & 9.9) and `promotion through employees personal touch' obtained 1.92 and 1.86 values (Bhattacharyay 1989) respectively from 95 and 80% customers. 99 and 95% JRB and SKGB respondents attributed 1.68 and 1.51 scores for `sufficient and informative advertisements' and 99% of both RRBs accorded 1.58 and 1.62 values to `frequent and effective promotional communication'. 79% SKGB respondents assigned 3.94 score (Table 9.11) for `employees assistance in completing bank formalities'. SKGB customers exhibited greater satisfaction (2.10) with regard to `promotion mix' in contrast to JRB (1.70) (Tables 6.1 & 9.1).

All this indicates that the hypothesis viz; marketing orientation in SKGB is greater than in JRB also stands accepted in case of developed areas as marketing status in SKGB branch (Baghpur) is higher (3.34) as compared to that in JRB branch (3.07) (Simbal Camp) operating in the developed areas (Tables 6.1 & 9.1). SKGB respondents highlighted higher satisfaction with respect to three marketing mix variables viz., product, price and promotion in contrast to JRB customers.

PROBLEMS AND STRATEGIC ACTION

The RRBs, whose primary objective is to uplift the status of rural masses by generating income and employment opportunities (Working Group 1975), have been engrossed with several problems and shortcomings. The major difficulties coming in the way of RRBs are the widespread illiteracy, poverty, ignorance, unawareness and helplessness among the Indian villagers (Kothai 1995; Hundekar 1991`; Kalkundrikar 1990; Sanjeevaiah 1988 and Bhatnagar 1983). In the light of aforesaid problems and research findings, there is a need to take appropriate strategic action which would help in building a sound marketing orientation in RRBs. Alongwith the identification of major problems coming in the way of marketing orientation in RRB various strategies have been suggested as under:

1. Need Based and Adequate Schemes

83 and 78% target and non-target customers of both RRBs have assigned 3.18 and 3.24 mean values to `adequacy and suitability of deposit and loan schemes'. Many a times well intentioned and carefully designed schemes failed because they are not addressed to customers' needs (Kalkundrikar

1990; Bhatnagar 1983). Some of the customers are not aware of deposit and loan schemes. Except saving accounts, usage of other deposit schemes is quite poor (Bhattacharyay 1989). Today even knowledgeable customers expect some assistance with regard to `when', `where' and `how' of parking their funds. Among credit related schemes, loan against deposits, cash credits, overdrafts, bill purchased and discounted and loans payable on demand are not common among rural customers (Bhattacharyay 1989).

R.B.I. should endeavour to widen the range of products offered (Mandanna and Chengappa 1993) and to modify unneeded and unprofitable services (Singh 1980) and understanding the specific needs of the rural people (Bhatt 1991; Menezes 1979).

2. Time Efficient and Hasslefree Procedure

All the loanees belonging to both target (63%) and non-target (23%) groups have exhibited their just `average' (2.9 & 3.0) level of satisfaction towards loan procedural complexities (Bhatnagar 1983). They have experienced lengthy and complicated loan formalities which result in unnecessary delay (Vijay Kumar and Gurunath 1991; Vaghul 1976). They have to enter into various agreements with the banks, fill numerous forms, letters, power of attorney etc. which create lot of inconvenience and dissatisfaction among them.

Loan proposals should be simultaneously submitted by bank branches to all the controlling offices (Goiporia 1996) ensure adequate and timely availability of credit (Rangarajan 1966). Readily and friendly assistance to illiterate customers in filing loan forms can help in establishing the popularity of the bank (Bhatnagar 1983) in this areas of operation. This would help weaker sections of the society to meet their emergencies and also to save themselves from the exploitations of village moneylenders/local traders.

3. Efficient and Adequate Bank Services

Both target and non-target respondents of JRB and SKGB have displayed their satisfaction (3.77 & 3.93) towards this component of rural banking. Some of the customers have complained about unnecessary delay on the counter, in encashment of cheques (Venkataramanan 1992), collection of cheques, issues of passbooks etc. (Vaghul 1976 and Varde 1976).

The bank's success depends on its ability to meet the needs of the customers and to render qualitative services to them (Venkateshwarlu 1987). RRBs should ensure that services are performed and delivered in the most effective way (Bhatt 1991, Bhattacharyay 1989) through timely and complete advice on financial prosperity of customers and effective communication (Kshirsagar 1976) with the clientele.

4. Reasonable and Attractive Interest Rates

`Below average' values (2.58 & 2.90) from majority of target (93%) and non-target (78%) respondents of two RRBs towards this aspect of rural banks indicate unattractiveness of deposit schemes to the customers. Due to illiteracy, customers are not aware of the fact that RRBs provide greater interest on deposits and charge lower interest on loans than any other commercial or co-operative banks (Rangarajan 1996; Savaraiah & Thirupalu 1985 and Shankar 1993).

With the deregulation of interest rates (Narasimham Committee 1994) rural banks should provide more and charge less keeping in view the socio-economic status of rural clientele. Timely credit at reasonable rates of interest should be made available to a large segment of rural population (Rangarajan 1996). RRBs main competition, with postoffices and co-operative banks. It is therefore, suggested that deposits of rural banks should be made more competitive as compared to interest and other incentives offered by aforesaid two institutions.

5. Timely Information on New Interest Rates and Accurate Interest Calculations

This aspect has generated 3.56 and 3.74 scores from the target and non-target customers contacted. They have highlighted their satisfaction between "3-4" range but no full satisfaction (5 point) which implies that employees are overburdened with routine jobs (Sankaranarayanan 1990) and they are unaware about rural problems like required timely information to the customers (Kothai 1995).

Since the customers are more conscious about the interest rates, any charge in the interest rate structure should be made known to the customers either by personal communication (Subramanian 1993) or by displaying the change on the notice board of the bank. Rural people are ignorant about the interest calculations. Therefore, emphasis should be laid on educating them regarding deposits as well as advances interest calculations. It would amount to increased faith of customers on employees, finally strengthening their relations.

6. Competent and Efficient Employees

Target and non-target respondents have attributed 3.59 and 3.75 values for the `competence and efficiency of employees'. Beside others, one major reason for high overdues in RRBs include inadequate appraisal of loan proposals insufficient follow up and poor collection efforts (Hundekar 1991) which indicates paucity of suitable work force (Kothai 1995) and lack of confidence (Sharma 1993).

Comprehensive induction programmes, refresher courses and workshops should be arranged in order to make employees more competitive (Verma 1992). Quality of training should be upgraded by paying greater attention to the process of understanding and successfully catering to the banking needs of the rural people (Goiporia 1996). Beside non-monetary, adequate monetary incentives should be provided to the employees, so that they feel motivated in providing prompt and responsive services to the customers (Hebbar 1988).

7. Adequate Staff and Satisfactory Performance

Target and non-target customers of JRB and SKGB have exhibited slight higher satisfaction than `average level' by according 3.36 and 3.39 scores for this aspect. However existing staff finds hardly any time for extending requisite information to their customers (management opinion in Chapter 10), due to work pressure on the counter.

The adequate manpower should be recruited to ensure need based availability of staff at branches (Goiporia 1996) so that lack to staff may not come in the way of achievement of banking targets (Singh 1987). With the adequacy of staff, burden of work would be shared by the staff members, they won't hesitate in extending their whole hearted co-operation.

8. Fieldworkers Promotional Skill

`Promotional effectiveness' of fieldworkers and their convincing skill has secured 1.58 and 1.67 scores from the target and non-target customers. The RRBs customers opined that fieldworkers lack commitment to impart door to door field services (Mandanna & Chengappa 1993; Bhattacharyay 1989). Therefore, due to the absence of adequate promotional skills in fieldworkers, RRBs have not been able to meet the banking needs of the weaker sections fully (Patel & Shete 1980).

Fieldworkers of RRBs should be motivated to visit the people at their residences for promoting the banking business. They should be imparted with the necessary training (Venkateswarlu 1987) and be well equipped with all the mechanisms to promote bank's schemes (Vijay Kumar & Gurunath 1991) and to make themselves capable of marketing bank services to the people.

9. Adequate and Educative Advertisement

76 and 88% target and non-target respondents respectively assigned 1.56 and 1.69 values for `sufficient and result-oriented advertisements'. Lack of advertisements (Bhattacharyay 1989; Hebbar 1989 and Varde 1976) about

bank's schemes, interest rates and overall performance has affected its business to a greater extent in terms of marketing orientation.

RRBs should highlight their performance and progress at least once or twice a month in the local newspapers (Goiporia 1996). New schemes and interest rates should be advertised repeatedly to enhance customer knowledgement.

10. Personnel Involvement and their Personal Touch

2.13 and 2.14 scores have been obtained for this component of RRBs from majority (93%) of target and non-target customers. Impolite behaviour (Pali 1987; Vaghul 1976 and Varde 1976), unfriendly and non-cooperative nature (Hebbar 1988) and negative attitude (Bhatacharyay 1989) of bank staff towards customers lead to the absence of personal contacts and relationships (Mandanna & Chengappa 1993 and Bhatnagar 1983) thereby affecting the goodwill of the bank.

Rural bank's staff should have local feel, knowledge and understanding of local problems (Verma 1992), as such success of an organisation is basically linked with creation of team spirit (Narver and Slater 1990) in rural banking.

11. Absence of Marketing Department

RRBs do not have separate marketing department to undertake marketing research for better banking schemes, reasonable interest rates, suitable branch location and promotional tools. It implies absence of proper initiatives to understand banking needs of the customers and to deliver services relevant to the areas of operation.

Independent marketing department should be created in RRBs so that adequate marketing culture can be made available to understand the banking requirements of rural people through extensive marketing research.

In this direction a marketing model (Figure 11.1) has been suggested which can be of great help in creating and enhancing marketing culture in RRBs. Rural banks main

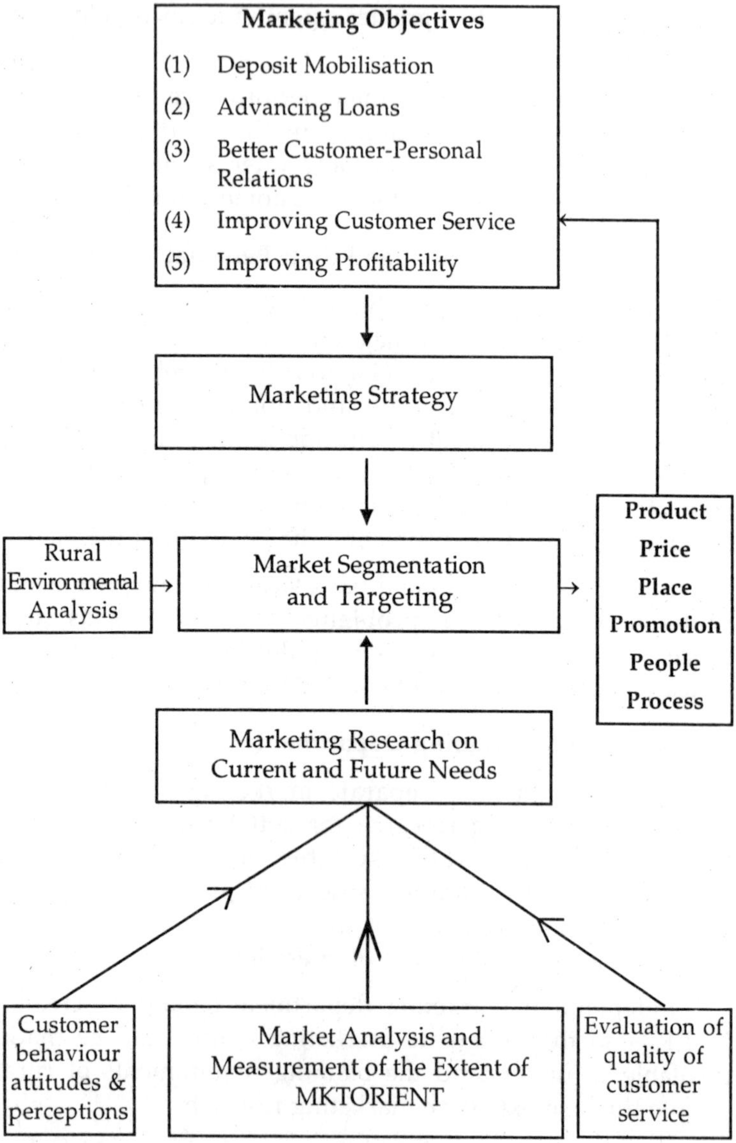

Figure - 11.1
Marketing Model for RRBs

objectives viz. deposit mobilisation, advancing loans, improving customer service and profitability can be achieved through the formulation of suitable marketing strategies. Continuous market research on current and future needs of target market should be conducted through the analysis of customer behaviour, attitudes and perceptions, measurement of present level of MKTORIENT and evaluation of quality of customer service. Finally on the basis of rural environment MKTORIENT in all mixs of `product adequacy', `price reasonability', `place effectiveness', `promotion optimality', `personal selling efforts' and `procedural effectiveness' should be maintained and increased on an ongoing basis.

12. Restrictions of R.B.I.

R.B.I's restrictions have been viewed separately for all the marketing mix elements; (a) Product-rural banking schemes are introduced, modified and dropped by R.B.I. and as such individual bank has limited liberty to deal with this aspect; (b) Price—Maximum and minimum limits to interest rates, which are same for commercial, co-operative and RRBs irrespective of the type of clientele served by them, are also (directed by R.B.I.; c) Place—Branch licensing power which was earlier in the hands of R.B.I. has now been passed on to NABARD for monitoring distribution pattern. NABARD has temporarily stopped issuing branch opening licences and thus unbanked areas and their banking needs have remained unaddressed; (d) Promotion—No committee has ever been set up by R.B.I. to deal particularly with the matters of various promotional tools available and their effective utilisation; (e) People—R.B.I. has banned recruitment in rural banks due to which their existing employees feel overburdened with the day to day work leading to monotony and boredom; f) Process—R.B.I. has laid down same procedures for commercial, co-operative and RRBs, inspite of various differences in their customers' educational level. Due to these complications, scope for enhancing marketing culture in RRBs is restricted.

Since RRBs have completed their 23 years of existence, they should be allowed to work independently, with the prior permission of R.B.I., in terms of introduction of schemes, opening of new branches, recruitment of necessary staff and less complicated procedures. Thus R.B.I. should encourage RRBs to design locally relevant and operationally effective banking schemes within the parameters of marketing orientation.

13. Control of Sponsor Banks

Though sponsor banks are mainly concerned with the formulation of short-term policies for RRBs but Chairmen and General managers of rural banks are deputed from sponsor banks only. A permanent employee of rural bank, who is well-versed with the bank and its problems, doesn't get the opportunity to participate in a meeting as he/she cannot be member in Board of Directors. Thus, the biggest problem is the greater dependence of RRBs on sponsor banks.

Regular Chairperson and General Managers of RRBs should be appointed on the basis of all India competition. Senior managers of rural banks, who have been associated for many years, should be given the opportunity to take part in the decision process.

14. Role of Central and State Governments

Beside sponsor banks, RRBs are also dependent on the decisions of Central and State governments. Change of Central/State government implies subsequent changes in RRBs policies.

RRBs should be provided with the rights of public sector companies, where there is a demarcation between management and owners. Rural banks should be freed from their shareholders and be extended greater freedom for successful operations. Central and State governments should participate in the working of RRBs by promoting their schemes and services; granting some concessions; assisting in the undertaking of marketing research; instructing all their departments, functioning in rural areas, to deal with RRBs and implementing such programmes which would help in meeting the needs of rural populace.

POLICY IMPLICATIONS

The findings of the study demand changes in the existing policies of R.B.I. and RRBs for the successful implementation of the suggestions, certain policy implications have to be examined. Policy implications pertaining to rural bank marketing have been listed as under:—

(1) R.B.I. will have to introduce new schemes after understanding the current and future needs of target people. In this respect, RRBs can assist R.B.I. by way of conducting regular marketing research.

(2) Loan formalities/complicated paper work will have to be curtailed. Direct and short cut policies have to be adopted in the disbursement of loans.

(3) RRBs will have to become more socially responsible by way of providing more and charging less on deposits and advances. It requires achievement of socio-economic objectives through social marketing.

(4) RRBs will have to make new policies for larger investments in the promotion of banking services. Promotion policy has to lay more emphasis on personal selling.

(5) Training programmes facilitated by sponsor banks will have to be passed on to the RRBs for better results.

(6) RRBs will have to keep in mind the educational level of rural people and thus will have to reduce large number of processes involved which create inconvenience.

(7) Sponsor banks will have to aid RRBs externally without jeopardising their daily operations. Top

officials will have to be recruited on permanent basis rather than the present policy of deputing chairman and general manager from sponsor banks.

(8) NABARD will have to issue more branch licences to rural banks so that the banking needs of rural masses, residing in unbanked areas, can be met effectively.

REFERENCES

1. Bapna, M.S. (1988). "RRBs—Their Working and Growth", *Rural India,* Sept., 180
2. Bhatnagar, Depti (1983), "Diffusion of Banking Innovations and Communication Strategies for Rural Areas", *Prajnan,* July-Sept., Vol. XII, 196-197.
3. Bhatt, Atul (1991), "Bank Marketing, Market Research and Indian Banks", *Prajnan,* Vol. XX, No. 1, 53-54.
4. Bhattacharyay, B.N. (1989), "Marketing Approach to Promoting Banking Services", *Vikalpa,* Apr.-June, Vol. 14, 39.
5. *Ibid.,* (1991), "Marketing Management and Innovations in the Light of Liberalisation", *Prajnan,* Vol. XX, No. 4, 419.
6. Chadha, B.L. (1994), "Towards Quality in Rural Banking", *Economic Review,* Feb.-Apr., Vol. 38, 11.
7. Goiporia Committee (1996), "Customer Service in Banks", *Planning Bulletin,* June-July, 286-297.
8. Hebbar, C. Kusumakara (1988), "Bank Marketing Strategy in Commercial Banks", *Southern Economist,* Oct., Vol. 27, 17-18.
9. Hebbar, A.R.K. (1989), "Problems of RRBs", *Yojana,* April, Vol. 33, 24.
10. Hundekar, S.G. (1991), "Rural Banking Scenario", *Khadi Gramodyog,* June, 342.
11. Kalkundrikar, A.B. (1990), "RRBs and Economic Development", *Prajnan,* July-Sept., Vol. XIX, 319.
12. Khandelwal, Anil. C. (1987), *Handbook on Personnel Management and Industrial Relations for Rural Banks,* Rawat Publication, Jaipur, 61-63.
13. Kohli, Ajay K. and Bernard J. Jaworski (1990), "Market Orientation. The Construct, Research, Propositions and Managerial Implications", *Journal of Marketing,* Vol. 54, April, 1-2.

14. Kothai, Krishna (1955), "HRD-Rural Banking", *Economic Review,* March, Vol. 35, 11-12.
15. Krishnan, C (1990), "RRBs and Rural Development", *Yojana,* Jan., Vol. 33, 32.
16. Kshirsagar (1976), "Improving Customer Services of Banks", *Prajnan,* Apr-June, Vol. VI, 146-155.
17. Lal, G.S. (1985), "RRBs", *Journal of Banking Studies,* July-Sept., Vol. VII, No. 3, 154-156.
18. Mandanna, P.K. and P.G. Chengappa (1993), "Marketing Approach in Rural Banking", *Economic Review,* June, 6.
19. Mark, V.V. (1988), "Deposit Mobilisation and Marketing of Bank Services", *Economic Review,* June, Vol. 33, 03.
20. Menezes, J.S. William (1979), "Marketing of Bank Services", *Prajnan,* Apr-June, Vol. VIII, 135-137.
21. Narasinhmam, M (1992), Financial Sector Reforms", *Economic Review,* June, Vol. 37, No. 103.
22. Pai, M.R. (1987), "Customer Service in Banks", *Southern Economist,* Feb., Vol. 25, 21.
23. Patel, K.V. and N.B. Shete (1980), "RRBs: Performance and Prospects", *Prajnan,* Jan.-Mar, Vol. IX, No. 1, 9-11.
24. Rangarajan, C (1996), "Rural India: The Role of Credit", *The Banker,* March, 15-17.
25. Sanjeevaiah, B.C. (1988), *"Rural Banking—A Comparative Study of the Performance of Rural Based Credit Institutions, Co-operative Credit Societies, Farmers Service Societies and RRBs"*, Unpublished Thesis, Dept. of Commerce and Management, Bangalore University, 01.
26. Sankaranarayanan, V. (1990), "Viability of RRBs", *Economic Review,* Vol. 35, March, 3.
27. Savaraiah, G & N. Thirupalu (1985), "RRBs—Marching in Rural Development", *Khadi Gramodyog,* Dec., 182.
28. Shankar, K (1993), "RRBs: At the Cross Roads", *Indian Banking Today and Tomorrow,* May, 4.
29. Sharma, Manoj (1993), "Bank Marketing and Customer Service", *Indian Banking Today and Tomorrow,* June, 25.
30. Sharma, S.C. and A.K.S. Tomar (1987), "Progress of RRBs in India", *Southern Economist,* April, Vol. 25, 15-16.
31. Singh, R.K.P. (1987), "Business Planning in RRBs." *Khadi Gramodyog,* Jan., 192.

32. Singh, Sampat. P. (1980), "Unbundling Bank Services: A Problems in Bank Marketing", *Prajnan*, Jan.-Mar., Vol. IX, No. 2, 238.

33. Subramaniam, C. (1993), "Team Spirit—Key to Customer Service and Deposit Mobilisation", *The Banker*, May, 35-36.

34. Sundaresan, R (1994), "Indian Banking in Retrospect—A Prospective View", *Economic Review*, Feb-Apr., Vol. 38, No. 3, 2-3.

35. Thingalaya, N.K. (1991), "The Dynamics of Bank Marketing", *Economic Review*, June, 5-6.

36. Vaghul, N (1976), "Employees Development for Efficient Customer Service", *Prajnan*, Apr-June, Vol. VI, 172-175.

37. Varde, S.D. (1976), "Customer Service of Banks", *Prajnan*, Jan.-Mar, Vol. V, No. 1, 134-137.

38. Varma, S.D. (1992), "RRBs—A Case for their Revival", *IBA Bulletin*, Dec., Vol. XIV, No. 2, 10-11.

39. Vaz, I.T (1992), "Rural Planning and Credit Department", *Economic Review*, Dec., Vol. 38, No. 4 & 5, 01.

40. Venkateswarlu, P.K. (1987), "Customer Service in Commercial Banks", *Southern Economist*, Oct., Vol. 26, 5-6.

41. Vijay Kumar, M.N. and H.J. Gurunath (1991), "RRBs: An Analysis", *Southern Economist*, Mar., Vol. 29, 17.

42. Working Group (1986), "RRBs—A Resume", G.O.I., Department of Economic Affairs, New Delhi, 19-22.

Bibliography

Books

Beri, G.C. (1994), *Marketing Research,* Tata McGraw Hill, New Delhi.

Bellur, V.V. (1987), *Marketing Research: Theory and Practice,* Himalaya Publishing House, Mumbai.

Berry William D. and Stanley Feldman (1985), *Multiple Regression in Practice,* Sage Publication, Inc.

Boyd, Harper W; Ralph Westfall and Stanley F. Stasch (1988), *Marketing Research—Text and Cases,* Richard D, Irwin Inc, Illinois.

Cattell, R.B. (1952), *Factor Analysis: An Introduction and Manual for the Psychological and Social Scientist,* New York, Harper.

Chabra, Trilok N. and Prem L. Taneja (1988), *Rural Banking in India,* Dhanpat Rai and Sons, Delhi.

Cundiff, Edward W.; Richard R. Still and Norman A.P. Govoni (1980), *Fundamentals of Modern Marketing,* Prentice Hall of India, New Delhi.

Enis, Ben M. (1980), *Marketing Principles,* Goodyear Publishing Co. Inc, California.

Fox, Edward J. and Edward W. Wheatley (1978), *Modern Marketing: Principles and Practice,* Scott, Foresman and Col. Glenview, Illinois.

Hosamani, S.B. (2002), *Performance* of *Regional Rural Banks,* Anmol Publications Pvt. Ltd., New Delhi.

Hughes, David G. (1980), *Marketing Management,* Addisonwesley Publishing Co., Philippines.

Khandelwal, Anil K. (1987), *Handbook on Personal Management and Industrial Relations for Rural Banks,* Rawat Publications, Jaipur.

Khemani, C.L. and B. Yerranraju (1987), *How and Why of Rural Banking,* Sagar Publications, New Delhi.

Kotler, Philip (1966), *Marketing Management: Analysis, Planning, Implementation and Control,* Prentice Hall of India, New Delhi.

Leader, W.G. and N. Kyritsis (1989), *Fundamentals of Marketing,* Hutchinson Education, London.

Luck, David J. and Ronald S. Rubin (1987), *Marketing Research,* Prentice Hall of India, New Delhi.

Maheshwari, S.N. (1991), *Banking: Law and Practice,* Kalyani Publisher, New Delhi.

McCarthy, E. Jerome; John F. Grashot and Andrew A. Brogowicz (1978), *Readings in Basic Marketing,* Richard D. Irwin Inc.

Mithani, D.M. (1989), *The Anatomy of Indian Banking,* Himalaya Publishing House, New Delhi.

Myer, Raymond H. (1990), *Classical and Modern Regression with Applications,* PWS-KENT Publishing Co., Boston.

Patnaik, U.C. and R.N. Mishra (1993), *Rural Banking in India,* Anmol Publications Pvt. Ltd., New Delhi.

Rao, C. Someswara (1998), *Economics of Rural Banking,* Anmol Publications Pvt. Ltd. New Delhi.

Sancheti, D.C. and V.K. Kapoor (1983), *Statistics: Theory, Method and Application,* Sultan Chand and Sons, New Delhi.

Shiffman, Leon. G and Leslie. Lazer Knuk (1995), *Consumer Behaviour,* Prentice Hall of India, New Delhi.

Sonara, C.K., *Regional Rural Banics in India,* Anmol Publications Pvt. Ltd., New Delhi.

Stanton, William J; Michael J. Etzel and Bruce J. Walker (1991), *Fundamentals of Marketing,* McGraw Hill, Inc.

Tull, Donald S. and Del I. Hawkins (1993), *Marketing Research—Measurement and Method,* Macmillan Publishing Company, New Delhi.

Verma, M.L. (1998), *Rural Banking in India,* Rawat Publications, Jaipur.

Wadhwa, Charan D. (1980), *Rural Banks and Rural Development,* Macmillan Co., Madras.

Zikmund, William G. (198), *Business Research Methods,* College Publishing, Oriando, Dryden Press.

Journals, Magazines, Newspapers and Reports

Agricultural Credit Department (1935), "Role of Reserve Bank in Promoting Rural Development", *R.B.I. Bulletin,* Dec. (Suppl.)

Agricultural Refinance and Development Corporation (1963), "Role of Reserve Bank in Promoting Rural Development", *R.B.I. Bulletin*, Dec., (Suppl.).

Ansari, Mohd. Salman (1987), "Working of RRBs in Eastern U.P.", Unpublished Thesis, Dept. of Commerce and Business Administration, University of Allahabad.

Badne, G.C. (1990), *"The Changing Profile of Banking in India—Structure and Working of RRBs"*, Yashwant Mahavidhyalaya, Maharashtra.

Balaji, N. and H.L. Rai (1986), "RRBs: An Evaluation", *Indian Banking Today and Tomorrow*, March.

Balasubramanian, C.S. (1995), "Bank Marketing and Public Relations", *IBA Bulletin*, Sept.

Balishter (1985), "Role of RRBs", *Co-operative Perspective*, Oct.-Dec., Vol. 20.

Balishter (1989), *An Evaluation of Performance of RRBs in Agra District of U.P.*, Unpublished Thesis, Dept. of Agricultural Economics, R.B.S. College, Bichpuri, U.P.

Bapna, M.S. (1998), "RRBs—Their Working and Growth", *Rural India*, Sept.

Bedi, Suresh (1992), *Factors of Deteriorating Economic Viability of RRBs—A Case Study of Haryana*, Unpublished Thesis, Dept. of Economics, Maharshi Dayanand University, Rohtak.

Bhatnagar, Deepti (1983), "Diffusion of Banking Innovations and Communication Strategies for Rural Areas", *Prajnan*, July-Sept., Vol. XII.

Bhatt, Atul (191), "Bank Marketing, Market Research, and Indian Banks", *Prajnan*, Vol. XX, No. 1.

Bhattacharya, B.N. (1989), "Marketing Approach to Promoting Banking Services", *Vikalpa*, April-June, Vol. 14.

Bhattacharyay, B.N (1991), "Marketing Management and Innovations in the Light of Liberalisation", *Prajnan*, Vol. XX, No. 4.

Budget (1999), "Yashwant Sinha Attempts A Please", *Hindustan Times, Sunday*, 28th Feb

Chadha, B.L. (1994), "Towards Quality in Rural Banking", *Economic Review*, Feb.,-Apr., Vol. 38.

Chahal, Hardeep (1994), "Customer Satisfaction in Public Health System—A Case Study of Jammu District", Unpublished Thesis, Dept. of Commerce, University of Jammu, Jammu.

Chairmen's Conference (1980), "RRBs—A Report", *Prajnan,* Jan-Mar., Vol. XI, No. 2.

College of Agricultural Banking (1969), "Role of Reserve Bank in Promoting Rural Development", *R.B.I. Bulletin,* Dec., (Suppl.).

Farmers Service Societies (1971), *Report of National Committee on Agriculture,* G.O.I., New Delhi.

Goiporia, M.N (1991), "Committee on Customer Service", *R.B.I. Bulletin,* Jan.

Goiporia, M.N. (1996), "Customer Service in Banks", *Planning Bulletin,* June-July.

Gupta, Krishan Gopal and Rajendra Singh (1985), "A New Look to Regional Rural Banks", *Khadi Gramodyog,* Dec.

Gupta, Mamta (1992), *"Marketing Effectiveness of Banking Services: A Case Study of S.B.I. in Jammu City"*, Unpublished M. Phil. Dissertation, University of Jammu.

Gupta, R.V. (1998), "Committee on Agricultural Credit", *R.B.I. Bulletin,* June.

Gupta, Yashpal and Ghalamreza Torkzadeh (1988), "Redesigning Bank Services System for Effective Marketing", *Long Range Planning,* Dec., Vol. 21, No. 6.

Hanspal, Savita (1998), "Lifestyles of the Middle Class in Delhi—Implications for Marketing Strategies", Unpublished Thesis, Dept. of Commerce, Delhi School for Economics, Univ. of Delhi.

Hebbar, A.R.K. (1989), "Problems of RRBs", *Yojana,* Apr., Vol. 33.

Hebbar, C. Kusumakara (1998), "Bank Marketing Strategy in Commercial Banks," *Southern Economist,* Oct., Vol. 27.

Hotelling, H (1983), "Analysis of Complex of Statistical Variables into Principal Components", *Journal of Education Psychology,* Vol. 24.

Hundekar, S.G. (1991), "Rural Banking Scenario", *Khadi Gramodyog,* June.

Javalgi, Rajshekhar G. (1992), "Marketing Financial Services to Affluent Consumers", *The Journal of Services Marketing,* Spring, Vol. 6.

Jaworski, Bernard J. and Ajay K. Kohli (1993), "Market Orientation: Antecedents and Consequences", *Journal of Marketing,* Vol. 57 (July).

Joshi, M.K. (1984), "RRBs: Provisions and Review of Progress", *Financing Agriculture,* April-June, Vol. 16.

Kaiser, H.F. (1958), "The Varimax Criterion for Analytic Rotation in Factor Analysis", *Psychology*, Vol. 23.

Kalkundrikar, A.B. (1990), "RRBs: An Analysis", *Southern Economist.*, Mar. Vol. 29.

Kanvinde, D.J. (1984), "Bank as a Lever for Rural Development", *Monthly Review*, Jan.

Kaur, Gurjeet (1996), *"Marketing Strategy to Bring Jammu Rural Bank Out of Red—A Case Study of Village GhoManhasan"*, Unpublished Dissertation, Dept. of Commerce, University of Jammu.

Kohli, Ajay. K and Bernard J. Jaworski (1990), Market Orientation: The Construct, Research Propositions and Managerial Implications", *Journal of Marketing*, Vol. 54 (April).

Kohli, Ajay. K and Bernard J. Jaworski (1993), "Market Orientation: Antecendents and Consequences", *Journal of Marketing*, July, Vol. 57.

Kohli, Ajay K. Bernard J. Jaworski and Ajith Kumar (1992), "A Measure of Market Orientation", *Journal of Marketing*, Dec.

Kothai, Krishna (1995), "HRD—Rural Banking", *Economic Review*, March, Vol. 35.

Krishnan C. (1980), "RRBs and Rural Development", *Yojana*, Jan., Vol. 33.

Kshirsagar (1976), "Improving Customer Services of Banks", *Prajnan*, Apr.-June, Vol. VI.

Kumar, Naresh (1988), "Role of RRBs in Rural Finance—A Case Study of Eastern U.P.", *Co-operative Perspective*, July-Sept., Vol. 18.

Lall, G.S. (1984), "Regional Rural Banks", *Journal of Banking Studies*, July-Sept., Vol. XII, No. 3.

Madhukar, R.K. (1990), "Dynamics of Bank Marketing", *Southern Economist*, Nov., Vol. 29.

Mandanna P.K. and P.G. Chengappa (1993), "Marketing Approach in Rural Banking", *Economic Review*, June.

Mark, V.V. (1988), "Deposit Mobilisation and Marketing of Bank Services", *Economic Review*, June, Vol. 33.

Mehta, Ravi; R. Singh (1988), "Personal Banking Services: U.K. Examples", *Prajnan*, Apr.-June, Vol. XVII, No. 2.

Menezes, J.S. William (1979), "Marketing of Bank Services", *Prajnan*, Apr.-June, Vol. VIII.

Multipurpose Co-operative Societies (1971), R.B.I. Bombay, Vol. II, Chapters VIII & XI.

Naidu, *et al.* (1984), "RRBs in Andhra Pradesh--A Review", *Khadi Gramodyog*, Sept., Vol. 30.

Narasimham, M (1992), "Financial Sector Reforms", *Economic Review*, June, Vol. 37, No. 1.

Narasimham, M (1992), "Report of the Committee on Financial System", *R.B.I. Bulletin*, Feb.

Narver, John C. and Stanley F. Slater (1990), "The Effect of a Market Orientation on Business Profitability", *Journal of Marketing*, Oct.

National Agricultural Credit Fund (1956), "Role of Reserve Bank in Promoting Rural Development", *R.B.I. Bulletin*, Dec., (Suppl.).

National Bank for Agriculture and Rural Development (1982), "Role of Reserve Bank in Promoting Rural Development", *R.B.I. Bulletin*, Dec., (Suppl.).

Nayak Committee (1994), "Adequacy of Institutional Credit to the Small Scale Industrial Sector", *R.B.I. Bulletin*, Mar.

Niranjana, N (1992), "Operational Efficiency of RRBs in India", *Rural India*, Apr.

Noorbasha, Abdul and M. Jyothi (1989), "Viability of RRBs—A Case Study", *Yojana*, May, Vol. 33.

Noorbasha, Abdul and M. Jyothi (1990), "Funds Management in RRBs—A Case Study", *Yojana*, Oct.

Pai, M.R. (1987), "Customer Service in Banks", *Southern Economist*, Feb., Vol. 25.

Patel, A.R. (1974), "Problems and Challenges of Rural Credit—A Case for Nationalised Banks", *Prajnan*, July-Sept.

Patel, K.V. and N.B Shete (1980), "Liberalisation and Rural Development in India: Role of Banking Sector in the Changing Environment", *Prajnan*, Oct.-Dec., Vol. XX, No. 4.

Patel, K.V. and N.B. Shete (1980), "RRBs: Performance and Prospect", *Prajnan*, Jan.-Mar., Vol. XI, No. 1.

Podwal, S and R. Bandyopadhya (1973), "Bank Branch Location in Rural Areas", *Prajnan*, Apr.-June.

Rangarajan, C. (1993), "Banking Education and Training", *R.B.I. Bulletin*, Nov.

Rangarajan, C. (1994), "Committee for Intensive Use of Technology in Payment System", *R.B.I. Bulletin*, Dec.

Rangarajan, C. (1996), "Banking Sector Reforms", *R.B.I. Bulletin*, March.

Rangarajan, C. (1996), "Rural India: The Role of Credit", *The Banker*, March.

Rao, K.D. (1980), "Some Planning Issues for RRBs", *Prajnan,* April.

Roa, Nageswar and Pramod Pathak (1990), "Customer Service and Banks", *Prajnan,* July, Vol. 34.

Rasotra, Poonam (1995), *"Consumer Satisfaction in Insurance",* Unpublished Thesis, Dept. of Commerce, University of Jammu.

Reddy, B. Darardharni and M.Z. Hussain (1983), "Rural Banks in India", *Capital,* Jan., Vol. 189.

Reddy, K. Negi and S. Rathnakumari (1987), "Farm Credit Utilisation—A Comparative Study of RRBs and ADB of S.B.I." *Southern Economist,* Feb., Vol. 25.

Regional Rural Banks (1975), "Role of Reserve Bank in Promoting Rural Development", *R.B.I. Bulletin.* Dec., (Suppl).

Report of Agricultural Finance Corporation (1989), *Financial Express,* 24th April.

Report of the Agricultural Sub-Finance Committee (1945), G.O.I., New Delhi.

Report of the All India Rural Credit Survey (1954), R.B.I. Bombay, Vol. II, Chapters VIII and IX.

Report of the Banking Commission (1972), G.O.I., New Delhi.

Report of the Committee on Rural Banks (1975), Working Group, G.O.I., New Delhi.

Report of the Committee to Review Arrangements for Institutional Credit for Agriculture and Rural Development (CRAFICARD) (1982), R.B.I., Bombay.

Report of Kelkar Committee on RRBs (1989), R.B.I., Bombay.

Report of the Review Committee on RRBs (1977), Dantwala Committee, R.B.I., Bombay.

Report on Viability of RRBs (1987), *R.B.I., Bulletin* Bombay.

Report of the Working Group (1975), Regional Rural Banks, G.O.I., New Delhi.

Ross Christopher A. (1997), "The Practice of Marketing in Newly Industrialised and Developing Countries, A Survey", *A Questionnaire.*

R.B.I. Bulletin (1998), "Banking Development and Policy Perspective", Report on Trend and Progress of Banking in India, November.

R.B.I. Bulletin (1976) "Credit Control and other Measures", Jan.

R.B.I. Bulletin (1976) "Credit Control and other Measures", June.

R.B.I. Bulletin (1990) "Credit Control and other Measures", Dec.

R.B.I. Bulletin (1991) "Credit Control and other Measures", Oct.

R.B.I. Bulletin (1992) "Credit Control and other Measures", Mar.

R.B.I. Bulletin (1992) "Credit Control and other Measures", July.

R.B.I. Bulletin (1993) "Credit Control and other Measures", Apr.

R.B.I. Bulletin (1994) "Credit Control and other Measures", Mar.

R.B.I. Bulletin (1994) "Credit Control and other Measures", Aug.

R.B.I. Bulletin (1995) "Credit Control and other Measures", Jan.

R.B.I. Bulletin (1995) "Credit Control and other Measures", July.

R.B.I. Bulletin (1995) "Credit Control and other Measures", Sept.

R.B.I. Bulletin (1997) "Credit Control and other Measures", Jan.

R.B.I. Bulletin (1997) "Credit Control and other Measures", Dec.

R.B.I. Bulletin (1998) "Credit Control and other Measures", Feb.

R.B.I. Bulletin (1997) "Development of Banking Technology in India", January.

R.B.I. Bulletin "15-Point Programme", July.

R.B.I. Bulletin (1996), "On Sound Bank Management", March.

Sangwan, S.S. (1989), "Viability of Rural Credit Structure—A Case Study of RRBs", *Prajnan*, Vol. 18.

Sanjeevaiah, B.C. (1988), "*Rural Banking: A Comparative Study of the Performance of Rural Based Credit Institution—Co—operative Credit Societies, Farmers' Service Societies and RRBs*", Unpublished Thesis, Dept., of Commerce and Management, Bangalore University.

Sankaranarayanan, V. (1990), "Viability of RRBs" *Economic Review*, Mar., Vol. 35.

Sarkar, B.K. (1983), "Bank Marketing for the Target Groups in the Priority Sector", *Prajnan*, July-Sept., Vol. XII, No. 4.

Satya, Sundaram (1984), "Strengthening RRBs", "*Financing Agriculture*, Apr.-June.

Savaraiah, G. and N. Narmalamani (1988), "Rural Banking for the Rural Milieu", *Indian Co-operative Review*, Oct., Vol. 26.

Savaraiah, G. and N. Thirupalu (1985), "RRBs—Marching in Rural Development", *Khadi Gramodyog*, Dec.

Shankar, K. (1993), "RRBs: At the Crossroads", *Indian Banking Today and Tomorrow*, May.

Sharda, H.M. (1980), "A Study of RRBs", *Lok Udyog,* June, Vol. 14.

Sharma, Manoj (1993), "Bank Marketing and Customer Service", *Indian Banking Today and Tomorrow,* June.

Sharma, R.D. (1995), "Marketing Effectiveness in American Banks", *Prajnan*, Vol. XXIV.

Sharma, R.D. (1996), MKTEFFECT: A Multiple Item Scale for Measuring Marketing Effectiveness in American Consumer Banking Through Customer Judgement", *Vikalpa*, Jan.-Mar., Vol. 21, No. 1.

Sharma, R.D.; Desh Bandhu and Gurjeet Kaur (1998), "Strategy for Marketing Orientation in Rural Banks—A Caste Study", *Prajnan*, Apr.-June, Vol. XXVII, No. 1.

Sharma, R.D; Desh Bandhu and Gurjeet Kaur (1998), "Nature and Extent of Marketing Orientation in Rural Banks", *Prajnan*, July, Vol. 1, No. 2.

Sharma, S.C. and A.K.S. Tomar (1987), "Progress of RRBs in India", *Southern Economist*, Apr., Vol. 25.

Singh, Harpal (1976), "Regional Rural Banks", Yojana, Vol. XXIII, Dec., (16).

Singh, R.K.P. (1983), "Profitability of RRBs in Bihar", Indian institute of Bankers", Apr.-June, Vol. 54.

Singh, R.K.P. (1983), "Profitability of RRBs in Bihar", Indian Institute of Bankers", Apr.-June, Vol. 54.

Singh, R.K.P. (1987), "Business Planning in RRBs", *Khadi Gramodyog,* Jan.

Singh, R.K. and K.M. Upadhaya (1984), "A Study of Loan Recovery of RRBs in Bihar", *Financing Agriculture*, Apr.-June.

Singh, R.K.P. *et al.* (1986), "Financial Viability of Commercial and RRBs in Bihar—A Case Study", *Indian Institute of Bankers*, Apr.-June, Vol. 58.

Standing Advisory Committee on Agricultural Credit (1951), "Role of Reserve Bank in Promoting Rural Development, C. (1993), "Team Spirit—Key to Customer Service and Deposit Mobilisation", *The Banker*, May.

Standing Advisory Committee on Agricultural Credit (1951), "Role of Reserve Bank in Promoting Rural Development", *R.B.I. Bulletin*, Dec. (Suppl.)

Subramaniam, C (1993), "Team Spirit—Key to Customers Service and Deposit Mobilisation", *The Banker,* May.

Sundarsan, R (1994), "Indian Banking in Retrospect—A Prospective View", *Economic Review,* Feb.-Apr., Vol. 38, No. 3.

Thingalaya, N.K. (1984), Revamping Rural Banks", *Economic Review,* Oct., Vol. 30.

Thingalaya, N.K. (1991), "The Dynamics of Bank Marketing", *Economic Revive,* June.

Thingalaya, N.K. (1993), "Role Responsibilities of Financial Institution vis-a-vis Programmes of Panchayat Raj Institutions", *Economic Review,* Aug.-Oct., Vol. 38, No. 1.

Vaghul, N. (1976), "Employees Development for Efficient Customer Services", *Prajnan,* Apr.-Jan., Vol. VI.

Vaishnaw, Bajranglal (1984), *"RRBs in India—An Appraisal with Special Reference to Rajasthan,"* Unpublished Thesis, Dept. of Commerce, University of Jodhpur.

Varde, S.D. (1976), "Customer Service of Banks", *Prajnan,* Jan.-Mar., Vol. V, No. 1.

Varde, Varsha S. and Sampat Singh (1982), "Profitability Performance of RRBs", *Prajnan,* Oct.-Dec.

Varma, S.D. (1992), "RRBs—A Case for their Revival", *IBA Bulletin,* Dec., Vol. XIV, No. 2.

Vaz. I.T. (1992), "Rural Planning and Credit Department", *Economic Review,* Dec., Vol. 38, No. 4 & 5.

Venkateswarlu, P.K. (1987), "Customer Service in Commercial Banks", *Southern Economist,* Oct., Vol. 26.

Vijay Kumar M.N. and H.J. Gurunath (1991), "RRBs: An Analysis", *Southern Economist,* Mar., Vol. 29.

Viswanathan, C.V. and Rajeev K. Seth (1991), "Changing Scenario of Bank Marketing: Challenges and Strategies", *Vichar.*

Vyas, Vijayshanker (1991), *"Marketing Management in Commercial Banks with Special Reference to Customer Service"*, Dept. of Commerce and Management Studies, University of Jodhpur.

Working Group (1989), *"RRBs—A Resume"*, G.O.I., Department of Economic Affairs, New Delhi.

ANNEXURE—I

Schedule for the Collection of Data from Customers

Demographic Profile

(1) Gender: ....

(2) Age: ....

(3) Qualification: ....

(4) Occupation: ....

(5) Family Size: ....

(6) Family Earnings: ....

(7) Residential Status: ....

(8) Landholdings: ....

(a) Irrigated: ....

(b) Non-Irrigated: ....

General Information

(1) Name of the bank: ....

(2) Association with the bank: ....

(3) Nature of account: ....

(4) If term deposit, period: ....

(5) Rate of Interest: ....

(a) Saving: ....

(b) Current: ....

(c) Fixed Deposit:...........................

(6) Have you availed credit from RRB. Yes/No

(7) If yes, fill in the following blanks

(a) Purpose of Loan: ....

(b) Amount applied:...

(c) Amount sanctioned: ....

(d) Loan sanctioning time: ....

(e) Loan disbursement time:......................................

(f) Source from where balance obtained:.................

(g) Satisfied with amount sanctioned: ....

(h) Kind of security demanded:.................................

Abbreviations Used

SA	=	Strongly Agree
A	=	Agree
N	=	Neutral
D	=	Disagree
SD	=	Strongly Disagree
NK	=	Not Known

Customers' Opinion Regarding Six Ps of Bank Marketing-Mix—

(A) Product

1. Bank deposit schemes are suitable to you. SA A N D SD NK
2. You are satisfied with existing deposit schemes. SA A N D SD NK
3. You are satisfied by depositing your savings with this bank only. SA A N D SD NK
4. Bank's advance schemes are suitable to you. SA A N D SD NK

5. You are satisfied with present number of advance schemes.	SA	A	N	D	SD	NK
6. Loan schemes need unnecessary time to cover all formalities.	SA	A	N	D	SD	NK
7. Bank demands reasonable security and guarantee.	SA	A	N	D	SD	NK
8. In future also this bank would be preferred to avail loan schemes.	SA	A	N	D	SD	NK
9. Bank's policy of providing product instead of money, is suitable to you.	SA	A	N	D	SD	NK
10. You are satisfied with the products supplied.	SA	A	N	D	SD	NK
11. For a layman, getting loan from this bank is a difficult task.	SA	A	N	D	SD	NK
12. Bank's policy of recovering the loan is not troublesome.	SA	A	N	D	SD	NK
13. You don't find any difficulty in paying instalments in time.	SA	A	N	D	SD	NK
14. Schemes are addressed to the needs of different sections.	SA	A	N	D	SD	NK
15. G.O.I./R.B.I. undertakes regular research to assess the target people needs.	SA	A	N	D	SD	NK
16. Pass book entries are absolutely correct.	SA	A	N	D	SD	NK
17. Immediate updating of passbook is done.	SA	A	N	D	SD	NK
18. Immediate encashment of cheques is done.	SA	A	N	D	SD	NK
19. Unnecessary time is involved in withdrawing the cash	SA	A	N	D	SD	NK
20. No delay is caused in depositing money.	SA	A	N	D	SD	NK
21. Formal procedure involved in getting the amount fixed for some duration is troublesome.	SA	A	N	D	SD	NK
22. Account opening formalities are difficult.	SA	A	N	D	SD	NK
23. New cheque or passbooks are issued as and when asked for.	SA	A	N	D	SD	NK
24. Procedure involved in getting product through loan is quite lengthy.	SA	A	N	D	SD	NK
25. Cheque/drafts clearance takes less time.	SA	A	N	D	SD	NK

26. Withdrawal of large sum requires considerable time. SA A N D SD NK
27. Working of bank is efficient and effective. SA A N D SD NK

B. Price

1. Interest rates paid and charged by the bank are attractive and adequate to you. SA A N D SD NK
2. Interest charged on advances is reasonable. SA A N D SD NK
3. Interest provided by this bank is motivating. SA A N D SD NK
4. Interest calculations are correct. SA A N D SD NK
5. Interest provided by post-office is comparatively satisfactory than this bank. SA A N D SD NK
6. Interest charged by the bank on advances is economical than charged by the money-lenders. SA A N D SD NK
7. Obtaining information regarding new interest rates requires lot of time. SA A N D SD NK

(C) Place

1. Bank's location is convenient. SA A N D SD NK
2. This is the only bank in your area. SA A N D SD NK
3. As compared to other banks this bank is nearest to you. SA A N D SD NK
4. Bank is located within the purview of 4-5 villages. SA A N D SD NK
5. Bank is easily approachable in emergencies. SA A N D SD NK
6. There is inadequate number of staff members. SA A N D SD NK
7. Employees of bank are competent and efficient. SA A N D SD NK
8. Employees of bank are co-operative and friendly. SA A N D SD NK
9. Employees possess information regarding banking matters. SA A N D SD NK
10. You are satisfied with present bank's staff. SA A N D SD NK

(D) Promotion

1. Bank advertises its schemes frequently. SA A N D SD NK
2. Bank effectively promotes schemes through T.V. and Radio. SA A N D SD NK
3. Bank heavily promotes its schemes through newspapers and magazines. SA A N D SD NK
4. Promotion of schemes through posters is appealing. SA A N D SD NK
5. Bank advertises its new interest rates more heavily. SA A N D SD NK
6. Bank promotes schemes through personal involvement. SA A N D SD NK
7. Fieldworkers promote various schemes of bank. SA A N D SD NK
8. Fieldworkers are effective in motivating customers to avail services of the bank. SA A N D SD NK
9. Customers receives attractive incentives in the form of gifts. SA A N D SD NK
10. Meetings are regularly held advertise new schemes. SA A N D SD NK
11. Employees are helpful in disseminating information regarding new schemes. SA A N D SD NK
12. Employees assist in filling the withdrawal/deposit forms. SA A N D SD NK
13. Employees help in filing all the formalities involved in obtaining loans. SA A N D SD NK
14. Employees inform the customer about new interest rate. SA A N D SD NK
15. Bank's counter services are satisfactory. SA A N D SD NK
16. Employees transfer creates lot of inconvenience. SA A N D SD NK

Customer's Suggestions Regarding Six Ps of Bank Marketing-Mix—

1. Some new and attractive schemes of deposit need to be introduced. SA A N D SD NK
2. Few new and effective schemes of advances need to be introduced. SA A N D SD NK

3. There is a need to make alterations in current interest rate structure.	SA A N D SD NK
4. There is a need to shift the branches of bank to more convenient places.	SA A N D SD NK
5. Few more branches need to be opened.	SA A N D SD NK
6. There is a need to increase present number of staff members.	SA A N D SD NK
7. There is a need to advertise existing and new schemes of the bank more effectively.	SA A N D SD NK
8. There is a need to give additional incentives to employees so that they feel motivated in extending required information.	SA A N D SD NK
9. Process for obtaining loan should be made more easy.	SA A N D SD NK
10. New interest rates should be heavily advertised.	SA A N D SD NK
11. Customers should be invited to participate in the affairs of bank.	SA A N D SD NK
12. Greater availability of credit rather than lower cost of credit should be bank's policy.	SA A N D SD NK
13. Computer should be installed for quick operation of bank.	SA A N D SD NK
14. There is a need to change the working hours of the bank.	SA A N D SD NK
15. Bank should also provide other facilities such as demand drafts, cash overdrafts, insurance premium, lockers availability etc.	SA A N D SD NK

Is there any complaint/suggestion box in the bank. If yes, have you ever complaint and what was the bank's reaction towards it.

ANNEXURE—II

Questionnaire for the Collection of Data from Managers

1. Designation in RRB: ______________________
2. Years of Association with RRB: ____________

Managements Opinion Regarding Six Ps of Bank Marketing—

A. Product

1. Bank's deposit schemes are suitable to its customers. SA A N D SD NK
2. Customers are satisfied with existing deposit schemes. SA A N D SD NK
3. Customers are satisfied by depositing their saving with this bank only. SA A N D SD NK
4. Bank's advance schemes are suitable to its customers. SA A N D SD NK
5. Customers are satisfied with present number of advance schemes. SA A N D SD NK
6. Bank's policy of financing the purchase of products instead of releasing cash in their favour is suitable to its customers. SA A N D SD NK
7. Bank's policy of recovering loan is troublesome. SA A N D SD NK
8. Bank admires the government policy of waiving off the loan. SA A N D SD NK

9. For illiterate customers, getting loan from this bank is difficult task. SA A N D SD NK
10. Customers have availed loan for more than once. SA A N D SD NK

B. Price

1. Bank charges reasonable interest on advances. SA A N D SD NK
2. Bank provides attractive interest on deposits. SA A N D SD NK
3. Customers are satisfied with interest rate provided and charged by the bank. SA A N D SD NK
4. Interest calculations are correct as per the customers knowledge. SA A N D SD NK
5. Present interest rate structure fully meet, the customers requirement. SA A N D SD NK
6. Deregulation of interest rates favours the customers. SA A N D SD NK
7. Bank's policy of providing more interest on deposit has increased the number of customers. SA A N D SD NK

C. Place

1. Bank's location is convenient to its customers. SA A N D SD NK
2. Service Area Approach has restricted the customers movement from one bank to another. SA A N D SD NK
3. Customers find this bank nearest to all other banks. SA A N D SD NK
4. Present branches meet the customers locational requirements. SA A N D SD NK
5. Present branches fulfil the profitability aspect of the bank. SA A N D SD NK
6. Far location of the branches is a problem for rural customers. SA A N D SD NK

D. Promotion

1.	Bank is using promotional tools in the light of customers educational level.	SA	A	N	D	SD	NK
2.	Advertisements have increased the number of customers.	SA	A	N	D	SD	NK
3.	Promotion of schemes and interest rates through posters is appealing to customers.	SA	A	N	D	SD	NK
4.	Promotion through personal involvement suits the bank's customers.	SA	A	N	D	SD	NK
5.	Meetings are held regularly to know various banking needs of the customers.	SA	A	N	D	SD	NK
6.	Fieldworkers are successful in motivating the customers to avail services of the bank.	SA	A	N	D	SD	NK

E. People

1.	Employees are trained to meet the customers' requirements.	SA	A	N	D	SD	NK
2.	Customers feel satisfied with present bank's staff.	SA	A	N	D	SD	NK
3.	Employees are fully aware of customers financial and non-financial needs.	SA	A	N	D	SD	NK
4.	Employees have less time to look after the needs of the customers.	SA	A	N	D	SD	NK
5.	Employees are extending their full co-operation to help the customers.	SA	A	N	D	SD	NK
6.	Employees welcome interaction with the customers.	SA	A	N	D	SD	NK

F. Process

1.	Present banking process fulfils the customers' requirements.	SA	A	N	D	SD	NK
2.	Rural banking process are simpler in comparison to other Commercial Co-operative Banks.	SA	A	N	D	SD	NK
3.	Customers are satisfied with the number of processes involved in the bank.	SA	A	N	D	SD	NK
4.	Account opening formalities are complex for rural people.	SA	A	N	D	SD	NK

5. Withdrawal of cash requires more time. SA A N D SD NK
6. Depositing of cash is done within no time. SA A N D SD NK
7. Issuance of passbooks and chequebooks involve a considerable time. SA A N D SD NK

Management's Suggestions Regarding Six Ps of Bank Marketing-Mix—

1. There is a need to have more deposit schemes. SA A N D SD NK
2. New advance schemes need to be introduced. SA A N D SD NK
3. Schemes should be introduced as per the customer's requirements. SA A N D SD NK
4. Profitability should be a consideration for introducing new schemes. SA A N D SD NK
5. Market research need to be undertaken before introducing new schemes. SA A N D SD NK
6. New interest rates need to be structured. SA A N D SD NK
7. Interest rate structure should be designed to fulfil customers need. SA A N D SD NK
8. New interest rates should lead to bank's profitability. SA A N D SD NK
9. Market research need to be undertaken before declaring new interest rates. SA A N D SD NK
10. Branches need to be located in new areas. SA A N D SD NK
11. Customers convenience should be considered before locating new branches. SA A N D SD NK
12. Location of new branches should reflect the profitability of that area. SA A N D SD NK
13. Market research need to be undertaken before locating new branches. SA A N D SD NK
14. All promotional tools need to be employed effectively. SA A N D SD NK
15. Advertising should be rural oriented. SA A N D SD NK
16. Sales promotional techniques would prove more effective in meeting customers needs. SA A N D SD NK
17. Banker-customers meeting should be held regularly. SA A N D SD NK

18. There is a need to make fieldworkers more customer-conscious.	SA A N D SD NK
19. Market research must be undertaken before employing promotional tools.	SA A N D SD NK
20. Employees should be given practical training in the rural atmosphere.	SA A N D SD NK
21. More employees need to be recruited.	SA A N D SD NK
22. Processes involved in rural banks should be simplified.	SA A N D SD NK
23. Processes should be designed after considering rural literacy level.	SA A N D SD NK
24. Working hours of the bank need to be changed.	SA A N D SD NK

ANNEXURE—III

Questionnaire for the Collection of Data from Chairmen Specific Queries of Marketing Orientation

(A) Product

1.	R.B.I. introduces new schemes after recognising target customers' needs.	SA	A	N	D	SD	NK
2.	Bank suggests schemes to R.B.I. which suits customers financial requirements.	SA	A	N	D	SD	NK
3.	R.B.I. successfully implemented the schemes suggested by your bank.	SA	A	N	D	SD	NK
4.	R.B.I. introduced different schemes for different set of customers.	SA	A	N	D	SD	NK
5.	Bank conducts regular market research studies to assist R.B.I. in introducing new schemes.	SA	A	N	D	SD	NK
6.	Bank knows the profitability of its different schemes.	SA	A	N	D	SD	NK
7.	Bank does not attempt to identify schemes which should be screened out from its scheme lines.	SA	A	N	D	SD	NK
8.	Bank does not attempt to identify schemes which should be added to its scheme lines.	SA	A	N	D	SD	NK
9.	Banks sometimes introduces short-term or specific schemes.	SA	A	N	D	SD	NK
10.	Bank's schemes always come from R.B.I.	SA	A	N	D	SD	NK

11. Bank's schemes come from the sponsoring bank. SA A N D SD NK
12. Schemes of sponsoring bank/R.B.I. are mostly subject to amendment by management of rural banks. SA A N D SD NK

(B) Place

1. R.B.I. considered profitability before the location of your bank's branches. SA A N D SD NK
2. Bank's location meet the requirements of different categories of customers. SA A N D SD NK
3. Bank conducts regular market research studies in a search of new location. SA A N D SD NK
4. Bank has adequate market coverage and services. SA A N D SD NK
5. R.B.I. dictates the location of the branch. SA A N D SD NK
6. Sponsor bank dictates the location of the branch. SA A N D SD NK
7. Bank itself submits the proposal for opening the new branches. SA A N D SD NK
8. It is the top management which decides the opening of new branches. SA A N D SD NK
9. In opening of new branch, opinion of subordinate staff is given due recognition. SA A N D SD NK

(C) Price

1. Interest rate structure designed is reasonable. SA A N D SD NK
2. Bank conducts regular market research studies in presenting new interest rate. SA A N D SD NK
3. Bank recognises the need for interest rate objectives and strategies. SA A N D SD NK
4. Bank sets its interest rates on the basis of rural environment. SA A N D SD NK
5. Bank knows about competitors interest rate and other charges. SA A N D SD NK
6. Bank's interest rates have been designed to fulfil the profitability objective. SA A N D SD NK
7. Interest rate fixed by R.B.I. is reasonable. SA A N D SD NK

8. Bank has its own pricing schemes. SA A N D SD NK

(D) Promotion

1. Promotional tools have been employed after considering customers level of education. SA A N D SD NK
2. Bank conducts regular market research studies in employing new promotional tools. SA A N D SD NK
3. Bank recognises the need to have clear advertising objectives. SA A N D SD NK
4. Bank has adequate sales promotion budget. SA A N D SD NK
5. Bank makes effective use of sales promotion tools such as loan melas. SA A N D SD NK
6. Bank has adequate procedures for evaluating the performance of its sales force. SA A N D SD NK
7. Bank does compensate its sales force well. SA A N D SD NK
8. Bank's promotional policies are carried
   - a> through advertising SA A N D SD NK
   - b> through field staff SA A N D SD NK
   - c> through brochures SA A N D SD NK
   - d> through loan melas. SA A N D SD NK

(E) People

1. Employees have been trained to serve the needs of customers. SA A N D SD NK
2. Bank employees need to be evaluated more frequently. SA A N D SD NK
3. Bank undertakes regular market research studies in conducting employees training programme. SA A N D SD NK
4. Employees have been successful in meeting the market requirements. SA A N D SD NK
5. Customers' needs are communicated to the employees for effective implementation. SA A N D SD NK
6. Marketing staff works in coordination with the employees of other managerial areas. SA A N D SD NK

7. Marketing intelligence system of the bank is effective. SA A N D SD NK

(F) Process

1. R.B.I. has designed your banking services to satisfy the requirements of customers. SA A N D SD NK
2. Various banking processes have been framed in the rural atmosphere. SA A N D SD NK
3. R.B.I has a well organised new process development for your bank. SA A N D SD NK
4. Bank conducts regular market research studies in assisting R.B.I. to introduce new processes. SA A N D SD NK
5. Loan procedure has been designed after due consideration of rural educational level. SA A N D SD NK
6. In banking processes standard guidelines by R.B.I. are to be followed by the bank. SA A N D SD NK

General Queries of Marketing Orientation

1. Bank integrates and controls its major marketing functions at a very senior level. SA A N D SD NK
2. Bank does not have formal marketing planning. SA A N D SD NK
3. Bank understands the importance of having a clear, well reasoned marketing strategy. SA A N D SD NK
4. In a bank, marketing thinking and orientation at the top is well communicated down the line. SA A N D SD NK
5. Marketing thinking and orientation at the top is implemented down the line. SA A N D SD NK
6. Bank makes effective use of its marketing resources. SA A N D SD NK
7. Bank has business mission that is clearly stated in market oriented terms. SA A N D SD NK
8. Bank has difficulty in allocating resources to the major elements of the marketing mix (product, place, price, promotion). SA A N D SD NK

9. The marketing officer has inadequate authority over banking activities that affect customer satisfaction. SA A N D SD NK

10. Top decision-makers regularly use the results of market research studies. SA A N D SD NK

11. Top decision-makers regularly ask for the conduct of market research. SA A N D SD NK

12. Bank has a marketing intelligence system which produces accurate, timely and sufficient information. SA A N D SD NK

13. Most people believe that marketing has little value in rural banks. SA A N D SD NK
    SA A N D SD NK

14. In banks, the traditional marketing management framework with its emphasis on 4P's (product, place, price, promotion) is not well suited because most of these variables are controllable. SA A N D SD NK

15. Is there any handbook on strategies for the implementation of Development Action Plan.

Yes/No.

Index

❑❑❑